THE FRATERNALIST

The Remarkable Life of Virgil C. Dechant

THE 12TH SUPREME KNIGHT OF THE KNIGHTS OF COLUMBUS

....

by John Dechant

Legacy Preservation LLC

The first edition of *The Fraternalist* was published in 2017 in Omaha, Nebraska, USA

ISBN 978-0-9842954-3-2

Published in 2017 by Legacy Preservation LLC, Omaha, Nebraska

John Dechant, Legacy Preservation LLC, writer and editor, Omaha, Nebraska

Wayne Kobza, Pencil to Press, publication design, Omaha, Nebraska

Printed and bound in USA.

Cover artwork: A portrait of Virgil Dechant by renowned American portrait artist John Howard Sanden (used with the permission of Sanden and the Knights of Columbus Museum).

For Ann Dechant,
the longtime first lady of the Knights of Columbus.

And for the wives of the K of C everywhere,
who quietly support their husbands in carrying out
the Order's good works.

CONTENTS

FOREWORD   IX

CHAPTER ONE   1

CHAPTER TWO   17

CHAPTER THREE   35

CHAPTER FOUR   59

CHAPTER FIVE   83

CHAPTER SIX   109

CHAPTER SEVEN   131

CHAPTER EIGHT   155

CHAPTER NINE   183

CHAPTER TEN   221

CHAPTER ELEVEN   257

CHAPTER TWELVE   287

ACKNOWLEDGMENTS   317

FINAL TRIBUTE   321

APPENDIX   325

SUPREME KNIGHT CARL A. ANDERSON

S ince its origins, the Knights of Columbus has been blessed with a number of remarkable leaders, and Virgil Dechant, the twelfth supreme knight, will always be counted among the best of these for his vision, congeniality, and dedication to brother Knights and their families.

In 1900, a priest praised the Knights of Columbus' founder, Father Michael McGivney, for boldly attempting what none at the time would dare to do: form a spiritual society of men, for men, with a "religious requirement"—namely, being a practicing Catholic.

A century later, when Virgil Dechant retired as supreme knight, he passed on to all of us a band of brothers profoundly shaped by his similar boldness. Like Father McGivney, he both understood deeply the needs of Catholic men—especially the need for brothers in the same faith—as well as envisioned their abilities which Catholic men themselves were unware of. It was a privilege for me to have worked closely with Virgil for so many years and an honor to succeed him as supreme knight of the Knights of Columbus.

In many ways, the need for true fraternity is underappreciated today. "Connectedness," often with a technological manifestation, is spoken of far more often than such a venerable quality like "fraternity."

In Pope Francis' very first message for the World Day of Peace, he echoed sentiments dear to Virgil's heart, when he chose to expound on fraternity—a quality perhaps unusual to many Catholics, but familiar to Knights, who claim it as one of the four principles of the Order. The pope lauded fraternity as "the foundation and pathway to peace," and called it an "essential human quality" which is "generally learned first in the family."

Long before this statement, Virgil had already recognized the tremendous need for Catholic community-building, especially among men. Indeed, for decades before these, Virgil both lived those words and led the largest group of Catholic laymen in the world into learning and living this "essential human quality." Equally to his credit, long before Pope Francis highlighted the link between fraternity and the family, Virgil was already fostering this essential tie in the Order, spearheading the effort to advance the Knights of Columbus' identity as an organization for Catholic families, not only for the benefit of families' men. He did this both by increasing the ways in which families were involved with the Knights, and by substantially increasing the Order's insurance program, bringing financial security to more and more Catholic families.

In his role as supreme knight, he also brought the Order to new heights by developing a close, supportive relationship with the Holy See, working closely with Pope John Paul II, who like him, focused heavily on supporting families and integrating them in the life of the Church.

Leading one of the largest lay Catholic organizations, it is no exaggeration to state that Virgil shaped not only the lives of millions, but shaped even the very character and experience of the Catholic Church in the United States.

Despite his prominence in his public role, so much of Virgil's work and vision happened behind the scenes, and so this book does a tremendous service to preserving and revealing not only the work, but the man who lived so personally Christ's command to love God and love our neighbor. He was, to both people familiar with him and newly acquainted, replete with not only neighborly friendliness, but brotherly attention, protection, and warmth.

Virgil often said that it was his job to leave the Order better than he found it. This book shows how he did just that.

THE FRATERNALIST

n a sense, it all began in a hospital room. It was a sterile setting, complete with an uncomfortable bed, an uncertain future, and all the tapioca pudding a patient could eat. It seems like an odd place to develop a strong affinity for almost anything, especially a fraternal organization, but that's what happened to Virgil C. Dechant.

Dechant was 18 and working for Kansas auto and farm equipment dealer Bill Weigand in 1949 when he and a co-worker survived a nasty car wreck one evening near Antonino, the town of his birth, located south of Hays, the area's major municipality and the crown jewel of the western half of the state.

Dechant was rushed to St. Anthony's Hospital in Hays. There he was treated for a series of injuries, including a broken hip that required the insertion of five pins during surgery. Having noticed his propensity for fast driving, his mother Ursula had always worried about the possibility of a wreck. That very day she had warned Virgil to be careful. Now he was facing a long, grueling recovery, and he would stay in the hospital convalescing for 60 days. His cast would stay on for three months. It would have seemed even longer if not for a dedicated group of men from the St. Augustine Council of the Knights of Columbus (#2340) in Liebenthal, which Dechant had recently joined. Every night, like clockwork, that group from the fraternal order of Catholic men came by the hospital to check up on him. At the time, he was dating Ann Schafer, a Liebenthal girl, who also visited regularly to check on his recovery. It's true that there were moments when Dechant wished his brother Knights would curtail their visits so he could spend more time talking to Ann. But they were a hearty bunch that never seemed to have anywhere else to be, and he did enjoy their company. Eventually Dechant was discharged, but an allergic reaction to the pins in his hip sent him back to the hospital. And still, the brother Knights kept coming to visit.

When he finally left the hospital for good, Dechant was so touched by the concern shown by his fellow Knights of Columbus that he decided to give the organization more of his time and energy. He figured it was the least he could do.

"I thought, 'Well, if that's what the Knights of Columbus is all about, with that sort of fraternal spirit, I should become more involved,'"

Virgil C. Dechant, St. Joseph's Military Academy.

Dechant recalled. "So I decided to attend a meeting."

And thus began a career with the Knights that would span more than six decades. Both Dechant and the Order would forever be changed.

Shortly before his car accident, Dechant had been encouraged to join the Order by Phillip Dreher, a Kansas farmer and K of C member. He had also been spurred on by a touch of envy; every year the council held a party on Columbus Day that was the toast of the Liebenthal community. Dechant's friends who were Knights or the sons of Knights could attend, but he never could. Year after year he would serve as an altar boy during Columbus Day Mass at St. Joseph Church, but the party was off limits because his father was not then a member of the council. When he turned 18, the opportunity came up to join. It was his ticket to the annual party.

"I think I'll ask my dad, and if he agrees I'll join," Dechant told Dreher, 30 years his senior. The conversation between Dechant and his father Cornel, who went by "C.J.," took place under a blackberry tree on the family's property, adjacent to the local Catholic church. Since Dechant was not yet 26 years old, he was required by the Order's laws to sign up for $1,000 worth of life insurance at a premium of approximately $26 per year, a 20-year whole-life plan.

"Go ahead and take it," the elder Dechant told his son, nodding affirmatively. Virgil knew very little about insurance then, only that it would pay off when he died. In time he would learn it and, eventually, master it.

At his first meeting with the St. Augustine Council after his recovery, Dechant was elected outside guard. The job's responsibilities were a mystery to him so he decided to stay close to Dreher, his proposer, who by then had been promoted to council grand knight after his predecessor re-enlisted into armed service for the Korean conflict.

During another meeting that first year with the Order, Dechant and others listened as Dreher made an announcement to the council. "I have a letter here from Supreme Secretary Joseph F. Lamb," Dreher said, "and I see that our brother John Schmidt has been chosen to receive honorary life status. So it is with great pride that I present him with this honorary life membership card."

Brother Schmidt, perhaps confused, stood to accept the honorary life card, but pretty soon Dechant overheard "a little bit of a German roar coming up from the crowd." A few of his brother Knights were claiming they had taken membership with the council before John Schmidt. Why weren't they candidates for honorary life status? Another man stood up and said, "I was also a charter member of this council, and brother Schmidt was not. Shouldn't I be entitled to a card?"

Sensing a brewing conflict, Dechant grabbed the letter and read it, more carefully than Dreher. The general position of the letter expressed that every council should start recognizing its longtime members, thus saluting them with honorary life status. Then the letter read, "I'm enclosing a sample card to show to your members, who each need to make personal applications to the Order." Dechant took another look at the membership card. It was made out to John Smith, a placeholder name similar to "John Doe." The card was just a sample. His discovery helped calm the German roar, at least for a while.

Having resolved his first major kerfuffle with the Knights of Columbus, Dechant in 1951 was elected grand knight of the St. Augustine Council. He was 21 years old.

The St. Augustine Council had been chartered on January 22, 1922, by 43 members. Those 43 men represented a significant portion of the tiny Liebenthal community, which had been founded in 1876 by some 60 Volga-German farmers who came to the United States after being forced out of Russia. They found the terrain and climate of the Liebenthal area suitable for growing winter wheat, as they had done in Russia. The first structure of any significance erected in Liebenthal was a Catholic church, completed in 1878 for just $200. A stronger and larger church made of Kansas limestone was built in 1905.

Within the confines of St. Joseph parish was a grade school, and there Virgil would get his first taste of formal education. His mother remembered him as a good baby and, as he grew up, a curious boy interested in the exchange of goods.

"He was a trader," Ursula Dechant once said of her son. "He traded with other boys marbles, pencils, and crayons, but he always got taken." During one such trade, he found himself having the upper hand with another boy, one of Barbara Herrman's sons. Virgil made out with something of greater value than the Herrman boy, and when Ursula found out about it she made him take it back. With tears running down his cheeks, Virgil returned whatever it was that he had traded for. According to Ursula, "That was the end of his trading."

In September 1944, Virgil's parents sent him to the Pontifical College Josephinum in Worthington, Ohio, home to a major and minor theological seminary. He was 14. Being sent away to the seminary was a sort of rite of passage in the Dechant household; Virgil's brothers Emerald and Harry would also attend the seminary in Ohio. Like many devoted Catholic families in that part of western Kansas, the Dechants were hopeful that at least one of their brood would choose a vocation to the priesthood. They felt a sense of obligation to provide their sons the sort of setting most conducive to receiving such a call. For Virgil, the priesthood was not to be, and he would return to Kansas to complete his high school education at St. Joseph's Military Academy in Hays, graduating in 1947. Following graduation, he took a course in business management at the Salt City School of Business in Hutchinson.

As a teenager he stood tall and slender, with large hands that could cradle a cigarette like a magician. Wide smiles came easily to him, and clothes were his friend. His St. Joseph's Military uniform fit him like a glove, and, for a farm boy, he sure looked comfortable in a suit and tie.

At the time Dechant joined the Knights of Columbus, Liebenthal's council had about 70 members. During his tenure as grand knight the council placed more emphasis on recruiting, and membership rose

The Dechant men, from left, top: LaVerne, Donald, Virgil; bottom: Harry, C.J., and Emerald.

to more than 120 within a few years. While the members of the St. Augustine Council were active in recruiting new members, money always seemed to remain a thorny issue. Annual dues, as Dechant remembers, were rather low, and nobody was willing to raise them.

"Everything we did was circled around money," Dechant recalled. "One night I had been to Hays to attend a council meeting where they provided wooden lecterns for the various officers to stand behind during meetings. Liebenthal didn't have any lecterns, or stations, like that, so I suggested that we should buy some or build some. In preparation for some disagreement, I had asked brother Al Herman, who had just finished building his home and had leftover lumber, to give me an estimate to make those stations out of that lumber. He volunteered to do this at no cost, and so I asked for a vote. Someone got up and said, 'Hey—not so fast. We have to check around because maybe somebody's willing to make them cheaper.'"

That bottom-line attitude was representative of the regional ethos of western Kansas and its large population of Volga German farmers. You couldn't pull the wool over anyone's eyes. If you wanted to get something accomplished, you had to either be a master at consensus building or content to do it yourself. This included the Dechants.

Following World War II, C.J. Dechant decided to try his hand at farming. He already owned land, but instead of continuing to rent it out to another farmer he elected to take on the risk himself. He bought a full line of machinery from Walter Jeffries, a retired farmer, to get the operation started. But the family also owned a general merchandise store in Liebenthal where Virgil and his brothers worked in childhood, and that business required a good portion of C.J.'s time and energy. The store opened for business on a snowy Saturday, February 24, 1934, under the name "Dechant's Feel at Home Store." Later it became known as the Dechant and Sons store. The family sold everything from corn flakes and coffee to cream, eggs, and sugar. You could even purchase men's and women's clothing at the store.

C.J. designated Virgil to manage the farming so he could focus on Dechant & Sons. Why C.J. chose Virgil, and not another child, is uncertain, but he wasn't without options. His progeny numbered twelve: Emerald, Harry, Bernice, Virgil, Mary Ann, La Verne, Peggy, Donald, Delores, Rosalyn, Carol Jean, and Jeanette.

In the late 1940s the Dechants bought a new Massey Harris 55 tractor from the Weigand Motor and Equipment Company in La Crosse, the county seat, located eight miles south of Liebenthal on Highway 183. Virgil helped his father negotiate the deal with Bill Weigand, the proprietor. The younger Dechant must have driven a hard bargain or looked like a natural salesman while doing so, because Weigand was so impressed with Virgil's negotiating savvy that he offered him a job working for his dealership on the spot. The deal was to sell cars and farm equipment on a commission basis with a weekly guarantee of $25. Dechant thought about the offer a moment, then said to himself, "Well, once I get the wheat in, I'd just as well learn that business." He took the job.

"So I started digging in," Dechant recalled. "We had Olds, Cadillac, and Massey Ferguson. And a few short-line implement companies. Pretty soon I was managing the place."

The fast track into management was due, in part, to his boss's political aspirations. Weigand was elected a senator in the Kansas legislature, thus limiting the time he had for his implement dealership. He named Dechant general manager in 1952. Weigand also asked Dechant to serve as co-chairman for one of his senatorial campaigns. In the process Dechant made the acquaintance of Al Albright, the other co-chair, who knew the ins and outs of Kansas politics. They became fast friends.

The Schafer family, from left: Geraldine, Joseph, Leola, Ann, Bert, Rosa, Rosemary, Coleta.

One evening Dechant accompanied Albright and Weigand to the Topeka home of Alf Landon, former Kansas governor and one-time candidate for president of the United States. Landon discussed his experiences with Kansas and national politics, and Dechant and the others listened carefully. It was incredible exposure for such a young man, and Dechant soaked it all up, not then knowing how valuable the advice would one day be in his own career.

On the subject of advice, perhaps the best he ever got came from his older sister Bernice, who suggested Virgil introduce himself to Ann Schafer, the girl who would wind up coming to visit him in the hospital. Like so many others on the Kansas plains, Ann had grown up on a farm. She was the youngest of six children of Joseph and Rosa Herrman Schafer, who lived five miles west of Liebenthal, near the Cordia settlement. Joe was a wheat farmer, and all his kids attended country school.

Before and after school, Ann and her siblings—four sisters and one brother—had chores to do around the farm. The Schafer homestead consisted of a farmhouse, machine shed, two garages, a chicken house, barn, and, of course, an outdoor toilet. A combination of German and English was spoken around the house, depending on who was talking. During World War II, the Schafers (and the Dechants) and other German families avoided speaking German in public, hoping to avoid suspicious looks from non-German neighbors. Times were tough but not as tough for the Schafers as some; many times Ann watched neighbors make dinner out of a few slices of bread dunked into a mixture of cream and corn syrup.

"I didn't think we were poor, but when I think about it now, we probably were," Ann recalled. "But we always had food and always had gasoline. Many times my aunts and uncles would come visit, and my dad

Ann Schafer, left, followed her sisters into the teaching profession after her education at Sacred Heart Academy in Wichita, Kansas.

Facing page: Virgil and Ann, around the time of their courtship.

would have to put gas in their cars so they could drive home. So I never thought we were poor. We were better off than most of our neighbors, so I thought we were really doing quite well."

Joe and Rosa Schafer believed passionately in education, so they sent their girls away for high school. Two attended school in Dodge City, while the others, including Ann, went to Sacred Heart Academy in Wichita, located 150 miles southeast of Liebenthal. Leola and Rosemary, the first two Schafer girls to attend Sacred Heart, did so by boarding with a doctor and his family. They rode a bus back and forth to school and helped care for the doctor's kids in the evenings. By the time Ann got to Sacred Heart, Rosemary was living on her own in Wichita, so Ann lived with her.

All the Schafer girls became schoolteachers. Ann was in charge of just five students her first year and seven the second. When she took a job teaching third and fourth grade in Liebenthal, the school was in the midst of a faculty changeover that made the school less dependent on the work of nuns. Changing times and social pressures had caught up with the nuns, and the school system decided that these ladies of the cloth shouldn't be the only teachers in a public school. For someone like Ann, this decision created a job opportunity.

Virgil and Ann were married on August 20, 1951, at St. Joseph Church in Liebenthal. They honeymooned in Colorado Springs, Colorado, where they saw the world from the top of Pike's Peak, at an elevation of more than 14,000 feet. They also toured other nearby attractions such as the Garden of the Gods before turning the car east and heading home. On the way back they spent a night in Denver, where they went out to dinner at a fancy restaurant.

A year after their wedding, they welcomed their first child, a son, Tom, into the world. Another son, Daniel, would come along in 1954.

Rainfall was sparse in 1953 and 1954, even by the bone-dry standards of the Kansas plains. As a consequence, crops around Liebenthal and La Crosse were especially poor. For an implement dealership, this was bad news. Weigand Motor and Equipment Company had excess used inventory, so Dechant conducted one of the first large-scale farm machinery auctions in the area. People came from all around, and the auction was a great success.

Activities at the St. Augustine Council of the Knights of Columbus were going even better for Virgil. As grand knight, he had the council thriving. He and his brother Knights held creative fundraisers and adopted new charities in the Liebenthal area. At the suggestion of a few members, the council held a turkey shoot at a local farm. Thomas Moeder, a member of the council, sat behind a shield of straw bales and loaded clay pigeons into a machine to fire out to the shooters. When the machine quit working, he threw them out by hand, earning him the nickname "Lefty." The turkey shoot was just one such event the council held; many others, including raffles and bake sales, brought in money for the council to spread throughout the community. It was all done in the spirit of helping your neighbor. The excitement aided recruiting; so did the hard work of Dechant's membership committee.

Virgil and Ann Dechant were married on August 20, 1951, in Liebenthal, Kansas.

Members pounded the pavement (or, in western Kansas parlance, "hit the dusty roads"), signing up new members one-by-one. The level of commitment to the cause shown by his fellow Knights—and friends—gave Dechant a tremendous level of enjoyment being grand knight.

"I must say, I had total support of all the members, particularly the older ones. I had my own fraternal brothers. They knew me inside and out. To get them to work together and pull down the same road, that took some doing, and I got great satisfaction out of that."

Other parts of the job also brought great satisfaction. During Dechant's first year as grand knight, he received a phone call at four o'clock on Columbus Day, shortly before the annual party that had given the council such local fame. On the line was Mrs. Adam Herrman, whose husband had recently died.

"Mr. Grand Knight, why is it that for the last 40 years I have been invited to every Columbus Day program and every other social event run by the council, and now that my Adam is gone, nothing?" she asked. "He had been a member of this council all this time. Does this mean that I can't come to any Knights of Columbus event?"

"Mrs. Herrman, you come," Dechant told her.

Dechant never forgot the phone call from Mrs. Herrman or the importance of looking out for widows and families of the Order, both their financial and familial needs.

In 1956, Dechant decided to take a leap. He had learned the implement business from his boss and mentor Bill Weigand, and as Weigand's political opportunities kept him away from day-to-day business, Dechant had acquired a good sense of running the business on his own. Now he was ready to go it alone. He opened

A large crowd gathered on the steps in front of St. Joseph Church in Liebenthal to greet the newly married couple.

Dechant Motor Company on Main Street in La Crosse. In time Dechant Motors would add a line of farm implements, but the company began by selling cars. Dechant acquired the rights to sell the American Motors line, known for its popular Rambler car. The chairman and president of American Motors was George Romney, future Michigan governor, with whom Dechant would one day work to promote charitable activities.

Just 26 years old, Virgil Dechant was now a Main Street business owner, a farmer, a husband, a grand knight in the Knights of Columbus, and a father of two. He was a busy man. In time he would only get busier.

CHAPTER TWO

The drive from La Crosse to Wichita, even by the pancake-flat standards of western Kansas, is mostly unexciting. It's a trip that covers roughly 150 miles of Kansas prairie, and most 1950s drivers made the jaunt in just under three hours. Other than seeing the sites in a few notable outposts such as Great Bend, Sterling, and Hutchinson, there was a lot of time to let your mind wander. Folks in this part of the world often refer to it as windshield time. If you were a talker, there were plenty of opportunities to talk; and if you were quiet, silence could last a long time. So you have to wonder: how many miles had passed before Phillip Dreher, Virgil Dechant's passenger on this particular day, worked up the nerve to ask his young grand knight what he was planning on doing with his new bride, Ann, who sat in the back seat?

The three of them were heading to Wichita for the annual statewide convention of the Kansas State Council of the Knights of Columbus, the first such statewide meeting for the Dechants. Women typically did not attend these meetings, a fact that had escaped Virgil. Somewhere between La Crosse and the Wichita Broadview Hotel where the meeting was to be held, Dreher leaned over and whispered into Dechant's ear, quietly enough that only Virgil would hear.

"Say, Virg, you're not bringing your wife to the convention, are ya?" Dreher asked.

Dechant was baffled. "Yeah—why wouldn't I?"

"Well, it's mostly for men," Dreher confessed.

This was news to Dechant. To Dreher's credit, he had broached the unpleasant topic politely, but that didn't erase the surprise still ringing in Dechant's ear. Thinking quickly, when they arrived in Wichita, the group made plans for Ann to stay with her sister Rosemary, who lived nearby. Dechant attended the meeting with Dreher and learned the ropes from other Kansas Knights in the process. He also made the acquaintance of a few young grand knights who, in the future, hoped to bring their wives along to socialize at K of C meetings. Like Dechant, they thought their predecessors' outdated thinking was due for an overhaul, and they aimed to do something about it.

The Knights of Columbus had been founded in New Haven, Connecticut, in 1882 by a Catholic priest, Father Michael J. McGivney, assistant pastor of St. Mary's Church in New Haven. McGivney's father had died at 48 when McGivney was in his first year of studies at a Jesuit seminary in Montreal, Canada, and the aspiring cleric worried that his dream of priesthood might have died right along with his father. Money was tight in the McGivney household, and Michael suspected he would have to abandon his dreams of holy orders to earn money his family desperately needed for survival. Fortunately, the bishop of Hartford arranged for aid so McGivney could continue his studies and, ultimately,

Virgil Dechant made it his crusade to include his wife Ann and other spouses at K of C functions.

become a priest. McGivney was ordained in 1877 in Baltimore's Cathedral of the Assumption by Baltimore's well-known Archbishop (later Cardinal) James Gibbons.

As a young priest in New Haven, McGivney all too often saw family dramas similar to his own repeated among his parishioners. Families would unexpectedly lose their breadwinner and patriarch, with devastating consequences. In those days, it was not easy for a Catholic immigrant to buy life insurance just anywhere. McGivney longed to do something about this problem; it was one of the world's wrongs he wished to right. He also began noticing significant growth in secret societies, which sometimes competed with organized religion for the time and attention of men he would rather have seen in his church pews and confessionals each week.

In the fall of 1881, McGivney reached out to young Catholic men in New Haven, hoping to entice them to join him in his newest venture, a Catholic fraternal organization that would provide a death benefit to the families of its members. A special meeting was held in the basement of St. Mary's Church on Hillhouse Avenue to discuss the plan.

Eighty men attended that meeting, including a large contingent that had formerly belonged to the Red Knights, a society formed by members of an Irish-Catholic militia shortly after the Civil War. However, like many fraternal organizations, the Red Knights hadn't been able to sustain their operations, and they broke up before the first meeting of McGivney's new order. Shortly after the meeting, McGivney's new group took the name "the Knights of Columbus." In 1882, the Order received a charter from the Connecticut General Assembly. That same year Father McGivney became the group's first insured member. It's noteworthy that McGivney, a child of Irish immigrants, and his compatriots chose as their patron such a universally well-regarded

American icon—Christopher Columbus—especially in an era when so many secret societies chose to honor heroes from "the old country" as a means of clinging to the last vestiges of their native identities. McGivney, perhaps, was looking to inaugurate an American society.

McGivney worked hard to grow his membership by reaching out across the diocese to plant the seed of his idea: to provide a $1,000 death benefit to the family of deceased members and a $5 weekly benefit to members who were unable to work because of illness. The former was, obviously, what we today call life insurance. The latter was essentially an early day disability policy.

By 1885, the Order suffered its first death and paid $963 to the family of Dennis J. O'Brien.

The O'Brien death was proof: McGivney's idea could work.

While McGivney's primary focus was taking care of family members by providing insurance, over time, as the Order grew and prospered, the fraternal activity of the Knights of Columbus expanded, too. This came with pluses and minuses. Fraternal spirit was strong, and brotherhood and camaraderie pushed many Knights of Columbus to assist in countless acts of charity and philanthropy in communities across the country and around the world. But somewhere along the way, McGivney's original intent, on occasion, had gotten lost. It had not been forgotten, simply misplaced. Thus, by the time Virgil Dechant became a member, the Knights of Columbus found itself functioning more like a men's club and less like a family driven fraternal organization, with some its members known for spending too much time in the club room and not enough time fixing the ills of society. Make no mistake—the Order still did great work in communities worldwide—but emphasis on the family had gotten lost in the shuffle.

Why? How? The answers to these questions are complicated. It's

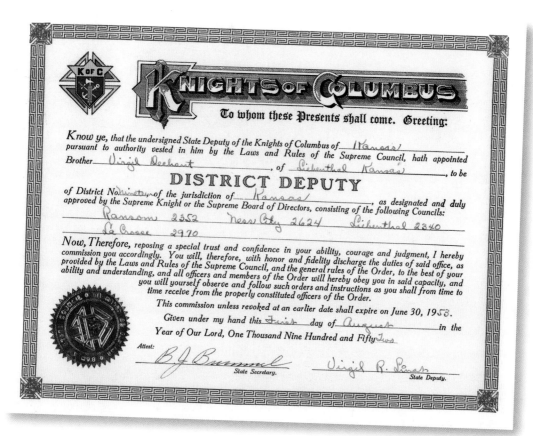

likely the era of Prohibition in the United States (1920-1933) incentivized membership in fraternal groups, which sometimes had alcohol stockpiled in speakeasies or other gathering spots. If one then follows the progression of major events in the history of the country, the next two such events are the Great Depression and World War II. The horrors of both left men looking for somewhere to go, away from their daily responsibilities, where they could bond with like-minded fellas and leave their real-world problems at the door. Answers to these problems, they thought, could be found at the local club, hall, or fraternal lodge. The many great works of the Knights of Columbus throughout these eras could mask what was going on at the foundation of the Order—and

Above: Charming and clean-cut, Virgil Dechant had a magnetic quality as a young grand knight in Kansas.

make no mistake, the Order's works were far-reaching—but over time, the Knights of Columbus had been pulled away, at least slightly, from its core mission, to care for all the needs of families.

So when a young Virgil Dechant and other fresh-faced grand knights from Kansas met at the Wichita meeting and discussed ending the unspoken code that forbade women from Knights of Columbus functions, this was no small step. This would be a major shakeup. But Dechant and his colleagues didn't let the potential consequences stop them.

"The following year, a few other young grand knights and I made up our minds that we were going to change that situation," Dechant said. "So we started bringing our wives to the conventions. And it shocked a few members. But, I must say, within a matter of a few years, everybody started thinking about bringing their wives too. Ever since that time, wives have been included as part of the Order. That started to transform the Order, at least in Kansas, into what it is today, a family organization. Along with the wives came the children, and it's been so much better for the whole Order.

"A council, to survive—especially in a town like La Crosse or Liebenthal but even in metropolitan areas like New York City—really needs to have families active. They need three legs: one is the member, another is his spouse, and then the parish priest or council chaplain. You'll get a lot of things done if they're all involved. So our actions weren't so much in rebellion to what the old guard was doing, but even then, at that time, the appeal for men to go out on their own like they did when the Order was founded had declined. A lot of wives were starting to work. These men felt more comfortable if their wives were also getting some benefit out of the Order. If they were getting benefit, they'd contribute much more than they'd receive. So it worked."

At Dechant's first state convention in Wichita, he was appointed as chairman of the Necrology Committee. On Sunday morning of the convention, State Secretary Mike Kamer approached Dechant and asked, "Do you have your report ready? At one o'clock we'll begin the memorial service."

Dechant was unaware that he was supposed to have prepared a report. Fortunately, the Necrology report was nothing more than a list of names (the Necrology Committee kept track of the deceased members of the Order in Kansas) that he would read during the ceremony.

"You better come with me," Kamer told Dechant.

Dechant followed Kamer up to his hotel room, and together they prepared a list of all the deceased members of the Knights in Kansas. Kamer typed the names while Dechant practiced pronouncing them. That afternoon, wearing his blue wool wedding suit, Dechant stepped up onto the stage and read the list without error—thanks to the Latin he had been exposed to at the seminary.

During Dechant's second year serving as grand knight of the Liebenthal Council, he was asked to serve as one of the state's district deputies, in charge of district 19. He was appointed by State Deputy Virgil R. Linot on August 1, 1952. It was an office he would hold until 1957. His district consisted of councils from Liebenthal, La Crosse, Ransom, and Ness City. In 1953, having moved into La Crosse with his wife Ann to start a family and operate his business, Dechant decided to transfer his membership to the council in La Crosse, #2970.

In comparison with their neighbors in the Liebenthal Council, the La Crosse Knights were Johnny-come-latelies. In the early days of the council, meetings were held in the basement of an old church. Degrees and other ceremonies were held on the second floor of an old grocery store. It would be decades before a parish center was built to hold

Above: Virgil and Ann joined other convention goers to celebrate his 1960 election as state deputy.

meetings and other parish functions. For Dechant, this presented an opportunity to help a young, up-and-coming council find its footing.

In 1956 Dechant took the Fourth Degree in Hays. By 1957, he was elected state treasurer of the Kansas State Council, a post he would hold for two years before he was appointed state membership director. Clearly, he was establishing a track record as someone who could rise fast within an organization. But what happened next came faster than anyone, even Dechant, could have predicted.

In 1960, Dechant was being considered for the position of state secretary; however, two of the men preparing to step into the role of state deputy, the state's highest office, had to bow out of consideration, one due to a health problem and the other because his employer moved him out of Kansas. Suddenly, the Kansas State Council needed a viable candidate for state deputy. Dechant was drafted for the office by a group of past state deputies, who recommended him to the convention delegation. He was in the right place at the right time.

Delegates to the Kansas State Convention in Hutchinson in 1960 elected Dechant state deputy. Just 29, he was one of the youngest men to ever hold the office in the entire Order.

On stationery from Hutchinson's Baker Hotel, Dechant scribbled down a few notes in preparation for his acceptance speech. Today, the notes are in a collection of materials at the Knights of Columbus Museum in New Haven. He wrote, "It's with deepest humility that I accept your tremendous vote of confidence...at this time, [this is] probably the greatest moment of my life. I wish to say this: God willing, I'll try to the best of my ability to make you a good state deputy."

The Knights of Columbus had been organized in Kansas in 1900, just 18 years after the Order had been founded in Connecticut. The state's first council, #534, started in Topeka, the capital, and others sprouted up in many of the state's small towns. Liebenthal's council began in 1922, and La Crosse came along in 1946.

By 1957, the Order in Kansas had grown to 18,000 members, but delighting over this number was fool's gold. At least that was the view of Bernard Brungardt, then chairman of the state's Committee on Lapsations. According to Roy Bird's 2000 history, *Fraternalism and Leadership: The Second Fifty Years of the Knights of Columbus in Kansas*, Brungardt used his platform at the 1956 state convention to take Kansas's state and local leadership to task for the growing number of inactive and absentee members. Brungardt's bottom-line position on the matter was that it was the fault of these supposed leaders when a

Top photo: A. H. "Tony" Knoeber, Francis Donnelly, and Virgil Dechant proudly sport their Kansas sunflowers.

Above: From left, Virgil Dechant, Ann Dechant, State Chaplain Fr. Donald J. Weber, Mary Donnelly, Francis Donnelly.

Above: Virgil Dechant, left, and Tony Knoeber, right, found time to sightsee during their 1960 visit to Atlanta for the supreme convention.

brother Knight suddenly lost interest in participation; it was the fault of the grand knights and district deputies and state officers for not making some part of the Order attractive to the common member. Bird speculated that Brungardt was only partially correct in his assessment of the membership situation. Another factor was a changing American culture, which included a large population of World War II veterans whose ideals and priorities had shifted in the aftermath of such a tremendous conflict.

Membership was just one hurdle the Kansas Knights would have to overcome in the second half of the 20th century. Another was a changing insurance market. Insurance growth began to plateau in the mid-1960s, likely because of the growth of other professional insurance forces that competed with the Knights of Columbus.

Bernard Brungardt, known to Dechant and other friends as "Ben," served as state deputy from 1950-1952. He was one of many Knights of Columbus who Dechant looked up to as he worked his way through the ranks in Kansas. While there may have been other men worth emulating, it was Brungardt whom Dechant idolized, and Dechant later said as much, referring to him as his mentor. There was much to admire about Brungardt, even in the professional world, where he worked as an attorney. He was from Hays, located 23 miles north of La Crosse, and was a member of Saint Joseph Council #1325, one of the state's oldest and largest, having been chartered in 1908. During his years serving the Knights, Brungardt was involved at many levels, including his aforementioned stint as the lapsation and reinstatement chairman (1954-1956). He also served as chairman of council development (1962-1964). Shortly after Dechant's election to state deputy, Brungardt invited him and other past state deputies for a celebration dinner at Al's Chickenette, a fried chicken hotspot on the south end of Hays. The dinner invitation made it clear that their relationship was built upon mutual admiration.

Another brother Knight whom Dechant admired was Jack Dowd, who served at all levels of the Order before his election as state deputy in 1948. Dowd, an employee of the Internal Revenue Service (IRS), later served the Order at the level of the Supreme Council in New Haven, where he began as a program consultant and later became the office director of the Catholic Information Service, where he worked with Father John McGuire. In 1963, Dowd would be named a Knight of the Order of St. Gregory the Great by Pope John XXIII—an honor also bestowed upon Brungardt.

Men like Brungardt and Dowd gave Dechant examples of leadership and a sense of how business was supposed to be run. So did Clarence Malone, whose work for the Supreme Council showed Dechant that someone from Kansas could reach those heights, if that person had the acumen and there was a need.

There were other Kansas Knights even closer in age than Brungardt, Dowd, and other past state deputies that Dechant became close with, including Dr. Harry Klenda, Emmet Blaes, Michael Kamer, Virgil Linot, Wilfred Schuler, Tony Knoeber, Vic Wasinger, Don Dreiling, and general insurance agents Ernie Tajchman, Gus Ley, John Rupp, and Ray Gottschalk, Dechant's brother-in-law.

"They were all very successful and very enthusiastic," Dechant said. "And they made a great team."

Camaraderie and fellowship bonded K of C members young and old in Kansas, including this group at Al's Chickenette.

Around the time of his election as state deputy, Dechant's business and personal affairs were moving almost as fast as his fraternal life. He and Ann added two children to the family: Karen, in 1959, and Robert, or "Bobby," in 1961. Tom and Dan, the older children, started school at St. Michael's parochial school in La Crosse, located within walking distance of the Dechant house.

By the time Tom and Dan enrolled at St. Michael's, the school was like new. A fire had destroyed the previous one-story frame school in 1953, but the parishioners of St. Michael's decided to rebuild. Dechant attended a meeting just two weeks after the fire to hear a contractor's proposal for building a new school, which was later approved by the parish. Construction began almost immediately, and just

Above: Dressed in white, Ann and Virgil prepare to leave for the States' Dinner in New Orleans in 1964.

seven months after the fire, the new St. Michael's parochial school was open for business. There, Tom and Dan, and later Karen, would get their start. The school, now closed, stands today and is used exclusively for religious education (CCD) classes.

Dechant Motors, Virgil's primary business interest, was doing well. He first operated the business out of a Standard Oil gas and service station on Main Street in La Crosse, but eventually the business outgrew that facility. Dechant needed something bigger, so he bought a factory on Highway 4, on the north end of La Crosse, which had been used to manufacture steel wagons. A significant build-out was needed, but the new facility was a clear step up for his growing concern. Dechant added a showroom and numerous upgrades to the building before reopening. In addition to the Rambler Motors franchise, Dechant began acquiring various short-line farm equipment franchises, an industry term used to describe smaller manufacturers that specialized in tillage and planting equipment. The short lines included Krause Plow, Hesston, New Holland, Crustbuster, and Richardson/Sunflower. Eventually the company would

Above: Young Dechants, from left, Karen, Danny, and Tom.

acquire the rights to sell Massey Ferguson implements, a full-line farm equipment manufacturer that was based in Canada.

Car sales would ebb and flow, sometimes in unpredictable flurries and barren dry spells, but over the long haul, especially in western Kansas, where the economy was driven principally by agriculture, implements were the lifeblood of the business. Dechant also hired new staff, including Elmer J. Meder, his brother-in-law (who had married Virgil's sister Mary Ann), who served as manager of parts and sales. Meder was a trustworthy, no-nonsense type who knew the La Crosse business community well, and he would prove to be one of the best hires Dechant ever made, as he would remain part of the business for decades.

Beyond cars and tractors, there was farming. This aspect of Dechant's business portfolio would, naturally, take longer to grow than his car business, but in time it would surpass the dealership in scale. At first, Dechant farmed land that he rented from his father, C.J., but he soon realized he needed to acquire his own land to grow the enterprise. In 1957, Virgil's parents gifted him and Ann a quarter section, or 160 acres, of farmland west of Liebenthal. The following year, Ann's parents gave the couple an 80-acre tract near the Dechant land. These start-up parcels gave Dechant the boost he was looking for. It would be nearly a decade before he could afford his first significant land purchase, but now he had gotten his foot in the door of the industry.

With decent cash flow from Dechant Motors, Dechant diversified his real estate interests. He began purchasing and developing various Main Street properties, including an IGA grocery store, a tavern, a law office, a parking lot, and a bank. He also developed an addition on the east end of town, which provided a few dozen lots where new housing could take root. This became known as the Dechant Addition to the City of La Crosse.

In the 1950s and '60s, the population of La Crosse hovered around 1,800 people. That number may seem small, but that period of time accounted for the largest population in the town's history, which dated back to 1876. Despite such seemingly limited resources, the community was the county seat of Rush County, which in those days included between 6,000 and 7,000 residents. When those people descended upon La Crosse, a fair amount of business was transacted, particularly for a small town. In that sense, it was a great setting to learn how to run a business. Your successes may have been modest in scale, but your failures didn't have to spell doom. And the young car dealer, with interests in farming and real estate, was proving to be one of Rush County's most zealous businessmen.

CHAPTER THREE

Sometimes it just pays to be in the car business.

That's especially true when you're a state deputy in the Knights of Columbus. Ask any state deputy in most any state and they'll likely tell you, if nothing else, the job requires near-daily correspondence and lots of driving. Access to a reliable car was a must. If you were the owner of Dechant Motors in La Crosse, Kansas, that car was often a Cadillac. The dealership may have sold American Motors Ramblers, but its head man knew the value of optics, especially in a small town.

A quick glance into Virgil Dechant's 1960 daily planner reveals just how busy the job of state deputy can keep you. Take the month of July, for example: On the 14th he was in Hays for an insurance meeting; on the 16th he traveled 300 miles to Kansas City for another meeting; he

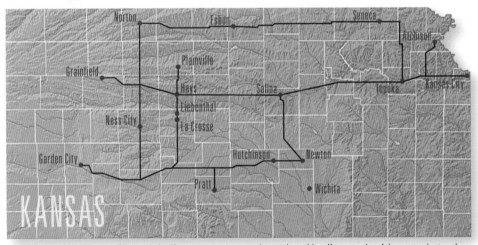

Virgil Dechant visited all corners of Kansas during his two-year term as state deputy; these cities offer a snapshot of those extensive travels.

attended a degree at Topeka council #2608 the following day, then an evening banquet at Pratt on the 23rd. He concluded the busy month by attending a corporate communion in Seneca on the 31st.

The rest of the summer (and fall) wasn't much different. His destinations included Garden City, Grainfield, Atchison, Newton, Norton, Ness City, Plainville, Esbon, and others. It seemed that whenever two or more Knights of Columbus were gathered, Dechant was there.

Paul Lenherr, from St. Mary's Council #657, who served as Kansas state deputy three decades after Dechant, said that part of the job description—the non-stop schedule of events—stayed the same, even many years later. "There were lots of after-hours phone calls," Lenherr said. "And traveling, every weekend. Of the 52 weekends, I was probably on the road 40 or 48 of them. I think I put 46,000 miles on my car over those two years."

The letter writing was nearly as time consuming. Almost daily, Dechant was sending off inquiries, answering questions, and accepting or declining invitations of all kinds—all by good, old-fashioned U.S. Mail. With no secretary, he handled the correspondence himself or dictated letters to his wife Ann, who was handier than he with a typewriter.

Many of Dechant's letters were directed at three Knights of Columbus insurance agents with whom he was particularly close; Ray Gottschalk, Gus Ley, and Ernie Tajchman. Tajchman, from Wichita, worked as a general insurance agent in western Kansas, handling a territory of 40 councils and nearly 6,000 members; Gottschalk later took over that territory. In one such correspondence shared between Tajchman, Gottschalk, and Dechant, Tajchman expressed to Dechant that "it is so wonderful to find you always so willing to sit down with us agents and get our side of the insurance feature of our great Order."

Another successful field agent and Dechant confidant in that part of the state was John Rupp, who in 1974 would become state deputy. From these men Dechant learned the marketing side of the insurance industry; he also witnessed firsthand the value life insurance could provide to families, often in desperate times.

"Growing up in Kansas, while I was getting involved with the Knights, I worked very closely with the general agents and field agents," Dechant said. "Working so closely with them, I came to understand the basic concept that our founder, Father McGivney, had in mind: to promote the benevolent benefits of the Order and, at the same time, provide for family welfare."

Around this time, a document was circulated among the Order's insurance agents titled "The 11 Commandments of a Knights of Columbus Insurance Agent." Its author is unknown, but the commandments, which offer a tremendous insight into the mindset of an agent and the fabric of the insurance program, read as follows:

- THE KNIGHTS OF COLUMBUS MEMBER is the most important person in our business.

- THE KNIGHTS OF COLUMBUS MEMBER is not dependent on us—we are dependent on him.

- THE KNIGHTS OF COLUMBUS MEMBER is not an interruption of our work—he is the purpose of it.

- THE KNIGHTS OF COLUMBUS MEMBER does us a favor when he calls—we are not doing him a favor by serving him.

- THE KNIGHTS OF COLUMBUS MEMBER is part of our business—not an outsider.

- THE KNIGHTS OF COLUMBUS MEMBER is not a cold statistic—

he is flesh and blood—a human being with feelings and emotions like our own.

- THE KNIGHTS OF COLUMBUS MEMBER is not someone with whom we are to argue or with whom we are to match wits.

- THE KNIGHTS OF COLUMBUS MEMBER is a person who brings us his wants—it is our job to fill his wants.

- THE KNIGHTS OF COLUMBUS MEMBER is deserving of the most courteous and attentive treatment that we can give him.

- THE KNIGHTS OF COLUMBUS MEMBER is the fellow that pays us our commission.

- THE KNIGHTS OF COLUMBUS MEMBER is the lifeblood of our business.

Dechant's oldest son Tom, who by 1960 was old enough to understand how intense a commitment his father kept to the Knights of Columbus, said most days during Virgil's tenure as state deputy started and ended with K of C matters. "Ray Gottschalk would stop by our house every morning about 9:30 to drink coffee, and they'd talk about the Knights of Columbus," he said. "And it seemed like every night, Vic Wasinger, who was then state secretary, would come by to discuss Knights of Columbus business. And later, it was Don Dreiling."

Tom's brother Dan remembers the same. He also remembers his father keeping demanding hours managing his business and fraternal commitments. "Back then he worked long hours," Dan Dechant recalled. "Long hours. I remember he always slept late. He probably went to the shop [Dechant Motors] in the mid morning and came home at ten o'clock at night. Most of the time we were home in bed by the time he got back from work. He worked crazy hours building that business."

When Virgil did finally come home, the work didn't end. "He would sit at his desk for hours, every night, working," remembered his daughter Karen. "Every night, in his work clothes. He never put his pajamas on and sat down. He worked and then went to bed. That was how he'd unwind, go to bed."

With such demanding hours and frequent absences, how did Dechant prevent an in-house mutiny? He and his children credit Ann for her tireless concern for their well-being. And there was the added benefit of their next-door neighbors, Ann's parents, Joe and Rosa Schafer, who had moved from their farm into the city of La Crosse. Their house on Hargrave Street sat immediately next to Virgil and Ann's.

"That allowed Dad and Mom to do their Knights of Columbus traveling with no worries about a babysitter," said Tom Dechant. "Grandpa would stay at the house and babysit. Grandma Schafer cooked for us. They did a lot of free babysitting—and worry-free babysitting."

From left, Bobby, Tom, Karen, and Dan Dechant assist in the kitchen.

During the academic year when Ann worked as a teacher, before Dan was old enough to attend school, he would accompany Ann to work every morning and wait until Joe Schafer came by to pick him up. Joe would take Dan to the family farm, where he would complete various chores while Dan watched and sometimes helped. The near-daily time together created a strong bond between grandfather and grandson. In later years, when the three oldest Dechant children were enrolled in grade school at St. Michael's, many days they walked to the Schafer residence during their lunch break, where Rosa would have prepared a midday meal, often fried chicken and French fries, the kids' favorite.

As state deputy, one of Dechant's major undertakings was an effort by the Knights of Columbus to promote vocations to religious life. The

movement came about when Dechant received a phone call from Bishop Mark K. Carroll, the Bishop of Wichita, who told Dechant that he felt it was time for lay organizations such as the Knights to involve themselves in promoting vocations to the priesthood. In the early 1960s, this was a rather novel way of thinking. The word "promoting" was rarely, if ever, used in conjunction with recruitment efforts into religious life. Rather, it was commonly thought that if an individual had a future as a priest or nun, the Holy Spirit

Mark K. Carroll, Bishop of Wichita.

would call that person to such a choice individually. Having spent some time himself as a seminarian at the Pontifical College Josephinum, Dechant was familiar with this line of thinking. However, he was ready and able to embrace a new model, one that wasn't oblivious to the power of the Holy Spirit, but, rather, was grounded in practicality and a simple understanding that in modern society, most any career path required some level of encouragement, even the priesthood.

At the bishop's suggestion, Dechant met with Carroll's vocations director, Father Edward Steinberger. Together, they developed a program designed to build awareness of religious vocations that could be used at the council level within the Knights of Columbus. Subsequently, the program was implemented, and, as Dechant recalls, "going very well." But it took until Dechant's second year as state deputy before the vocations initiative picked up sufficient momentum, and even then, there weren't enough results for it to be deemed an essential piece of the state council's portfolio. Dechant's successor as state deputy subsequently did not continue the program.

Later, Dechant would get the chance to pitch his vocations program to members of the supreme council. Those efforts were also met with some resistance, at least initially.

In the case of the vocations program, at least in the early 1960s in Kansas, it seems Dechant, Carroll, and Steinberger were simply the victims of bad timing, having arrived on the front end of an idea. In time, Catholics en masse would join them.

Marion F. Forst, Bishop of Dodge City.

One thing Catholics en masse were rallying behind in the early 1960s was their U.S. President, John Fitzgerald Kennedy. Kennedy was representative of social change in the country, and this attitude of change made its way to the plains of Kansas. "The 1960s constituted a decade of change for the Knights of Columbus in Kansas: change in programs; change in public perception; change in attitude among the members; and change in the Order itself," wrote author Roy Bird in *Fraternalism and Leadership: The Second Fifty Years of the Knights of Columbus in Kansas*.

Kennedy was well supported by members of the K of C in Kansas; he was, after all, Catholic, and a Knight of Columbus. His election to the presidency signaled to Catholics that their views and beliefs, which for so many decades seemed to have been discriminated against at the highest levels of American politics, would now be heard.

Beyond the vocations initiative, the Knights of Columbus in Kansas worked closely with the state's four bishops: Edward J. Hunkeler, Archbishop of Kansas City; Mark K. Carroll, Bishop of Wichita; Frederick W. Freking, Bishop of Salina; and Marion F. Forst, Bishop of Dodge City. In the mid-1950s, the Kansas Knights had chartered the Charities Aid Foundation with the intention of promoting and supporting (financially) activities of a religious, charitable, and educational purpose throughout Kansas. The Foundation's first gift, in the amount of $10,000, helped fund Catholic student centers at state colleges in Kansas, after the state's four bishops appealed to Kansas State Deputy A.H. "Tony" Knoeber in 1959 about using the funds for this purpose. In 1960 and 1961, State Deputy Dechant continued the bishops' funding in the same amount. Dechant was joined in May 1961 by numerous past state deputies to present the offering to the four bishops.

Through these dealings and other mutual interests, Dechant got to know the Kansas bishops well. History would prove this true of most any state deputy who worked so closely with the clergy. In particular, he became especially close with Bishop Marion Forst of Dodge City. The pair made a natural connection; after all, La Crosse was located in the Dodge City Diocese. But beyond that they shared a mutual respect and a concern for Catholic activities in the sometimes-neglected plains of western Kansas. This strong bond would continue for decades.

The Pennies from Heaven program was closely allied with the Charities Aid Foundation. It had been developed by Emmet Blaes during his tenure as state deputy during the early 1940s. Pennies from Heaven was originally created to assist victims of a military airplane disaster

Virgil Dechant, back left, shares a meal with colleagues in the Kansas State Council of the Knights of Columbus.

in Wichita whose homes had been destroyed. By the time the Charities Aid Foundation came into being, the Pennies program was intended to help grow the foundation's funds through the contributions of pennies that had been saved by member Knights over the course of the year. In 1963 it took off under the leadership of Francis Donnelly, Dechant's successor. Today the program is used for disaster relief across the state and across the world.

Membership was another key initiative during Dechant's Kansas administration. During his tenure as membership director, the Kansas Knights had made increases in insurance and associate membership, significant enough to draw the attention of Supreme Knight Luke Hart. By the time Dechant became state deputy, the Order had instituted a program called "Every Council Active," and Dechant responded by fulfilling the charge, adding at least one new member to every council in the state during his two years as state deputy.

"Membership growth is so important," he said. "The more manpower you have, the more effective your programs will be. But it seems like the hardest thing for members to do is go out and recruit new members. They want to do it, but they seldom get it done, so you really have to motivate the membership to do that. With the Every Council Active program, I helped add at least one new member to every council in Kansas. That's a difficult achievement to attain, but I was blessed in having the assistance of some wonderful priests."

In early 1961, Dechant helped save a council from closing in Esbon, Kansas, a small town in Jewell County, located in the north central part of the state, near the Nebraska border. Esbon Council #1148 had stopped growing, and Dechant's predecessors as state deputy thought it should be closed. It had been one of the state's earliest councils, having been chartered in 1906 with 39 members, but by 1960 it had fallen on hard times.

The thought of closing a council was sacrilege to Supreme Knight Luke Hart, and Dechant was familiar with Hart's feelings on such matters. Hart believed that once a Knights of Columbus council was needed in a community, it would always be needed. So Dechant resolved to reactivate the council. He was aided by a willing parish priest, Father James Grennan of Esbon, who felt the same as Dechant. Together, they reactivated the council from insolvency.

The news of Esbon's revival caught the attention of Supreme Knight Hart in New Haven. Hart wrote to Dechant on March 3, 1961, telling him, "I am indeed delighted to know of the splendid result of your efforts to reestablish the above council and put it on an active footing. I congratulate you and I extend to you the thanks and appreciation of the Supreme Council."

Dechant's Esbon turnaround became an example for Hart to use Order wide. On occasion, state deputies from other states would be faced with similar circumstances, and he now had an archetype for how to save a council from the brink of failure. Hart wrote:

I wish that all the state deputies would have the same enthusiasm with their work that you have manifested in connection with this council. Yesterday I had a letter from a State Deputy in which he asked permission to arrange for the forfeiture of the charter of a council that had 51 members, of whom 29 are

---

HART
KNIGHT

File 1 - Item 34

Knights of Columbus

COLUMBUS PLAZA

NEW HAVEN 7, CONN.

March 3, 1961.

Mr. Virgil C. Dechant,
State Deputy,
LaCrosse,
Kansas.

Dear Brother Dechant:

The information contained in your letter to me of the 28th ult. that Esbon Council 1148 is being reactivated is indeed very gratifying.

Esbon Council has been in existence for more than half a century. It has had a part in all of the great works the Order has done for the Church and for the Catholic people throughout that entire period, including the endowment of the Catholic University, the great program of service for our armed forces during the First World War, the favorable decision with reference to the Oregon School Law, the relief of our co-religionists in Mexico, the amendment of the Pledge of Allegiance to the Flag whereby by the addition of the words "under God" thirty million people in our country daily acknowledge their dependence upon Almighty God, the cancellation of the invitation to Tito to visit this country and the saving of Artukovic from extradition and certain execution, the erection of the Bell Tower on the Campanile at the National Shrine of the Immaculate Conception and the Catholic Advertising Program, which has resulted in 3,968,831 inquiries concerning the Catholic religion, the enrollment of 419,165 persons for instruction in the Catholic religion and which last week alone brought 10,049 inquiries and 1,368 enrollments.

None of these things would have been possible except for the unity of the Catholic manhood of America through and under the auspices of the Knights of Columbus. Every Catholic man should want to have a part in this continuing activity on behalf of Holy Mother Church by our Order and I am sure that all of those who have been members of Esbon Council in the past must take pride in the fact that they have helped to make it possible.

The news of the reactivation of the council has given me a great thrill and I want to extend to you, to Father James Grennan, to all of those who have participated in this movement and to each and every member of the council my personal thanks and those of the Supreme Council.

Sincerely yours,

Supreme Knight.

LEH:meb

LUKE E. HART
SUPREME KNIGHT

File 1 - Item 32

Knights of Columbus

COLUMBUS PLAZA

NEW HAVEN 7, CONN.

March 3, 1961.

Mr. Virgil C. Dechant,
State Deputy,
LaCrosse,
Kansas.

Re: Esbon Council 1148

Dear Brother Dechant:

Your letter of the 28th ult. has just come to hand and I am indeed delighted to know of the splendid result of your efforts to re-establish the above council and put it on an active footing. I congratulate you and I extend to you the thanks and appreciation of the Supreme Council.

I wish that all the State Deputies would have the same enthusiasm with their work that you have manifested in connection with this council. Yesterday I had a letter from a State Deputy in which he asked permission to arrange for the forfeiture of the charter of a council that had 51 members, of whom 29 are insurance members. I am not sure that he will be pleased with what I said to him in my letter but I told him what God loves, the truth.

You are most fortunate in having the enthusiastic support of Father Grennan. This other State Deputy also had the support of the pastor. He wanted to run up the white flag and surrender.

I am glad to comply with your request for a letter of congratulation to the council and I am sending the same to you herewith. I am also writing to Father Grennan to thank him for his fine cooperation.

Sincerely yours,

Supreme Knight.

LEH:meb

insurance members. I am not sure that he will be pleased with what I said to him in my letter but I told him what God loves, the truth.

You are most fortunate in having the enthusiastic support of Father Grennan. This other state deputy also had the support of the pastor. He wanted to run up the white flag and surrender.

Dechant's Esbon triumph was more significant than just a notch on his belt. Time would prove it a wise decision for the state council and the Order. "In a time when communities in rural Kansas are struggling for survival, Knights of Columbus Council #1148 in Esbon, Kansas, has played a key role in keeping our Church and community vibrant," were the words used to describe the council's success in Roy Bird's 2000 history of the Knights in Kansas. Once it was back on solid footing, members of the Esbon council promoted youth and family activities within the parish community, helped with parish cleaning and cemetery upkeep, sponsored seminarians, and contributed charitable dollars to those most in need. The council also received the John F. Kennedy Award, three Father McGivney awards, and was recognized as a Star Council six times from 1980 to 2000.

In early 1962, Dechant took a hard look at his efforts to increase membership. The results did not please him. In 1961, he showed a net increase of 150 members (521 new members minus 371 suspended members), a number that he felt was disappointing, given the amount of emphasis he and the other state officers had placed on membership. So, Dechant doubled down. He held eight evening meetings with district deputies throughout the state over the winter of 1961-'62, intended primarily to emphasize the importance of increasing membership. He also wanted to hear from his district deputies about the problems they encountered trying to increase membership in the field. He deemed these meetings a success and felt confident that the results would start to show, given enough time. He and Membership Chairman Don Dreiling spent considerable time and effort planning open houses and other recruitment events. At some of these events, they played two films about the Order, "Noble Heritage" and "Living Traditions," to help spice up their presentation.

These efforts would yield significant gains. At the time Dechant took office, 21,417 men were members of the Kansas Knights of Columbus; by the conclusion of his tenure as state deputy, that membership had grown to 22,450, an increase of 1,033 members.

Related to the membership battle, Dechant probed deeper into the way councils were organized. He spent a day in Wichita in January 1962 to visit with pastors from various parishes about his membership worries. He also used these meetings to float an idea he'd been contemplating, parish councils.

While it might come as a surprise to the modern-day Knights of Columbus member, there was an era in which the

STATE DEPUTY
Virgil C. Dechant
CA 2-2791
La Crosse, Kansas

STATE SECRETARY
Victor Wasinger
1906 Marshall Road
Hays, Kansas

STATE TREASURER
Marcus A. Gottschalk
112 West 4th
Coffeyville, Kansas

Knights of Columbus

KANSAS STATE COUNCIL

Charity-Unity-Fraternity-Patriotism

STATE CHAPLAIN
Rev. Donald J. Weber
118 North Ninth Street
Salina, Kansas

STATE WARDEN
Nicholas Theis
Troy, Kansas

STATE ADVOCATE
Edwin J. Dreiling
4000 East Central
Wichita, Kansas

PAST STATE DEPUTY
A. H. Kneber
1111 Downing
Hays, Kansas

Dear Catholic Friend:

It is not by chance that I am writing you this letter, but rather through the recommendation of your Pastor and the fellow Catholic men of your parish.

The subject I am about to discuss with you may play an important role in your future life.

As the State Deputy of the Knights of Columbus in Kansas, I want to invite you to join the greatest Order of Catholic men in the world. The Knights of Columbus is an organization composed of over 1,000,000 Catholic men in the United States, Canada, Mexico, Cuba and the Philippines.

Since its origin over 75 years ago it has prospered on the principles of Charity, Unity, Fraternity, and Patriotism. The late Pope Pius XII referred to the Order as the "Strong Right Arm of the Catholic Church" because it has constantly been the maneuvering elbow of the Clergy and the Heirarchy in defending the fundamentals of our Faith. It has been particularly active in preserving the parochial school system and in preventing unfair taxation of our institutions. It has contributed greatly to stamping out, or at least neutralizing, religious prejudice through its Catholic Advertising Program. Through its project of microfilming of the Vatican documents it has contributed greatly to the study of the development of Western civilization.

The Knights of Columbus is one of the largest fraternal benefit societies in the world through its unique insurance program available to its members in many diversified plans.

We are enclosing several pieces of literature which will give you more detailed information about our Order.

We want you to know that we need you and that we would like for you to become a member of our great Order. Let's hope that we'll be able to call you "Brother Knight" in the near future.

Sincerely yours,

Virgil C. Dechant
State Deputy

Order's many councils existed separately from Catholic parishes. Councils would sprout up that were composed of members from one, two, three, or more different parishes. This created conflicts of interest. Consider, for example, a K of C council that included members from five or six different Catholic parishes. When it came time for the Knights of Columbus to initiate activities among the various parishes, where did they start? Oftentimes, the answer was nowhere. Their resources were insufficient to serve so many parishes, and, rather than risk offending any of the parishioners by conducting activities in some but not all of the parishes, they'd simply do nothing, or very little.

"We had a lot of councils that were composed of numerous parishes in those days," Dechant said. "I could see that all of their revenue and time was usually spent keeping the club room going. When they were asked what they had done for the parish, their excuse was, 'Well, we've got too many parishes, and what we do for one we must do for the others.' To get around that, it made sense to start the council at the parish level and meet within the parish boundaries. That way, the council could be the right arm of the parish priest."

Tom Zarda, who would later serve as the state deputy of Kansas, saw countless examples of council stagnation during his early days with his own council in Shawnee, Kansas, which included members from six or seven different parishes in the Kansas City area. Zarda joined the Order in 1952 at age 18. Immediately, he observed the same problems as Dechant. "We couldn't serve those six or seven different parishes," Zarda said. "If you were a council of, say, five parishes, you didn't know if this guy or that guy was going to church. You didn't know if you could influence him to go to church. So many times we didn't do anything because we were afraid of offending our members because we did one thing here and didn't do the same thing there."

The verdict from the four Wichita pastors was clear: three of the four welcomed the idea of starting parish-based councils and even asked that their parish serve as the host parish once the new councils were formed. It seemed Dechant's idea had merit.

In a 1962 letter to Supreme Knight Hart, Dechant described for Hart the three councils in Wichita, #691, #3677, and #4118. "Together these councils represent a total membership of 1,458 members," he wrote. "There are approximately 7,000 potential Catholic men living in this area. While all three councils are showing a definite improvement in the field of membership this year, they have actually not been able to scratch the surface."

Dechant also realized an inherent roadblock to his parish council theory: selling the concept to K of C members who were already rooted in a particular council and would be reluctant to switch on the grounds of parish affiliation. But Dechant didn't back off his idea, even asking Hart for data on a similar experiment with councils in St. Louis, Missouri. "It is my feeling that until we get more councils in this area, we will never realize the absorption that we should have," he wrote Hart.

True to form, Hart wrote to Dechant in response to his parish council idea. Hart was less critical of Dechant's membership efforts than Dechant was of himself, noting that he was "greatly pleased with the evidence of industry that you have given to the work of the Order in Kansas." Hart pointed out that on July 1, 1960, Kansas had 36 councils that had not produced a new member for more than a year, but in just six months under Dechant's leadership, that number had been trimmed to six. It was "a record of which you may well be proud," Hart wrote.

Regarding Dechant's idea of forming parish councils, it seemed that the supreme knight was intrigued by the idea but uncertain of the potential effects. "It might be well to let the membership of a parish

Virgil Dechant, right, received a commemorative gift (a gold ring) from District Deputy Paul Sramek upon the completion of his term as state deputy.

form the nucleus for a new council but I am not sure that it is a good thing to represent it as a parish council," Hart concluded.

It seems Hart was drawing on experience from his own council, Kenrick #686 in St. Louis, which had initially been organized from members of St. Ann's parish. By the time of his correspondence with Dechant, Hart figured that just five percent of the council's membership came from St. Ann's. Hart assumed the fluid nature of parish membership would contribute to a similar amalgamation of K of C councils, thus undermining the intent of parish councils. Dechant, on the other hand, was presuming the Order would add councils in more parishes, thus working toward a utopian 1:1 ratio of parishes and councils. In such a model, a Knights of Columbus member who moved his family into a different parish could then simply transfer his K of C membership to his new parish.

The letters between Hart and Dechant might be the first documented modern-day missives on the subject of forming councils by parish, but the genesis of the idea actually dates back to the Order's earliest days. In April 1882, Father Michael J. McGivney, acting as the financial and corresponding secretary of the Knights of Columbus, issued a letter to other priests in Connecticut to explain the formation of the Knights of Columbus and to encourage the formation of new councils. "Our primary object is to prevent our people from entering *Secret Societies*, by offering the same, if not better, advantages to our members," McGivney wrote. "Secondly, to unite the men of our Faith throughout the Diocese of Hartford, that we may thereby gain strength to *aid* each other in time of sickness; to *provide* for decent burial, and to render pecuniary assistance to the families of deceased members."

McGivney finished his letter with the following appeal, which seems to indicate his preference that councils form within Catholic parishes: "Hoping you will give this matter your kind consideration, and that you will exert your influence in the formation of a Council in your parish, we hold ourselves in readiness to forward any information desired."

Perhaps aided by their frequent correspondence—and a mutual passion to grow the Knights of Columbus—Dechant developed a strong admiration for Luke Hart and his leadership style. Hart was a lawyer, a political conservative, and the first man to occupy the office of supreme knight as a full-time job. His leadership style was decidedly throwback. When he was awarded the job he decided to move to New Haven so he'd be better equipped to handle his new duties from the head office of the supreme council. In doing so, he hoped to establish a precedent for future supreme knights to follow. History would prove this arrangement most effective.

Knights of Columbus historian Christopher Kauffman referred to Hart as "the most thoroughly prepared man ever to hold the highest office of the Order," and it was a hard point to refute. By the time he took the job in 1953, Hart had attended more than 30 supreme conventions—many as supreme advocate—and had been heavily involved with the Order for most of his life. In the process he had formulated his own ideas about how the Order would best function. Moving to New Haven was one such idea. Another one was helping modernize the Knights' insurance operations. Hart, with his legal expertise, had led the effort to adopt a universal code that governed fraternal benefit societies in all states. And he embraced a new investment philosophy, one that he had formed before he became supreme knight and one that the Order would continue after his years in New Haven. Rather than investing in low-yield bonds, Hart decided, at the

Dechant was all smiles as he played along with this initiation ritual into the Past State Deputies Club.

recommendation of friends in other comparable insurance companies, to invest in real estate. He embraced a lease-back real estate philosophy, in which the Knights would buy property and then lease it back to the seller. According to historian Kauffman, no such lease-back agreement was more noteworthy than the Order's 1953 purchase of the grounds upon which Yankee Stadium resided in the Bronx, New York. The Knights purchased the property for $2.5 million, then leased it back to the Yankees for an initial term of 28 years with options for an additional 60 years with a fixed-rate rent of $182,000 per year. Hart joked that the $2.5 million purchase check was the largest check he had ever signed.

Not all of Hart's changes were met with great enthusiasm, especially at the home office in New Haven. This only complicated his persona. For example, Hart felt that any business, even the Knights of Columbus, shouldn't have two paid holidays in a month.

"Hart toughened everything up, to a fault," said Bob Lane, then a recent high school graduate who had taken a summer job with the Knights. "That got everybody stirred up. These guys went out and solicited a union—an office union—so we had a strike. We had a strike in August of 1955, and I was in the union."

No sooner had Lane become a part of the union than he found himself standing in a picket line. His father, a career railroad painter, asked his son what he was doing. It was a question to which Lane had no response. Fortunately for Lane, Hart, and the rest of the Order, the strike was resolved in less than a week. But Hart had made his point: he could be

Ann and Virgil Dechant, facing page, board a bus with other convention delegates, including Mr. and Mrs. D. Francis Sullivan, supreme secretary, center.

tough in matters of business and negotiation, sometimes, even, to a fault. Lane would eventually parlay his startup job into a full-time position in the accounting department and later into the office of supreme secretary.

Dechant, the young state deputy from Kansas, saw Hart's business savvy and commitment to the Order and took notice. Of Hart, he said, "He ruled with an iron hand, but he knew the insurance program. He governed forcefully, but he still had compassion in some of his more difficult decisions. And he always had the members' good in mind."

To Dechant, Hart's model of leadership seemed like a good one to emulate.

Dechant first met Hart in 1956 as a delegate to the supreme convention in Detroit, Michigan. Over the next few years, the two shared other brief exchanges in person, including a 1960 meeting when Dechant, then state deputy, had invited Hart and his board of directors to hold a meeting in Topeka, Kansas, in honor of the retirement of Supreme Director Clarence Malone, a Kansan. At the retirement reception at Malone's home, Ben Brungardt visited with Hart and advised him to keep an eye on Dechant, who Brungardt felt was one of the Order's rising young stars. This was a significant encounter because Brungardt and Hart had long been at odds over various K of C matters, but at this meeting, the two put their past disagreements aside.

Then in 1961 Hart appointed Dechant chairman of the Good of the Order Committee. As part of his duties at the supreme convention in Denver, Colorado, Dechant was asked to deliver a report to the convention delegates on behalf of his committee. Before he gave his remarks, Dechant asked Hart to review his report. Hart agreed and asked Dechant to come see him in his room at the convention hotel in Denver.

Dechant came to Hart's suite, and the supreme knight asked him to take a seat while he reviewed his report. On the coffee table in front of Dechant's chair were two albums full of pictures that Hart had taken during a recent trip to Rome, Italy, where he and other members of the K of C board of directors had been received by Pope John XXIII. While Hart reviewed the report, Dechant looked through the albums, in awe at the photographs of Hart standing next to the leader of the Catholic Church.

Hart completed his review—as Dechant recalls, he corrected the document mostly for grammar—and gave Dechant his blessing to deliver

A well-traveled family: from left, Ann, Dan, Tom, Karen, Virgil, and Bobby Dechant.

it. The following year at the supreme convention in Massachusetts, Hart asked Deputy Supreme Knight Dr. John McDevitt to bring Dechant and his entire family—wife Ann and their four children—by his table for a formal introduction during a Boston baked bean supper for the convention delegates.

Admiration between Hart and Dechant appears to have been a two-way street, for obvious reasons. Dechant saw in Hart a model for leadership, a man of principle, with years of experience at all levels of the Order. In Dechant, Hart saw potential. The young state deputy from Kansas was a hard worker, entrepreneurial, and willing to make his Knights of Columbus commitment a way of life. Plus, he looked the part. While many of the men involved with the supreme council were of advancing age, Dechant was young and vibrant, with a charming wife and a growing family.

Having introduced his young family to the supreme knight in Boston, Dechant loaded his family into the car in the summer of 1962 and headed back to Kansas. Their 1,700-mile journey home would be one ideally suited to singing "Ninety-Nine Bottles of Beer on the Wall" and "King of the Road" until everyone in the car became hoarse. With a car full of children, it was a tall ask of any parents, but at least they'd be riding in the comfort of a Dechant Motors Rambler Ambassador.

As Dechant well knew, sometimes it just pays to be in the car business. Especially when you're a state deputy in the Knights of Columbus.

ight-year-old Dan Dechant looked helpless. The odor of charred steel and burning rubber was still fresh, wafting in the warm Kansas breeze. The busier-than-normal traffic flow on Highway 4 that morning was no coincidence.

There had been a fire.

Wearing a white T-shirt and blue jeans, Dan sat on an upside-down crate with his arms folded, just yards away from his father's implement dealership east of LaCrosse, and watched as firemen put out the remaining flames

In Building Only Short Time . . .

Implement Store Burns

An early morning fire Wednesday destroyed the Dechant Motor and Implement Company building on Highway 4 east of La Crosse.

Reported around 4:30 by Duane Zimmerman who had noticed smoke coming out of the building as he was preparing to leave home, the fire had gained enough headway

was noticed. Dechant reports that while the contents of his safe were saved, all his other records were destroyed.

The fire loss to building and contents has not been set, but unofficial estimates place the loss at around $50,000. Insurance adjusters were at the fire site Thursday morning working but report it will be several

from the blaze that had destroyed the building—and, potentially, the family's livelihood.

"What now?" he thought to himself.

A *Rush County News* photographer was on hand to capture the scene from the boy's point of view. The photo he snapped ran in the newspaper that week. The cutline read: "It was a sad show."

It was indeed a sad show that morning, June 27, 1963. How it had all come about was something of a mystery.

Virgil Dechant had been working at Dechant Motors until midnight, finishing up some business with Julius Pfeifer, a custom harvester from Cut Bank, Montana. When he left, everything at the business appeared in order. At 4:30 a.m., Duane Zimmerman was preparing to leave his house when he noticed smoke emitting from the building. When firemen showed up to battle the blaze, "heat was popping out the windows of the concrete and steel building," according to newspaper reports. It was a particularly hot fire, and the store's inventory of tires burned easily, which just made matters worse. Firemen battled the blaze for several hours before they got it under control.

When Dechant showed up to survey the damage the next morning, he found the contents of his safe were secure. However, all his other records had been destroyed. The building itself was destroyed. The newspaper unofficially estimated the loss at $50,000. The fire was determined to be the work of an arsonist drifter. Apparently this person had started the blaze during the four-

It Was A Sad Show

DANNY DECHANT, 8-year-old son of Mr. and Mrs. Virgil Dechant of La Crosse watches as firemen douse the last remaining embers in the early morning fire at his Daddy's implement building on Highway 4 just east of La Crosse. Unlike the natural fascination most small boys have for fires, this was one conflagration that young Danny didn't enjoy witnessing. (News Photo) hour window between Dechant's departure and Zimmerman first noticing smoke.

Dechant agreed to a settlement with the insurance company; as part of the deal he was able to keep whatever salvage existed. He arranged for the heavy parts to be cleaned and sold at a discount.

Between the insurance and the parts sale, Dechant was able to recover his loss. But one problem still persisted: what about the future of Dechant Motors?

Dechant's forgettable week turned downright horrible on July 3 when he learned his younger brother Donald, one day shy of his 26th birthday, had been killed in a tractor accident two miles east of Liebenthal. These sorts of accidents were not entirely uncommon in the farming communities of western Kansas, but that fact provided little solace.

The sudden and unexpected death left the family devastated.

Donald, like Virgil, was a member of the Knights of Columbus, having joined in 1955 at age 18 as an insurance member. He later became a Fourth Degree member of the Order. Donald was a husband and father of two young boys. His burial Mass was held at St. Joseph Church in Liebenthal, and he was then laid to rest in the Liebenthal Catholic Cemetery.

If ever there was an opportunity to leave the car business behind and seek out another career, this was it. Virgil Dechant could make a clean break. But he was not about to throw in the towel on the business he'd spent seven years building.

Dechant purchased a property on Main Street in La Crosse and built a new, modern, steel building to house his dealership. Then in December 1964 he acquired the franchise rights to sell Ford cars and trucks. He subsequently dropped the Rambler line. One noteworthy benefit of the

The Massey Ferguson line of implements was a perfect complement to Ford automobiles at Dechant Motors. Here, Virgil and Ann preview a new tractor line at an introductory show in Mexico City.

Ford franchise was its full truck line, which was a perfect complement to the farm equipment that the dealership already sold.

Dechant's timing seemed clairvoyant. That year Ford released its popular Mustang automobile, with a list price of $2,300. The Mustang would topple the Model-A as Ford's most successful automobile launch; sales were aided by numerous popular culture appearances, including the car's cameo in the 1964 James Bond film *Goldfinger*. Dechant capitalized on the Mustang's popularity by sponsoring the athletic teams at St. Michael's Grade School—aptly called the St. Michael's Mustangs. When he got together with his Knights of Columbus pals, it seemed they were more interested in asking Dechant about the Mustang than discussing fraternal matters.

As for fraternal matters, they were going about as well as the sales of the Ford Mustang. In August 1963, at the annual convention in Milwaukee, Wisconsin, Dechant was elected to the board of directors of the supreme council of the Knights of Columbus, having been recommended and strongly supported by Supreme Knight Luke E. Hart. A Kansan joining the national board was not unprecedented: Clarence Malone, one of Dechant's near contemporaries, had already earned such a distinction, serving from 1951-1963. So had James Gibbons and Michael Healy, two state deputies from Topeka, who served from 1923-'30 and 1930-'37, respectively. However, it was no small feat, especially considering Dechant's relative youth (he was 32 years old). It's worth noting that it was Malone who formally nominated Dechant to succeed him on the board, a moment that Malone later called "my biggest single thrill."

The most noticeable change to Dechant's lifestyle as a result of his board appointment was increased travel. Rather than simply driving the roads of the Kansas plains, Dechant now found himself visiting places such as Missouri, Nebraska, North Dakota, Oklahoma, Colorado and Utah. During these travels he came to know many of the Order's insurance agents in these states, just like those he befriended in Kansas. These men included Jim McCue of Missouri, Herb Kappel of North Dakota, Dave McKinney of Colorado, and Ed Peters of Nebraska.

"I got to know those agents, and I got to know of their difficulties," Dechant said. "And I learned the areas where the Order had to improve in providing services."

The added travel may have felt burdensome to Dechant, but his kids viewed it in a different light.

Dan Dechant said, "One of the big pluses that made our family unique in La Crosse was that every summer we took a vacation, i.e. the K of C supreme convention. I got to think that was the norm. Every year we drove to the supreme convention and had a fabulous vacation. Most people in La Crosse never even left Rush County. Every summer I had a week-long vacation that most of my friends didn't have, and I felt over privileged because we did that."

Denver. Boston. Baltimore. Miami Beach. Every year was a new destination. At the 1964 supreme convention in New Orleans, Louisiana, there was a special event one evening for kids. The Dechants were notified that the older kids—Tom and Dan—were expected to show up in formal attire, such as a sport coat. Virgil felt the optics of proper clothing were no different than a small-town businessman driving an attractive car, so he took Tom and Dan on an hours-long shopping excursion in New Orleans to find two sport coats that fit. The net cost of the whole ordeal was somewhere in the neighborhood of $40, recalled Tom Dechant.

Dechant's election to the board of directors was the last such elec-

The jet-setting family from Kansas. From left, Ann, Tom, Dan, and Virgil Dechant heading off to a supreme convention.

Dr. John McDevitt, right, offered Virgil Dechant, center, the chance to come to Connecticut and work full-time for the Knights of Columbus. Dr. John Griffin, left, and George Turner, far right, joined Dechant to congratulate McDevitt on his 1964 election to supreme knight in St. Louis.

tion during the Luke Hart era. Hart died on February 19, 1964, at the age of 84. Deputy Supreme Knight John W. McDevitt, from Massachusetts, who'd spent his career in the field of education as a teacher, principal, and school board member, would replace him. He was elected in St. Louis after Hart's funeral. McDevitt had also served as chairman of the Massachusetts State Board of Education.

Historian Christopher Kauffman noted that McDevitt was the first supreme knight born in the twentieth century. McDevitt had also been the first deputy supreme knight to hold the job from the home office in New Haven, taking a page from Hart's philosophy of running the Order from its place of origin.

The differences between McDevitt and Hart were clear. McDevitt seemed more capable than Hart of using consensus building as a business methodology and less prone to—using Dechant's words—ruling "with an iron hand." In time, Dechant recalled, McDevitt would prove to be "the right man at the right time after Vatican II."

"He was loyal to a 'T' to the magisterium of the church," Dechant said of McDevitt. "And he led the way for the Order to get involved in pro-life activities and various other social programs that helped bring about the future of the Order.

He opened the installation of state and council officers and memorial services to spouses."

McDevitt was instrumental in raising the racial awareness of the Knights of Columbus. In 1966, early in his tenure as supreme knight, McDevitt announced that the Knights would help sponsor the John La Farge Institute, named in honor of La Farge, a Jesuit priest, author, and longtime advocate for social awareness who had died in 1963. At the supreme convention a year later, McDevitt updated delegates on the progress of the institute and noted the importance of involving Christian moral principles in the many social dialogues of modern society.

One such example of the differences between Hart and McDevitt involved the Order's presence in Mexico. Late in his tenure as supreme knight, Hart, convinced that the insurance program managed by the Mexico State Council was not fully in compliance with the Order's rules, placed stronger controls over Mexican insurance operations. This was met with great resistance from the Mexico State Council and the Archbishop of Mexico City, Miguel Dario Miranda, who advised the state council to ignore the supreme knight's demands. Hart countered by urging the board of directors to suspend the entire Mexico State Council. The situation dragged on for nearly a year. In April 1963, the board suspended all the Mexican Knights who had managed the insurance program. Later, the entire Mexico State Council was suspended, including the archbishop. The Mexico State Council's response was to announce that it would no longer be affiliated with the supreme council.

Lines were being drawn in the sand.

Whether Hart's obstinacy only furthered the rift or more clearly indicated the fault of the Mexico State Council, when John McDevitt became supreme knight he aimed to fix the problem as quickly as possible, regardless of which party was more (or less) at fault. Less than two months after taking office, McDevitt and Supreme Chaplain, Bishop Charles P. Greco, visited Archbishop Miranda and other church officials in Mexico City to make peace. The Mexico State Council was reinstated, both sides outlined agreeable terms for running the insurance program in Mexico, and in little time McDevitt saw to it that a brother Knight from Mexico, Past State Deputy José Cardenas Stille, was named to the board of directors of the supreme council.

McDevitt's philosophy of catching "more flies with honey than you do with vinegar" may have simply been representative of the generational differences between him and Luke Hart, but it may also have been a product of McDevitt's career in education. Dechant suspected it was the latter, at least indicated by correspondence he shared with Bishop Marion Forst of Dodge City in the spring of 1964. In a revealing letter, Forst wrote to Supreme Director Dechant on the subject of attendance at Knights of Columbus meetings, a subject that had plagued the bishop for two decades.

Forst indicated to Dechant that his experience had taught him that most men were not interested in attending meetings at such regular intervals. Forst pointed out that in the new era of modern entertainment, buoyed specifically by the advent of television, men no longer needed to leave the home for a good time. They could now do it right in the comfort of their living room, in front of the television set. Such a dynamic, he believed, threatened fraternal orders like the Knights. Forst suggested that councils would be better served holding meetings just once or twice annually, thus leaving the rest of the work to committees.

Forst's suggestion included the following appeal:

The question is this: Could you be sufficiently sold on the idea yourself to enthuse the superior council of the Knights to finance a study of "Men and Meetings" and perhaps come up with a solution that would revitalize K of C activity on the local level, and perhaps even all men's organizations? If the idea has merit, I'm sure the expenditure of funds to pay this expert on men's meetings would be worth it both for the KCs—and all men. Any improvement that could be fostered would certainly be an invaluable aid to the faith of our men.

Dechant wrote back to Forst, expressing an open mind on the matter. "It appears to me that the basis of our problem lies in the fact that we tend to become so well organized that the interests and the good of the individual are completely overlooked," he wrote.

Most Reverend Marion F. Forst
Bishop of Dodge City Diocese
910 Central Avenue
Dodge City, Kansas

Your Excellency:

Since receiving your letter of March 24, 1964, I have given much thought to the problem with which you confronted me. Indeed as you so well stated, the most serious concern facing fraternal and service organizations today is that of attendance and participation by its members. This is a matter that concerns all men associated with the success and the future of such organizations.

It appears to me that the basis of our problem lies in the fact that we tend to become so well organized that the interests and the good of the individual are completely overlooked. Instead of approaching subject matter with the thought in mind as to what might be the best for our individual members, we are prone to approach it with the thought—what is the best for the group or the club.

Your proposal that the Supreme Council of the Knights of Columbus sponsor a study in this regard is most appropriate and very timely.

As you undoubtedly know, we have recently elected as a new Supreme Knight, John W. McDevitt, former Deputy Supreme Knight.

Brother McDevitt was formerly engaged in the field of education. It is my thinking that he might be very interested in this program.

I shall have the opportunity to present this to him on the 18th of this month, at our regular quarterly board meeting in New York. In the meantime I would appreciate any suggestion or help that you might wish to give.

With best wishes and personal regards, I remain

Respectfully yours,

Virgil C. Dechant
Supreme Director

Bishop's House
910 Central Avenue
Dodge City, Kansas
March 24, 1964

Mr. Virgil Dechant
LaCrosse, Kansas

Dear Virgil:

Seeing you — although I got to speak to neither you or the Mrs. — perhaps was the source of your being enough on my mind to enlist this letter. Then last night the Grand Knight and another officer of the local K of Cs presented me with a check for vocation promotion — and went on to bemoan how few attend meetings — etc.

Well, we talked about how to get better attendance at meetings. Later I thought about it — and I suppose the idea chased itself all night while I slept — and then this morning (while saying my Office, so maybe it was a good distraction) I determined to write to you.

The question is this: Could you be sufficiently sold on the idea yourself to enthuse the Superior Council of the Knights to finance a study of "Men and Meetings" and perhaps come up with a solution that would revitalize K of C activity on the local level, and perhaps even all men's organizations ? If the idea has merit, I'm sure the expenditure of funds to pay this expert on men's meetings would be worth it both for the KCs — and all men. Any improvement that could be fostered would certainly be an invaluable aid to the faith of our men.

This is something I've been thinking about for years — 20 or more anyway. Which is an admission that I haven't yet found the answer for myself — and also that I was not too successful in making something worthwhile out of a parish men's organization.

Most of my thinking has been negative: e.g. I feel that by far the majority of men are not interested in going to meetings; about the only ones who are faithful are the few who want to get out of the house; or want to play cards, etc. The dedicated ones are in other church or civic groups — mostly. Furthermore, the day of enticing the men to come out for a good program — talk, wrestling match, etc. is over, too, they can see and hear much better entertainment right at home on TV. Furthermore, the wife is tired of having the husband out every night — for VFW meetings; PTAs; KCs; Union or Kiwanis meetings; bowling leagues and whatnot. All these meetings also tire the man; and he's willing not to go. So you can't get him out anymore.

For positive suggestions, about which I am not positive: Many a priest feels that the day of the monthly meeting is over. He asks maybe an annual or semi-annual meeting is enough. So couldn't we, perhaps take hint from successful service organizations. If we have meetings, let them be mixers only — short and easy. Then let all the organizations work be done by committees. The Knights have a splendid six point program, mostly, though, unused. Could the stress be placed on program committees. The officers would meet monthly as a steering committee to ride herd on whatever other committees the Council fostered (and it needn't always have all six points going full blast.) The annual meetings could be limited to, say, a Communion breakfast meeting, with a full turnout worked for and demanded; and one business meeting for elections, etc. Again with a full turnout demanded. The Council's monthly bulletin would keep the membership informed on program work — and other activities — but the real work would be done in committee — and if they fostered a project (like a Day of Recollection, Cana Conferences, Get Out the Vote, Civil Rights, etc.) then the committee would have to for that project expand and advertise and produce.

Anyway, it is nice to have the chance to wish you and Mrs. Dechant a Happy Easter — and the best to you. Thanks for listening.

Marion F. Forst

Dechant pledged to pass along Forst's suggestion to new Supreme Knight John McDevitt, who, Dechant pointed out, "was formerly engaged in the field of education." Dechant suspected the professorial McDevitt would have great interest in such a study.

In 1965, Forst tabbed Dechant to chair the annual Dodge City Diocesan Development Drive. The diocese met its fundraising goal. Forst later presented Dechant with the diocesan Joanine Award and an engraved set of cufflinks, which Dechant kept the rest of his life.

John McDevitt's first few years as supreme knight saw various changes to the roster of supreme officers that had served under Luke Hart. Some of these moves were prompted by retirements, and one was even the result of a death. The Knights of Columbus boasted more than one million members throughout the world, so adequate leadership was key. McDevitt would indeed tackle challenges other than juggling personnel. These included the Order's policy on race relations and its effect on membership. In 1964, McDevitt's recommendation to the supreme council changed the way an applicant to the Order could be kept out, or "blackballed" from membership. Previously, it took just five such blackballs to keep an applicant from joining the Order; the new rule mandated that one-third of those present had to vote down a new member. That was again revised in 1972 to mandate that only a majority of the members present could squash a new applicant. McDevitt also led the Order through the turbulent times that accompanied changes in Catholicism from the Second Vatican Council—a whole separate and complex issue.

One other personnel matter that captured McDevitt's attention was of particular interest to Virgil Dechant.

Why? Because it involved his own future.

In June 1966, Supreme Knight McDevitt asked Dechant to consider moving to New Haven to work for the Knights of Columbus full-time as assistant supreme secretary and supreme master of the fourth degree. Dechant took the proposal under consideration.

During his discernment he weighed many factors. "Of course I had concerns because I had a young business that was doing very well. I knew that I would either have to abandon it or find new management for it. I didn't really know if it would be possible to manage it at arm's length from New Haven. Plus, I would be accepting new challenges. And it would not be an easy task because I would have to move a young family. All my children, except Tom, who was in his freshman year at the seminary, were in grade school or younger."

Dechant solicited advice from friends, relatives, and business-people he respected. And he sought the counsel of Bishop Forst in Dodge City. One day Dechant drove to Dodge City to see Forst to personally explain his flattering opportunity. Forst asked various questions during their discussion before succinctly concluding, "Look, if you feel you can do the job, I suggest you do it. Because if not, you'll never be the same. You'll forever regret that you bypassed that opportunity."

The bishop's recommendation solidified Dechant's thinking. He decided to take the job, and he wrote McDevitt to inform him of his decision.

Dechant's decision did not yield universal approval. His own father C.J. cautioned his son about the plunge he would be taking, telling Virgil, "Why don't you stay here? Here you're a big fish in a little pond. If you go up there, you'll be a little fish in a big pond."

Ann's father Joe Schafer felt the same way; he even wrote Virgil and Ann a letter after they completed the move in which he suggested the couple had probably made a mistake. The Dechants' friends seemed excited for them, but those who were unfamiliar with the Knights of Columbus wondered how moving across the country to work for a fraternal organization could be a wise career choice.

C.J. Dechant's fish-and-pond paradigm was partially correct. True, there are fish that flounder when they branch out into ponds too big for their own good. And there are big fish that spend their entire existence as dominant creatures in small ecosystems. But then there are simply big fish, creatures that find ways to exist and thrive in most any environment, big or small, foreign or familiar. His son was one such creature.

The mechanics of moving to Connecticut would prove more difficult than the simple act of accepting the job. First, Dechant had to draw up a plan to ensure the survival of Dechant Motors. To achieve this, Dechant sold a portion of stock in the business to his manager of parts and sales, Elmer Meder, with payment to be made from dividends. Dechant would still own control of the dealership, and Meder would run its operations. Subsequently, when Dechant's accountant, Dean Cooley, informed him that he would be moving his family to New Orleans, Dechant hired Alvin Legleiter to fill the accountant's position; Legleiter would in 1978 become a state deputy in Kansas with the Knights of Columbus. Legleiter was also sold stock to be paid from dividends. The complexity of the arrangement allowed Dechant a fallback plan if the new job didn't work out. He could simply return to La Crosse and resume his full-time management of the dealership, although he acknowledged that others would have probably deemed such turnabout a failure. Even Ann Dechant believed there was a definite possibility the move could last just two or three years, and then they'd return to La Crosse.

In March of 1966, Dechant had purchased 80 acres of farmland from the Fred Schuckman estate at auction for $19,000, an amount he called "an awful sum for those days." He kept the land, and in time he would continue to add to it. Conversely, he made arrangements with

Clarence Wilson, president and principal stockholder of the Home State Bank in La Crosse, to trade the remaining lots he owned as part of the Dechant Addition for stock in the bank. Dechant would also serve on the bank's board of directors for a number of years.

Then there was the family situation. This would prove most difficult.

"At first, it seemed kind of exciting, to move," said Ann Dechant. "But when I really got to thinking about it, I realized that we were well settled in La Crosse. Karen was in the second grade. Bobby was not even in school yet. Danny was in the seventh grade. Tom was at the seminary, Savior of the World, in Kansas City, Kansas. So I knew that we had to take the kids out of school. It was hard. We were packing, and my parents lived right next door, and they didn't appreciate at all that we were moving. My dad had played a lot with Bobby, and he knew that he'd be moving away. Of course he knew that it was our choice. I guess he thought, 'Why would they want to go to the east coast?' He also knew that we would have been there next door, and he could have helped take care of the kids as they got a little older."

Virgil went to New Haven alone to start his job at the beginning of the school year in September 1966, and Ann stayed back with the kids in Kansas so they could complete the fall semester before moving in January. During that five-month period, Dechant returned to La Crosse a handful of times. He used these visits to see his family, settle his business affairs, and help pack for the move.

Ann made one trip to New Haven to help Virgil shop for a house. He had already initiated a search with the help of Deputy Supreme Knight Dr. John H. Griffin and his wife, Mary Louise. That same year, Griffin would be appointed the Order's supreme physician.

The Dechants settled on a house in North Haven, Connecticut, with a big yard where the kids could play. The Griffins lived roughly a mile away, which would provide another benefit—a close ally in a strange community.

The week of the move arrived. "The kids almost couldn't imagine it, until it really happened," Ann Dechant remembered. "I remember when Karen came home from school on that last day, she said, 'I bet they've even moved my desk out.' She was kind of upset, and she had friends obviously. Of course when we moved, they all had to make new friends."

Virgil put the family's La Crosse house on the market. It would sell eventually, once they had gotten settled in Connecticut.

The family had a cat that Virgil and Ann decided would stay behind, so Virgil took the cat "out for a ride" the day before they left and abandoned it in a field outside of town. Having moved out of their house completely, the Dechants spent that night with Elmer and Annie Meder and family. When they were loading up the car the next morning, the cat reappeared, having navigated its way back from the field to the Meder's house, where it spotted the Dechant car in the driveway. With a front yard full of impressionable kids, Virgil had no choice but to take the cat with them. And off they went.

That day, January 15, 1967, was Super Bowl Sunday—the first Super Bowl Sunday. For Kansans, excited that their Kansas City Chiefs were part of such an important game, the night turned into a disappointment. The Green Bay Packers won, 35-10. The Dechants stopped in Salina to visit Knights of Columbus colleague Jack Dowd and his family, staying long enough to watch some of the game before continuing on.

The next stop was at Savior of the World Seminary near Kansas City, where they dropped Tom off for school. He would complete his semester there before joining the family in Connecticut that summer. Having already spent his first semester that fall away from his family, the arrangement didn't feel strange to Tom, only different in a matter of degree.

"I went from being 300 miles away from home to 1,500, so that was about a push," Tom said. "Other than I wondered, 'Where are they living? What's their house like?' But I had friends to keep me occupied."

However, his siblings missed him. "It was weird," Dan Dechant said. "We got in the car and drove, but now it was just three kids and two parents."

"The amazing thing about that move—and I was just five at the time—was you're so many miles away from home, but our dad still had a farm and the car dealership back in Kansas," said Bob Dechant. "Versus most moves, you're severing ties. But he still had his business in Kansas. And so every year we'd get new cars, but the only way to get them was to drive. So we would make this drive, and then do the drive back. That was two days in each direction."

Over the coming years the Dechants would make the drive between Kansas and Connecticut so many times that they became familiar with the best rest stops and restaurants along the way. The usual stops included Columbus, Ohio, which was roughly the halfway point, and a popular greasy spoon in Pennsylvania that the kids loved, The Country Chicken.

On this first trip, nobody was thinking about return trips or places to eat. They each had one eye on the road and the other in the rear view mirror, watching Kansas disappear in the distance, wondering how permanent their new life on the east coast would be.

* * *

In 1967, the supreme council of the Knights of Columbus was headquartered in an aging building on Meadow Street in downtown New

Haven that had formerly been occupied by the New York, New Haven and Hartford Railroad. While the railroad building was a significant step up from its smaller predecessor, 45 Wall Street, it lacked many of the charms that one would expect of a modern office. There was no air conditioning, and in the summer employees would have to open all the building's windows to get adequate relief from the Connecticut humidity.

Office spaces had been carved out of the old railroad offices in varying sizes, which was puzzling to new employees. Space was limited for the Order's growing staff. A noisy Addressograph machine would make "bangs" and "booms" that reverberated throughout the building, seemingly all day long. And in the days before his death, the building's most permanent tenant was the boss himself, Supreme Knight Luke Hart, who took residence on the fourth floor.

Luke Hart wasn't the only supreme knight with legendary quirks. John McDevitt, Hart's successor, drove a car with Massachusetts license plates that read "1492," a reference to the Order's namesake, Christopher Columbus. Employees could tell whether or not McDevitt was in with a simple glance through the parking stalls for "1492."

McDevitt, whose only three vices in the world—according to one former employee—were lobster, cigars, and poker, was always concerned with appearances, at least as far as they pertained to the Order. For example, he was especially conservative regarding office décor and fixtures out of respect for his members' premium dollars. McDevitt knew that the activities of the supreme council were supported by regular K of C members, and any excess could send the wrong message about the Order's true purpose. So most requests for new office furniture or decorations were put on hold.

The primitive office atmosphere was about to change. On May 2, 1967, the Knights broke ground on a new headquarters: a 23-story, modern-looking downtown building. When completed, the new build-ing—distinguishable by four 320-foot towers on its corners that were intended to represent four principal K of C ideals: charity, unity, frater-nity, and patriotism—would emerge as one of the New Haven skyline's most prominent sights. Hartford Auxillary Bishop John Hackett and New Haven Mayor Richard Lee joined McDevitt at the groundbreaking ceremony. The new office would take two full years to complete, but its construction was a sign of progress within the Order.

It was a proud moment for all involved in 1970 when the move to the new building was complete. Naturally, that event failed to escape controversy. In the years leading up to the move, the Order had hired an outside consultant—in fact, a man with a Ph.D.—to plan for the move so the home-office staff would be able to seamlessly occupy the new building and avoid a loss in productivity. A few weeks before the move, the consultant reported to the Order that he had suffered a nervous breakdown and would be un-able to complete his work. Worse yet, he had developed no files or system that someone else could replicate. So the task of planning the move into the new head-quarters fell into the lap of the new guy, Virgil Dechant. Re-lying mostly on his

EIGHT

K. of C. official to speak at anniversary fete

Virgil C. Dechant, supreme secretary of the Knights of Columbus, will be the guest speaker for the Diamond Jubilee dinner of Council 512 Saturday in the Knights of Columbus Home on U. S. 422 east.

The dinner will be the culmina-tion of a week long 75th anniver-sary that began with the confer-ing of Knighthood degrees on Sunday. Speaking with Dechant Saturday will be Carmen Capone of Pittsburgh, a supreme director of the National council, and guest for the gala dinner party, when special presentations to Council 512 will be made by both New Castle and Lawrence County of-ficials.

Dechant, who serves the head-quarters in New Haven, Conn., was elected to the board of the Supreme Council in August of 1963 after he had been an active member of Council 2340 of Liebenthal, Kan. since 1949. A

successful businessman and ad-ministrator, he is chairman of the board of Dechant Motor Co.

Dechant is a native of Liebenthal, Kan. but moved to LaCrosse and transferred his membership to LaCrosse Council 2970 in 1953, after serving as Grand Knight, and deputy direc-tor of the Leibenthal Council for five terms. He became a state treasurer and state deputy in Kansas. In 1967, Pope Paul VI named him a Knight of St. Gregory for recognition of his work for the Catholic Church. He has served as president of the Dodge City, Kan., Diocesan Development program, and was a member of the diocese's educa-tion committee.

The anniversary program of Council 512, continues today when the Council will present an "Appreciation Dinner," for priests and nuns of the Lawrence County Deanery at the K of C Home.

Virgil C. Dechant

Virgil Dechant, second from right, was the fresh face on the board of directors when he arrived on the scene in New Haven, Connecticut.

experience operating his own business—and a simple dose of common sense—Dechant was able to plot a strategy to move office furniture, files, and other necessities to the new headquarters without incident. Better yet, he and his help accomplished the bulk of the work over the course of a long weekend, as he remembers.

New Haven was a city rich in culture and political history. It claimed to be the home of the Frisbee, the Erector Set, and its own style of pizza. Its neighborhoods were as distinct as its residents, and, besides the Knights of Columbus, the city got its biggest economic boost from Yale University, the longtime Ivy League stalwart, located near the K of C.

In his role as assistant supreme secretary, Dechant brought home a salary of $22,000, as he recalls. In those days, it was a well-paying job, but for Dechant the salary was a slight cut in income from his career as a car dealer-farmer-real estate developer in Kansas. In 1967, the average annual household income in the United States was about $8,000. Dechant still received income from his Kansas operations. Soon he found out how much he needed it. A dollar didn't stretch as far in Connecticut as it did in Kansas.

The biggest adjustment for Ann and the kids, she recalls, was making new friends. "I didn't want to use babysitters because I didn't know anybody to babysit," she said. "So at first I couldn't really go out with Virgil to different things. I wasn't going to leave the kids with someone who'd just been suggested by somebody else. But eventually we got friendly with more people."

On the first day of school, Dan Dechant walked down the street to catch the school bus to North Haven Junior High School. That day he would have the pleasure of being "the new kid." So would Karen and Bobby, who attended St. Stephen School in Hamden.

"In La Crosse, I had been at St. Michael's School," Dan said. "And seventh and eighth grade were in the same classroom with one teacher. Then I went to public school at North Haven Junior High, and every class was in a different room with a different teacher. So I went from one nun who taught every subject to two grades to a big, giant school with thousands of kids. English was in one room, then the bell would ring and I'd go to math in another room. That was a culture shock. In the public school, the students were much more street smart than I was. I was a little naïve and sheltered in comparison, so it was a real culture shock for me."

Back in Kansas, things were going well for Tom Dechant at Savior of the World Seminary. That was until one day in the spring of 1967 when a priest informed him he had a phone call. Tom knew something was amiss.

"You never got phone calls," he remembered. "It just wasn't allowed."

On the line was his uncle, Emerald Dechant, Virgil's brother.

"Your dad's in bad shape," Emerald told him. "Grandma and Grandpa Dechant are flying up there to be with him."

"What's wrong?" Tom asked.

"Well, he's had some stomach problems. So be sure to pray—goodbye."

Tom hung up the phone, unsure what to make of the call. The priest standing nearby told him they would say a Mass for his father the following day.

"That's fine," Tom thought to himself. But it still didn't help answer the question: what was wrong with Virgil Dechant?

Virgil C. Dechant

C.J. Dechant did not like to travel. So when he and his wife Ursula turned up in Connecticut in the spring of 1967 to check in on their son Virgil, who had suddenly been admitted to the hospital, Virgil's kids knew the situation was serious.

"They thought he wasn't going to make it," Tom Dechant said. "But this was 1967."

This was 1967, and the mysterious illness that had put Virgil in the hospital was a bleeding stomach ulcer, an ailment that began plaguing him in Kansas. Stomach ulcers occur when disruptions in a person's digestive fluids cause damage to the lining of the stomach. In Dechant's case, the episode was likely brought on by a high level of stress—possibly due to his new job responsibilities—and a regrettable encounter one evening with lots of spicy Italian food, served by a well-meaning home office employee from the mailroom.

Properly treated, stomach ulcers are minor problems. But when left to fester, they can potentially lead to serious problems, including bleeding and perforation in the stomach. Dechant's doctors chose to operate, and they removed approximately one-third of his stomach. He was given 26 pints of blood during his hospital stay. The situation escalated when he developed a staph infection. The only treatment at that point was an experimental drug, dicloxacillin, a byproduct of the rash of bioprospecting that had taken place after penicillin came onto the medical scene. In 1967, dicloxacillin was brand new, and Dechant was monitored every hour as part of a test case to see how he responded to the drug. Ultimately, his body would react with favor.

Virgil and Ann's daughter Karen recalls that the family had set up a May altar in their living room at the time of the illness, and every day Ann and the kids would pray a rosary at the altar on Virgil's behalf. Karen called the whole experience "a solemn feeling." She had also noticed different treatment from the nuns at her Catholic grade school, who had been made aware of Virgil's illness. This went on for weeks, and all the while C.J. and Ursula stayed put in Connecticut, helping care for the kids. That year, Dechant missed his first Kansas state convention since joining the Order. The Kansas State Council authorized his friend Vic Wasinger to purchase a gift for their ailing pal, a silver bas relief of the Last Supper.

Weekend fixer-upper projects around the Dechant house sometimes included house painting, and nobody was exempt from the work—visitors included (longtime friend Vic Wasinger is pictured kneeling).

By the time Tom Dechant rejoined the family in Connecticut in late May, after his spring semester at the seminary had ended, Virgil had been discharged from the hospital. He was home recuperating and under strict instructions from his doctors to take it easy. Tom had been given scant details on his father's condition and was shocked to see Virgil looking pale and gaunt after his lengthy hospital stay.

With a full compliment of free labor under one roof, Dechant engaged his kids in a few household projects, including building a new patio out of plasti-crete. With fresh stitches in his stomach, Dechant assumed the role of project manager, but even so, he couldn't resist getting his hands dirty. While the family got settled, household projects such as the new patio became a regular pastime around the Dechant house on weekends.

"Saturdays were always for projects," said Bob Dechant, the youngest child. "And in the fall we'd always put the Notre Dame football game on the radio and listen while we were puttering around."

"We loved it," Karen said. "The whole family...even when we refinished those wood carvings from the old Knights of Columbus building. We all worked with tools to get all the varnish off."

Today those same wood carvings are on display at the Knights of Columbus Museum, shown in an exhibit which depicts a typical council chamber.

For Dan Dechant, the weekend projects in North Haven were a noticeable—and surprising—difference from life in Kansas.

"When we moved to Connecticut I was in the seventh grade," Dan said. "As I was starting to grow up, I liked to use tools and do mechanical stuff. But we had hardly any tools in La Crosse. If anything needed to be fixed around the house, somebody from the shop [Dechant Motors] would come by and fix it. I would always ask, 'Dad, can we get a tool to do this or fix that or something to do this or that?' He'd say, 'Too expensive, too expensive, too expensive.' So as privileged as I felt taking vacations all the time, I felt like, 'How come everyone else has these things? This is Kansas, everybody has tools. We have no tools.' So we moved to Connecticut, and now there were no guys from the shop to come by and fix stuff. So every Saturday there would be a project at our new house. And the builder of our house did some shoddy workmanship, so there were lots of projects that had to be done. Every Saturday, we'd work on these projects, and Dad and I would go buy tools to get the project done. And it started raining tools! There was no tool that cost too much. And the biggest surprise to me was that he knew how to use them all. I had never seen him use this stuff. So sometime as a kid in Liebenthal he had used these tools. I never saw him use these tools in La Crosse, but in North Haven he knew how to use them all."

Rejuvenated by time at home with his family and a growing familiarity with his new surroundings, Virgil Dechant returned to full health by July 1967, just in time to help run the supreme convention in Montreal, Canada, also the site of Expo 67, a world's fair. For the progression of his career trajectory, his timing, yet again, was providential. That year, Supreme Secretary D. Francis Sullivan developed cancer and decided to retire. His assistant, Dechant, was then tabbed to replace him as supreme secretary, a scenario "which nobody had contemplated so soon," Dechant conceded. The promotion became official during the October 1967 meeting of the board of directors, held in South Bend, Indiana. At that time, Dechant resigned as supreme master of the fourth degree, and Howard E. Murphy replaced him as assistant supreme secretary.

In his role as supreme secretary, Dechant experienced newfound exposure to members of the Order nationwide. Naturally, his travel com-

Away at school, Tom Dechant's visits home were always special moments, particularly for his younger siblings.

mitments grew. But ever the fraternalist, he enjoyed the opportunity to meet other members of the Order. Such opportunities allowed him to drive social change within the Knights of Columbus beyond the plains of Kansas. During his first tours through councils along the east coast, Dechant observed the same attitudes toward women and families that had existed in Kansas when he was a district deputy. Women rarely accompanied their husbands to K of C meetings, and if they did, at banquets, they sat apart from their husbands. If there was a dais, or head table, the men would sit there, and their wives would be seated elsewhere among the crowd. The same was true at supreme conventions.

At one event the Dechants attended, the evening's featured speaker was Philip Kenyon Chapman, the first Australian-born astronaut in the American space program. Chapman, a member of the Knights of Columbus and the Knights of the Southern Cross in Australia, sat at the head table with Virgil, and his wife sat in the crowd, next to Ann Dechant. At one point during the evening, Ann and Mrs. Chapman went up to the bar for a cocktail. They instructed the barkeep to "send the bill to the head table," a delicate but effective form of protest.

In time, Dechant and others helped change the attitudes toward women at K of C events. The old guard put up a modest amount of resistance, but soon, just like in Kansas, these attitudes gave way to a new wave of men committed to the inclusion of wives and children at K of C functions.

Sometimes the travel took Dechant back to Kansas, his homeland. His April

IMAGES COURTESY OF KNIGHTS OF COLUMBUS MUSEUM.

The old and the new: In 1970, the Knights of Columbus took a major step up in the world, leaving one headquarters behind and starting fresh in a brand-new building.

1967 visit included Supreme Knight McDevitt, who trekked to La Crosse to speak at a reception held in Dechant's honor. Additionally, Dechant attended the Kansas K of C state convention every year (except 1967, 2016, and 2017). And in the spring of 1970, Dechant would visit Hays to complete the negotiation of a K of C loan for the construction of a new St. Anthony's Hospital, the same hospital where 18-year-old Dechant had received such a spirited crowd of well wishers from the Order while recovering from a car accident.

The occasions to travel for meetings, banquets, and degrees also offered Dechant a chance to sharpen his public speaking skills.

In 1968, Dechant added a touch of verse to his usual shtick to better describe how he envisioned his role with the Knights of Columbus and the role of the everyman dedicated to his local council, the sort who never missed the chance to help out at a parish fish fry or a council activity. Dechant chose to read *The Indispensable Man* by Idaho poet Saxon White Kessinger. The poem, all of 20 lines, instructs the reader to place his hand in a bucket of water and take note of the hole that remains once it's removed. "The hole that's remaining, is the measure of how you'll be missed," the poem reads. The instruction is clear: do good work, certainly, and be proud of what you do, but don't ever think that your contributions to the world are irreplaceable. "Remember, there is no indispensable man."

During one speech, after reciting the poem, Dechant told his audience, "The real credit for the work and success of the Order belongs to the man who is working at the grass root level. He is the man who faces the dust and sweat needed to make the Order grow. It is on his devotion, his enthusiasm, his enterprise and his dedication that my success as supreme secretary is and will be built. If he fails, I fail. We shall always have a supreme secretary. He is easily replaceable. It is the man dedicating himself to the work of the Order at the local level who is so difficult to replace. He is the man who deserves our real honor, our genuine tribute, our eternal gratitude."

Dechant's tenure as supreme secretary would last 10 years, taking him well into the 1970s. It was a tenure that would ultimately prove successful, but there were some rocky moments along the way, and it all came to a head in 1969.

Dechant recalled that "in 1969, things were not going well. Membership was down. Insurance sales were down. And it seemed like we weren't doing anything correct."

Many nights, Supreme Physician Dr. John Griffin, and sometimes other supreme council staffers, would stop by the Dechant house to discuss the internal politics of the New Haven office. Griffin was one of Dechant's closest allies in New Haven. These evening sessions were eerily similar to the sort Dechant had hosted back in Kansas, meeting with Ray Gottschalk, Don Dreiling, and Vic Wasinger. But in New Haven, the tone of these meetings was different. The discussions had a harder edge, reflective of complex personalities and differing business philosophies within the Order. Clearly, Dechant had a vision of where he thought the Knights of Columbus should go, and he felt stymied by seemingly poor results. He was anxious to do more.

Dechant requested a meeting with Supreme Knight John McDevitt. His primary purpose, in the simplest terms, was to ask his boss for more responsibility. Whether or not McDevitt could sense Dechant's unease is unknown, but Dechant felt that it was time to draw a line in the sand.

"I didn't come up here to ride a sinking ship," Dechant told McDevitt at their sit-down. "And unless we make some changes—if we can't turn it around—I'll consider tendering my resignation and returning to Kansas."

McDevitt said to Dechant, "Do you think you can do any better if I were to put the insurance program under your direction?"

"With my eyes closed," Dechant told his boss.

Certainly, in the entire history of the Supreme Council of the Knights of Columbus, there have been more candid, even cocksure, appeals to authority. But it's doubtful that any other such exchange would have a more lasting effect on the future of the organization.

Make no mistake, Dechant was not bluffing. A return to Kansas was indeed possible if things didn't improve.

Fortunately for Dechant, McDevitt heard him loud and clear. He

From left: Vic and Armella Wasinger, Virgil and Ann Dechant, John McDevitt, Bishop Charles Greco, and Mary McDevitt—prior to their 1971 Rome trip.

offered Dechant the chance to run the insurance operations—in addition to his duties as supreme secretary.

But Dechant didn't stop there.

"Before accepting his offer, I requested that I also be put in charge of the service department, which operated the membership division and the fraternal activities of the Order. My reason for requesting both duties was that I saw them—and still see them today—as going hand in hand, the insurance depending on paid professionals and the fraternal works and membership programs depending on volunteers that would use the professionalism of the agency field force to assist in the recruitment of members and the sales of insurance, guaranteeing the financial well-being of the Order. I knew the two areas would have to work together to make each one a success. I think I just had a feel for what the members expected. It was not very complicated. It was simple: provide them a service, and to do that, we had to have a professional field force that could make a good living doing that.

"Thanks be to God, Mr. McDevitt gave me the leeway to get that job done."

How had the insurance program eroded to such a poor state that Dechant was considering leaving his job altogether? To answer that question, it's important to understand the evolution of Knights of Columbus insurance, right from the very beginning of the Order.

The basic composition of the Knights of Columbus includes two key elements: insurance and fraternal services. The insurance side of the Order is today, in Dechant's own words, "a very professional company, known as a fraternal benefit society, that has its own laws and rules governed by the various states in which we do business."

The K of C insurance force has professional agents that market and sell the Order's various products of whole life, term, disability, and long-term care insurance. These men are paid on a commission basis, like most insurance agents in other companies, and the insurance portion of the K of C operations is its primary source of revenue.

The fraternal side of the Order exists to support volunteer-based activities in councils spread throughout the world. The Knights of Columbus operate countless programs that support families, parishes, and charitable causes. One noteworthy example: during World War I, the K of C sponsored army huts for servicemen in camps spread throughout America and the European theater. Modern day examples of fraternal activity include the Tootsie Roll drives to support people with disabilities, free throw and other athletic contests for youth, and assistance to causes such as the Special Olympics.

In 1892, the Knights of Columbus had established a "Reserve Fund" to guarantee that its insurance operations would be sustainable during epidemics, then a major concern. In those days, the Order offered three classes of insurance, with benefits of $1,000, $2,000, and $3,000. Up until that time, the only way a man could join the Order was to purchase insurance; this changed in 1893 when the Order began permitting associate members, but any man under age 26 was still required to purchase a life insurance policy with a minimum benefit of $1,000—a condition that Virgil Dechant had to abide by when he joined the Knights in 1949.

In 1898, the Knights established a committee on insurance rates, which led to the hiring of the Order's first consulting actuary, David Parks Fackler. Moving to an actuarial basis seemed to legitimize the Order's insurance business because it put the Knights on equal footing, professionally speaking, with other insurance carriers who also used actuaries.

In 1940, the Knights took another important step toward becoming a professional insurance company by implementing an agency system. These men—professional agents—sold insurance on the Order's behalf and were compensated on a commission basis—like they still are today—for their sales. Prior to professional agents, members could buy their insurance from, it seemed, just about anyone in their local council, including the financial secretary. In the earliest days of

AN INDEPENDENT 1970

COMPARATIVE REPORT

KNIGHTS OF COLUMBUS
Supreme Council
Columbus Plaza
New Haven, Connecticut

IT IS A FACT . . . That the financial structure and operation its strength. In this regard we believe the The following is an INDEPENDENT **KNIGHTS** with the 25 largest insurance concerns in average of 103 years of life insurance experience, own 73 p panies and hold 64 percent of all life insurance in force, a tive of good general management and financial stability.

BASIC SIGNIFICANT FACTORS — AS OF DECEMBER 3 (The 25 Life Companies listed below are the largest by the amoun

SOLVENCY:

A wide margin of assets over liabilities is a significant safety factor. This indicates financial soundness and a Company's ability to meet all obligations as they become due.

Assets for each $100 of liabilities as of Dec. 31, 1969

Aetna Life Insurance Company, Conn.	$108.04
American National Insurance Company, Texas	118.00
Bankers Life Company, Iowa	104.80
Connecticut General Life Ins. Co., Conn.	106.56
Connecticut Mutual Life Ins. Co., Conn.	107.31
Continental Assurance Company, Illinois	109.26
Equitable Life Assurance Society, New York	105.47
John Hancock Mutual Life Ins. Co., Mass.	106.03
Lincoln National Life Insurance Co., Indiana	119.25
Massachusetts Mutual Life Insurance Co., Mass.	106.28
Metropolitan Life Insurance Company, N. Y.	106.84
Mutual Benefit Life Insurance Co., New Jersey	104.60
Mutual Life Insurance Company of New York	107.49
National Life and Accident Ins. Co. of Tenn.	123.89
National Life Insurance Company, Vermont	106.13
New England Mutual Life Ins. Co., Mass.	107.25
New York Life Insurance Company, New York	106.42
Northwestern Mutual Life Ins. Co., Wisconsin	105.76
Occidental Life Insurance Company of Calif.	115.73
Penn Mutual Life Insurance Company, Pa.	105.23
Phoenix Mutual Life Insurance Co., Conn.	107.34
Prudential Insurance Co. of America, N. J.	106.13
State Mutual Life Assur. Co. of America, Mass.	108.89
Travelers Insurance Company, Connecticut	110.59
Western and Southern Life Insurance Co., Ohio	108.34

AVERAGE 25 LARGEST LIFE COMPANIES	**$107.11**
KNIGHTS OF COLUMBUS	**$121.85**

— CONCL

The comparative analysis made of the above organization in COMPANIES in our opinion is very favorable. BASED ON THE PRESENT FINANCIAL POSITION, WE BELIEVE IT TO BE A RELIA

© Standard Analytical Service, Inc., 1970

the agency system, one of the agents' primary objectives was to try to convert associate members to insurance members, a goal that remains in place today.

Even with an agency system in place, the insurance program was rife with flaws. For example, many times an agent would make a sale, and in those days the member would make his premium payments through his local council's financial secretary. Many times these men failed to report the payments or keep accurate records. If a member failed to make his payments, his policy would lapse, but oftentimes the financial secretary would fail to notice or report the lapse. Meanwhile, the agent who had sold the policy would have received commission payments for the policy as part of his regular working income. Years later the Order brought in computers to track insurance cases, and these machines revealed irregularities between premiums due and commissions paid to agents.

The Order's solution to the problem only created more friction with the field force. Debt accounts were assessed to these agents against future commissions, and suddenly their monthly commission checks were much smaller than before. They were left complaining how they now owed money back to the Knights of Columbus. The debt accounts made for a sometimes-hostile working relationship.

In 1944, the Knights added juvenile insurance, marketable to fathers who wished to purchase life insurance for their sons who were under 18. When the insured sons of K of C members then reached 18 years of age, they would be eligible to join the Order and were already insured, thus incentivizing their membership. In 1958, after much debate, a plan was introduced to allow members to purchase insurance for their wives and daughters.

Steadily, albeit slowly, the insurance side of the Order grew. In 1960 the Order reached an important milestone: $1 billion of insurance in force and assets of more than $170 million. Supreme Knight Luke Hart's commitment to and knowledge of the insurance business had much to do with the program's constant growth. He had helped write the fraternal code that governed the Knights and other fraternal benefit organizations, and his annual reports reflected the regular progress the Knights were making in growing the insurance arm.

When John McDevitt took over, he and his board of directors felt it wise to hire an outsider to the Knights of Columbus to manage the insurance program. Why? Perhaps the changing times and an era of professional specialization had something to do with it. More importantly, McDevitt was a career educator, unlike his predecessor, Hart, who knew insurance as part of his professional acumen. While he recognized the importance of the insurance program, Dechant said, McDevitt knew it wasn't his bailiwick. The board wanted a pro, and McDevitt agreed.

However, McDevitt's savvy for insurance operations shouldn't be sold short. In the late 1940s, McDevitt lobbied the Massachusetts State Legislature on behalf of the Knights of Columbus, whose license to sell insurance in the state had been suspended at the hands of an in-house uprising. Two Massachusetts Knights had accused the Order of improperly managing its mortuary reserve fund for insurance purposes, thus, they claimed, damaging the integrity of its product.

Research would prove that the Knights had accessed their mortuary reserve fund in accordance with standard operating procedures used by all fraternals. According to historian Christopher Kauffman, the Knights were back in good standing in less than a year, thanks mostly to McDevitt's persistence and political acumen, and agents in Massachusetts could resume selling K of C insurance.

Thomas Gillooly, a former insurance commissioner from West Virginia, was brought in to run insurance operations under McDevitt. Gillooly was given a term contract, which stipulated he would be paid an amount greater than the supreme knight. The board of directors felt such an offer was necessary to entice a man of Gillooly's credentials to take on the job, and their vote approving the contract reflected this attitude.

Virgil Dechant felt otherwise. "This will never work," he advised the board. He very simply stated, "You can't pay an employee more than you pay the chief [McDevitt]."

Dechant's feelings on the matter were based on principle, not his personal feelings for Gillooly.

Shortly after Gillooly's hiring, Dechant's warning to the board proved prophetic. During an April 1966 board meeting in San Juan, Puerto Rico, Gillooly gave a report to the board, in which he essentially made a strong pitch that, in his role, he should have more control over insurance and money matters than the supreme knight. That night, on a bus ride to an event sponsored by the host council in San Juan, Dechant pulled Gillooly aside and told him his remarks may have rubbed some people the wrong way. Dechant advised Gillooly to apologize to McDevitt to smooth things over.

Later that night, while dining at a restaurant with Gillooly and his wife and Elmer VonFeldt—a Kansan who was then the editor of *Columbia*, the Order's monthly magazine—Dechant brought up the issue again. He advised Gillooly to reconsider his position and try to make things work with McDevitt under the current arrangement.

Gillooly's wife told Dechant that it was too late for Tom to change his mind. She was right. Gillooly refused.

By August, Gillooly and the Knights of Columbus had parted ways. His replacement was Mike Flynn, from New Jersey, who, like Gillooly, came to the Order with an insurance background with a commercial company. One of the first things Flynn did in his new role was hire Joseph Mauro as his assistant. Mauro was a suave, successful agent from New York who had previously worked for the Metropolitan Life Insurance Company. He was impressed with the potential of the Knights of Columbus insurance program, which he viewed as rather fledgling, especially after a decade working with a premier agency in New York. So impressed was Mauro with the new job's potential, he uprooted his large family from the city and moved to Madison, a New Haven suburb, a move which, at the time, felt like relocating to a "hill-billy place," he said.

When Mauro came to New Haven, he was struck by more than just untapped potential in the K of C. There were many obstacles, real and figurative, that stood in his way.

"I walked into the building, the old railroad building, on the first day and I was stepping over wires and plugs on the floor, and I thought, 'Oh my God, people work like this,'" Mauro said. "There were a couple of things that were so archaic, thank goodness we got them changed.

"To think, in 86 years, they had not even put two billion dollars of life insurance on the books. When I arrived there it was something like $1.7 billion. I'm saying, 'There's got to be such a potential there.'"

Among the archaic methods that Mauro pointed out, at one time the Order's insurance could not be sold to any person connected to the liquor industry. Bar owner, distributor, deliveryman—it didn't matter. Another oddity: if a bachelor purchased a policy and named his mother as the beneficiary and subsequently got married, the policy automatically listed his wife as the beneficiary. This, too, would eventually change.

During 1967 and '68, Dechant played an active role on the committee working with actuaries to develop a new agency contract for Knights of Columbus insurance agents, which also introduced, as he put it, "an updated and generous dividend scale." In 1968, at a general agents meeting in Boston, Mike Flynn presented the new contract and dividend scale to the agents.

What should have been a proud moment for the Order and an inspiring moment for the agents turned out to be a dud. Rather than accepting their new agreement with excitement, the agents left the meeting confused and demoralized. Flynn's presentation style did little to alleviate their confusion. As Dechant recalls, "what should have been a banner year, 1969, was a disaster. Total sales amounted to $161 million with a net gain of only $64.5 million. Today we have individual field agents writing more than the entire Order did in that year."

Also in 1968, the Order did away with the "Under 26 rule," which stipulated that members under 26 years of age were required to purchase a minimum amount of $1,000 of life insurance.

Why eliminate a guaranteed stream of insurance premiums?

According to Joe Mauro, it was a necessary step to motivate agents to sell the member the insurance that he needed to protect his family, rather than to sell just the minimum amount.

"I think it's one of the smartest things the board of directors ever did," he said. "Because of this, we had to build a professional field force, no more part-time agents. Part-time agents do nothing except wait for something to come their way. A full-time agent has to go out and learn

Supreme Physician, Dr. John H. Griffin, far left, and his wife Mary Louise, helped the Dechants get acclimated to their new surroundings in Connecticut.

how to prospect, and he has to learn how to develop leads and do all that. The turnover rate in the insurance business is unbelievable. It's a matter of hiring 300 people a year, hoping to net about 30. That's the way it goes."

An unsteady field force. Despondent agents. Archaic business rules. This was the environment Virgil Dechant was stepping into when he asked to take over the insurance operations. Maybe McDevitt just figured "why the heck not?"

After all, Dechant had earned a solid reputation as a businessman in Kansas. And he sought to learn the insurance business from the bottom up. He wasn't afraid to ask questions.

Bob Lane said the same. "One thing about Virgil: he read everything. If he didn't know it, he'd learn it. And I'm telling you, he learned it. He was a hands-on guy. Everybody knew it. And he knew our insurance operation needed to be modernized."

Dechant's turnaround plan began with the agents.

His first objective was to enlarge the field force and build up their morale.

The decision was made to replace Flynn as the director of agencies with a general agent from the Knights of Columbus field force. This strategy was purely motivational; if other agents in the field saw one of their own elevated to such a position of leadership, surely they would hold such a person in high regard and aspire to one day do the same.

Dechant and McDevitt held a series of interviews in New York with numerous high-producing, successful K of C agents, most of whom were from the eastern seaboard, to gauge their interest in and compatibility for the job. After a thorough search, John O'Brien, from Dallas, Texas, was selected for the position. O'Brien successfully ran an agency in Dallas. With the promotion, his son Terrance would step into his father's role in charge of the Texas agency.

O'Brien, Dechant, and McDevitt, who agreed on Joe Mauro's value at the home office, made the decision to keep Mauro working with O'Brien. This would help provide continuity.

The next step was to incentivize the agents for a job well done.

"At the time John O'Brien took over the agency department, we had approximately 250 career agents and others who were not full-time," Dechant said. "To build a field force and to promote sales, I was able to persuade the supreme knight to permit me to launch an incentive trip to Rome for all the general agents that met their quota for the year in 1970."

McDevitt, as a rule, did not believe in incentives. However, he decided to give Dechant some leeway—and give the promotion a chance. At the time, incentives used to promote insurance sales or recruitment of new members were not allowed under the Order's bylaws, the reason being that previous power brokers within the Order felt incen-

Virgil Dechant, at podium, during a visit to Puerto Rico.

tives, particularly with regards to membership, would lead to a spike in undesirable members, thus creating long-term problems. This line of thinking may have one day had its place, but by 1969, that era had passed. So in order for the Rome trip to occur, the Order's bylaws were amended to permit incentives for both fraternal and insurance matters.

Joe Mauro felt the incentive trip for agents was about one thing particularly important in the insurance business: "Salesmanship! That was Virgil."

The incentive trip to Rome took place in early October 1971. Twelve Knights of Columbus insurance agents and their spouses and family members made the trip, and they were joined by Bishop Charles P. Greco, supreme chaplain of the Order; Mary McDevitt, wife of Supreme Knight John McDevitt; and Virgil and Ann Dechant.

The 1971 trip to Rome was significant for the Order and for Dechant, for numerous reasons. First, its success was an endorsement of the incentive program and justification to continue it going forward. Second, it began what would ultimately become a lengthy and prestigious career for Dechant in Rome. In the process, the trip, and others like it in coming years, helped solidify the relationship between the Knights of Columbus and the Vatican. Third, and perhaps most importantly for Dechant, it introduced him to a man in Rome who, over time, would exert as much influence and offer as much counsel to his career as any other, Count Enrico Pietro Galeazzi.

Count Galeazzi had been a close, personal friend of Pope Pius XII; the relationship dated back to the Holy Father's days as Cardinal Eugenio Maria Pacelli. Galeazzi, born into a noble family from Perugia, served as the chief architect and engineer of Vatican City; he had even been its lay governor for many years. In this capacity he became involved with a major Knights of Columbus initiative, the construction of six youth centers throughout Rome, which began at the request of Pope Benedict XV during a K of C pilgrimage to Rome in 1920.

Galeazzi would serve as the Knights' Rome representative until his death, but that only begins to describe his tremendous impact on the Order.

Galeazzi was largely responsible for the creation and maintenance of the youth centers, which became known as "playgrounds." During World War II, he made three trips to the White House as a personal envoy of Pope Pius XII. On one such visit he carried a letter from the Holy Father addressed to President Roosevelt, in which the Pope asked that Rome be spared from more bombing, which it mostly was. Today that handwritten letter is on display at the Knights of Columbus museum in New Haven.

Galeazzi was also a close friend of Joseph P. Kennedy, father of U.S. President John F. Kennedy. When the elder Kennedy or any member of his sizable clan made a trip to Europe, he called upon Galeazzi to make arrangements for their stay, sometimes including papal audiences. Over the years, the two traded frequent letters, and Galeazzi became a confidant when relations between Kennedy's prominent political family and Cardinal Francis Spellman, archbishop of New York and a close friend of Galeazzi and the pope, began to wane.

King Umberto II, the last reigning King of Italy, had bestowed the title of "count" upon Galeazzi in 1945, with the understanding that it would one day be handed down to his first-born male descendant. That man would be Galeazzi's grandson, Count Enrico Pietro Demajo, who today heads Knights of Columbus activities in Rome.

During the first agents' trip to Rome, Galeazzi greeted the American insurance contingent on the ramp outside their plane in Rome. From there, he guided the group to the Hotel Intercontinental, where they would stay. Throughout their trip he left nothing to chance for his American friends.

Count Enrico Galeazzi, center, became a mentor for Dechant in Rome and with the Vatican.

"He took care of our every need from morning until night," Dechant recalled. "He made sure that our pilgrimage would go as planned in every detail. He was able to arrange for our delegation to have front-row seats in St. Peter's Basilica during the Holy Father's weekly audience."

In addition to that audience, Galeazzi arranged for the Dechants, Bishop Greco, and Mrs. McDevitt to be received by the Holy Father, Pope Paul VI; it was a greeting known in Rome as a "bacia-mano," which means "hand kiss" or "greeting of the hand."

Dechant called his first meeting with the Pope "a tremendous experience."

He was instantly taken with his new friend Galeazzi and the wealth of experience he had to share: "It was only natural that I developed an admiration for him. How blessed I was that he became my mentor and tutor in all ways, especially in dealing with the Vatican and heads of state. I tried to be a good student with the hope that I would acquire a small part of his diplomatic skills."

In time—in fact, very little time—the incentive trip and other changes to the insurance program that Dechant helped initiate would prove effective for the Knights and their members.

While the Order's insurance operations may have been imperfect, one thing the sales force had working in its favor was the actual product, Knights of Columbus insurance. It was always solid and actuarily sound.

In 1970 the Knights published the results of an independent comparative report conducted by Standard Analytics Service. In the report, the Knights of Columbus were compared against the 25 largest insurance companies in the country. The Knights' ratio of surplus funds was found to be more than three times the average of the largest life insurers; their cash liquidity was far greater than average; and their sol-

The Order's top insurance general agents were rewarded for their achievements with an October 1971 trip to Rome, Italy.

vency—a measure of assets over liabilities—was deemed stronger than every other carrier in comparison. The report concluded that Knights of Columbus insurance, when compared with its competition, came out "very favorable." Furthermore, it stated, "We believe it to be a reliable institution, and it warrants public confidence."

Having in 1960 reached one billion dollars of insurance in force, the field force surged through the next decade, reaching $2 billion in force by 1971. By 1975, that number would grow to $3 billion. The number of field agents also rose and would continue to do so for many years. The Knights also absorbed insurance members from the Catholic Benevolent Legion, or C.B.L.

Dechant recalled: "Under O'Brien, insurance sales began to increase at a rapid pace. The morale of our agents made a 100 percent turnaround. They had confidence in their leadership and placed total trust in John [O'Brien] and Joe [Mauro]." By year end 1975, the insurance in force amounted to $3.2 billion.

When O'Brien retired (more than a decade later), Mauro would replace him. He chose Ed Nutter, a general agent and former state deputy from South Carolina, as his assistant. The combination of Nutter's fraternal experience and Mauro's insurance expertise gave the K of C the best of both worlds. Mauro believed just as strongly in conserving existing policies as adding new ones, which proved key in building a company that could benefit its members.

Fraternal changes also proved impactful. In 1970 the Knights introduced Surge with Service, a program intended to take the Order's activities, as Dechant put it, "out into the public square, whereby the programs would benefit the needy, the outcast, and the forgotten."

According to Christopher Kauffman's *Faith and Fraternalism*, Surge with Service aimed "to stimulate local programs in Church, community, council, family, youth, and membership activities." Surge with Service would be modified multiple times over the next decade, but at the heart of all these modifications was a need to more precisely brand the Knights of Columbus as a Catholic family fraternal service organization instead of an organization of Catholic men.

In short, Surge with Service represented what Dechant believed the Order could and should stand for all those years ago as a newly married grand knight in Kansas.

The rebound from the difficult times of 1969 now seemed complete. Dechant and the Knights of Columbus had now put their house in order, and they had started by revamping the Order's most basic function: to adequately provide a death benefit to the families of its members. Bigger things and greater responsibilities awaited Dechant and the Order in the next decade.

CHAPTER SIX

W all to wall, every man in the ballroom of New York's famous Waldorf Astoria hotel was wearing a white dinner jacket. At least it seemed that way. On the dais, three rows deep, sat more Catholic men in white jackets. On this night, their wives were scattered among the crowd of thousands, sitting with delegates from their own jurisdictions.

The only ones not wearing white jackets were the Catholic priests in attendance and, of course, the evening's principal speaker, President Richard M. Nixon, who had chosen a black tuxedo for his attire.

Nixon was proof that there are exceptions to every rule.

It was this night, August 17, 1971, at the annual Knights of Columbus supreme convention, that Nixon delivered the main address at the annual States' Dinner. The president took the lectern and spoke on a variety of topics. He referenced football coach Vince Lombardi, a Knights of Columbus member, as an example of great character. He discussed his affinity for Catholic schools, pledged his support to prevent their closing, and even mentioned that his secretary was the beneficiary of a Catholic education. Years later that secretary, Rose Mary Woods, accepted blame for erasing a portion of an audio recording that may have included details of the Watergate break-in which eventually led to Nixon's resignation as president.

But on this night, it's unlikely anyone in the room had ever heard the word "Watergate."

Supreme Knight John McDevitt sat next to Nixon. McDevitt pointed out to the crowd that, for the first time ever, a president would address the crowd at the States' Dinner. To the president's right sat Supreme Chaplain, Bishop Charles Greco. Two seats farther right sat Virgil Dechant, the Order's youthful-looking and bespectacled supreme secretary, wearing—you guessed it—a white tuxedo jacket. To his right sat Attorney General John Mitchell, later of Watergate fame; to his left, Archbishop of Hartford John Whealon. Dechant later described the president's speech as a "stirring address."

Earlier that night, Dechant's youngest son Bobby had nabbed the president's autograph. After the speech, Dan Dechant confiscated the saucer and spoon that Nixon used to drink his cup of coffee.

It was a tremendous night for the Order, but for the Dechants, the excitement was just beginning.

The Dechants had sent Bobby, 9, up to their Waldorf hotel room early for bed. "This is New York City," they told him, "so be extra careful." He heeded their advice by double bolting and chaining the door shut.

"And then," as Bobby recalled, "I went down for the count."

A few hours later, after the dinner, the Dechants came up to the room only to discover that they couldn't open the door because Bobby had locked it with enough scrutiny to secure the main gate at Fort Knox. Virgil and Ann knocked and knocked on the door and yelled as loudly as they could, but Bobby never came to open it. For all they knew, something could be terribly wrong inside the room.

Virgil went to get help.

The security presence that night was unusually high for a Knights of Columbus event, and he returned to the room with representatives from the Secret Service to help unlock the door. They used magnets to flip the double-bolt lock, but the chain made it impossible to open the door more than a few inches.

President Richard Nixon addressed the K of C at the States' Dinner in 1971. Virgil Dechant, front row, had a bird's eye view.

"Bobby! Bobby!" Ann yelled.

Still no response.

Then the Secret Service used a saw to cut through the chain and open the door. Once open, Virgil and Ann burst into the room. Bobby was asleep on the bed, snoring. When he woke up he wondered what all the fuss was about.

After all, this was New York City. He was just doing as he was told—being "extra careful."

As convention hijinks went, that night at the Waldorf may have been the high-water mark for the Dechants. But there were other moments, certainly, especially as the children entered their pre-teen years. Once in Montreal, Canada, the children and some friends purchased boxing gloves, which resulted in more than one dangerous thump to the head. Another time, they lobbed a large water-soaked glob of toilet paper out the window of their hotel room, some 30 floors up. It landed on the steering wheel of a convertible parked on the street below with enough force to cause the car's horn to honk, much to the surprise of the hotel's flock of unsuspecting bellmen. In every case, the children came out of these capers unscathed; only Virgil and Ann had to suffer with worry.

THE WHITE HOUSE
WASHINGTON

November 20, 1969

Dear Mr. Dechant:

President Nixon has received your letter embodying the resolution adopted by your organization. Your courtesy in bringing this expression of views to his attention is appreciated.

The President is pleased to know that you share his high regard for the Honorable J. Edgar Hoover.

With the President's best wishes to you and your membership,

Sincerely,

Noble M. Melencamp
Staff Assistant
to the President

Mr. Virgil C. Dechant
Supreme Secretary
Knights of Columbus
Columbus Plaza
New Haven, Connecticut 06507

RECEIVED
NOV 28 1969
MAIL ROOM

Dechant's interactions with presidents of the United States included this Columbus Day meeting with Gerald Ford, center.

But as pre-teen pranks go, the Dechant kids were relatively tame. One could even argue their sometimes-rowdy convention behavior was fair payback for having to explain their father's job title to friends at school. The average fourth grader had a hard time grasping that a "supreme secretary" was a deeply involved business executive, not some sort of glorified stenographer.

In January 1972, Virgil Dechant returned to Kansas to help celebrate the Golden Jubilee (50 years) of Liebenthal's St. Augustine Council #2340, where he had joined the Order. Dechant delivered the main address at the banquet.

In 1973-'74, Dechant became heavily involved with the selection and installation of a new insurance administration system for the

Supreme Knight John McDevitt was able to meet Dechant's parents C.J. and Ursula during a visit to Kansas for K of C business.

Knights of Columbus. This involvement would ultimately revamp the entire record-keeping system of the K of C, including more than a half-million life insurance certificates. The Knights chose a modern, computerized system called "Life/70," developed by Continuum, a Texas company. Bob Lane was tabbed to manage the transfer to the new system. He would report directly to Dechant.

Continuum provided two consultants to help the Knights of Columbus convert to the new system, Pete Bailey and Barry Nickerson. The Knights would later hire Nickerson to a full-time job.

The conversion to Life/70, according to Dechant, was completed successfully and "in record time."

Bob Lane mostly agreed, saying, "we had to clean up some files that were unfortunately not quite accurate, and it took a team of people doing all that. As a user group we met regularly to run tests of products so that we could see if it would work for this, that, or the whole."

Most of all, Lane was most pleased that his boss, Dechant, "who was trying to run the whole damn operation," was happy with the new system. And he was.

"That system is still administering the operation for much of the Order's business," Dechant said decades later. "Although it's constantly being updated. Much time, money, and effort has been spent on other systems, but we have not found one that would surpass its simplicity and efficiency."

Converting to Life/70 did wonders for the insurance business. It also gave Dechant the opportunity to learn it in detail. The results would bear that out. In 1975, A.M. Best, for the first time, gave Knights of Columbus insurance its highest approval rating. Life insurance policies in force continued growing at a rapid pace. By the end of 1976, the Knights had almost 700,000 policies in force.

The year 1973 was also a landmark year for the Order's investment portfolio—or, at least, for its most famous piece, the grounds at Yankee Stadium, which it had owned since 1953. In 1970, New York City Mayor John Lindsay approached the Yankees about upgrading the stadium, which was showing significant signs of wear and tear (Yankee Stadium opened in 1923; it had been built for $2.4 million). A year later, the renovations would receive approval, contingent upon the city's purchase of the ballpark and the grounds on which it stood, all by virtue of eminent domain.

It's noteworthy that at the time New York City was on the verge of bankruptcy. Lindsay originally planned on spending $25 million to upgrade the stadium; he ended up spending closer to $125 million, Dechant recalled. With an election on the horizon, Lindsay certainly wanted no part of the criticism that would accompany such over-spending, particularly for a ballpark the city didn't even own. Through the use of eminent domain, the city was trying to strong-arm the Knights of Columbus out of their ownership agreement for less than top dollar. The matter came up at litigation in 1973 at the Bronx County Courthouse.

The parties at the litigation included Rice University, represented by prominent attorney and future Secretary of State Cyrus Vance. While the Knights of Columbus owned the grounds on which Yankee Stadium sat, Rice owned the stadium itself, having inherited it from John W. Cox, an alumnus, who had purchased it in 1955 from Arnold Johnson, who had purchased it two years before that from the team's co-owners Dan Topping and Del Webb.

Among the Knights' negotiating party was Bob Clair, chief coun-sel from Shearman and Sterling, a prominent New York law firm, and Charles Walden, who had just been hired a few months before as the director of the Knights' investment department.

Just 29, Walden was obviously the junior man in the room, and he knew it. Walden had been hired out of graduate school by a large trust bank to work on its investment operations. Soon after, a close friend asked to pass along his résumé to John McDevitt at the Knights of Columbus. Walden agreed, and he went through an interview process that included meeting Dechant and Supreme Knight John McDevitt. Walden was an Episcopalian, a fact that did little to dissuade the Order from hiring the young investment whiz.

A day before the Yankee Stadium litigation, Dechant tapped Walden on the shoulder and told him that his presence would help greatly at the proceedings in New York. The Yankee Stadium matter was mostly foreign to Walden, so he packed a leather valise with all the files he could find on the property and got into the car with the supreme secretary to head into the city.

Justice Wallace R. Cotton, considered an authority on real estate and the condemnation of property, would hear their argument that day. The purpose of the litigation was an appraisal that the Knights had gotten on the land, valued at $5 million. Under the terms of the city's proposed purchase

The Knights of Columbus had purchased the grounds on which Yankee Stadium sat during Luke Hart's tenure as supreme knight; this was one piece of real estate that the Order could not hold onto.

agreement, the Knights would receive just $3.5 million for the property. They were there to pursue the $1.5 million difference.

When they arrived at the Bronx County Courthouse, just two blocks from the stadium, they entered the clerk's office on the first floor but were told to meet upstairs in Justice Cotton's chambers. Cotton, a diminutive man, sat in a big, high-backed chair at the end of the conference table. The chair towered over his head.

The arguments began, and soon the tension in the room began to escalate. Justice Cotton held up his hand and, loudly enough to quiet the whole room, said, "Stop!" He pivoted around in his chair to look out his office window, where he could see the stadium in the distance.

"Nothing in the South Bronx is worth more than $4.2 million," he declared.

The room went silent. Cotton's tone was definitive.

When neither party could take the silence any longer, someone suggested that it was time for a recess. Out in the hallway, the K of C contingent huddled to discuss their next move. One of the men, Judge McNally, an advisor to Shearman and Sterling who had previously served as a condemnation judge, said, "He just gave us his ruling." As far as McNally was concerned, there was nothing else that could be done.

Later, the group adjourned for lunch in Manhattan, where they agreed their only move was to fold and accept the judge's opinion.

Cotton's ruling was final; the only justification for an appeal would be a discrepancy in the law, not his opinion. The Yankee Stadium deal may have been the most famous of the Knights of Columbus' lease-back real estate ventures, but Cotton's ruling made certain that it would not be its most profitable.

The Knights returned to New Haven, somewhat in defeat over the loss of the stadium (more than the price). However, young Charles

Walden came away from the matter impressed by what he had learned watching Virgil Dechant, both in his preparation for the meeting and his command of the material.

"He studied the Yankee Stadium deal to a 'T,'" Walden said. "And he would read that stuff. A lot of guys in his position at a life insurance organization would probably have said, 'you know what, we got ourselves in trouble on this deal.' Companies just charge things off and move on. But what I loved about Virgil is he would roll up his sleeves and not only mentally grasp what people like me, the operatives, should be doing, but he would get himself involved. That's what was so neat about it.

"I think he had a real innate ability for business, and particularly real estate. You know, buying a quarter section of farmland or a full section at auction is one thing when you make your judgment, but that translated for him."

On the surface, it seemed New York City and eminent domain may have gotten the better of the Knights of Columbus on the Yankee Stadium deal. But greater examination proves this wasn't necessarily so. The problem confronting the Order with the stadium on its books was the potential 73-year lease term, which included a fixed rent the Knights would be paid ($182,000 per year for the first 28 years of the lease and then $125,000 annually for the three 15-year terms promised for renewal). The figure reduced the economic value of the land substantially. Using their $4.2 million, Walden advised the Order to turn around and invest the amount at a rate of some 13 percent, thus netting the Order more than half a million dollars annually, an amount far greater than the ballpark rent.

Charles Walden wasn't the only man in the offices of One Columbus Plaza who trusted Dechant's judgment. By the middle part of the decade, it seemed clear to many that Virgil Dechant was the obvious choice to replace John McDevitt as supreme knight.

"Virgil wasn't supreme knight yet," Walden said, "but it was obvious to me that he was the guy John McDevitt would look to in every way, shape, or form."

"I had the feeling the first time I met him that he was going to be the future supreme knight," Bob Lane said. "I just had that gut reaction. He had a way about him, and the questions he'd always ask were right on the money. He didn't beat around. There wasn't anything that went on in that building that he didn't know about."

Lane's nephew, Ronald Tracz, began a career with the Knights of Columbus by working in the Order's printing plant during the summers as a college student. In 1976 Tracz accepted a full-time job overseeing the Order's federal insured student loan program and began a four-decade career with the Knights. Just like his uncle, Lane, Tracz sensed immediately that Dechant was destined for the Order's top job.

"It was obvious, I think, to everybody at that particular time, that Virgil was the heir apparent, going from the McDevitt administration to the new one," Tracz said. "He was kind of lining things up even before an actual transition took place."

That transition took place in January 1977 upon McDevitt's retirement. At their quarterly meeting in San Juan, Puerto Rico, the board of directors unanimously selected Virgil C. Dechant, 46, to succeed John McDevitt as supreme knight of the Knights of Columbus. Almost perfectly, the selection took place on January 22, marking—to the day—the 55th anniversary of the St. Augustine Council in Liebenthal. It also occurred two days after the inauguration of U.S. President Jimmy Carter.

What Dechant never even dreamed possible—to attain the

Virgil Dechant, front row, far left, joined other Knights of Columbus at this visit to the gravesite of President John F. Kennedy during the 1965 supreme convention in Baltimore, Maryland.

Kansan in Top K. of C. Post

By The Star's Own Service

New Haven, Conn.—A Kansas native, Virgil C. Dechant, last week assumed leadership of the Knights of Columbus, an organization of 1.25 million Catholic men in the United States, Canada, Mexico, the Philippines and Puerto Rico.

The new supreme knight, who is chairman of the board of Dechant Motor Company in LaCrosse although he now lives in Connecticut, said the most important task confronting him is to increase vocations to the religious life. Vocations have been declining, he said, but no one group is to blame. The Catholic laity—which includes members of his organization—is as much at fault as anyone, Dechant said, and the answer lies in Catholic family life. If there is reverence and encourage-

ment, he said, more children will choose to be priests or sisters.

Dechant, who was born in Antonino, Kan., joined the Knights in 1949 through the Liebenthal, Kan., Council. From 1960 to 1962 he was deputy of the state organization and then became state treasurer. In 1963 he was elected to the Supreme Board of Directors, the governing body of the national organization, and in 1967 became the board's supreme secretary.

VIRGIL C. DECHANT
. . . hails from LaCrosse

highest office of the fraternal Order he revered so much— was now a reality. The farmer and businessman from the plains of Kansas, who had joined the Order 28 years earlier, would now lead the Knights of Columbus.

News of Dechant's promotion spread far and wide. "Kansan in Top K. of C. Post" read one headline from the *Kansas City Star*. "A Kansas native, Virgil C. Dechant, last week assumed leadership of the Knights of Columbus, an organization of 1.25 million Catholic men in the United States, Canada, Mexico, the Philippines and Puerto Rico," the article read.

In Hays, Kansas, Jack Schramm, alumni director of Dechant's alma mater, St. Joseph Military Academy, which by then was known as Thomas More Prep High School, called Dechant's election "the biggest public relations benefit ever in the history of TMP." Schramm continued, "It is probably the highest Christian leadership post in the world that can be held by a layman."

Dechant would return to Kansas in April for a K of C board meeting and to attend a testimonial dinner in his honor on the campus of

Fort Hays State University in Hays. Many of Dechant's longtime friends from the Kansas State Council were there that night, as was his predecessor, John McDevitt, who spoke in praise of Dechant. Also in attendance was another mentor, the Most Reverend Marion Forst, Bishop of Dodge City, who had advised Dechant to make the move to New Haven in the first place. Dechant had stayed in close contact with Bishop Forst from New Haven, sharing letters and asking about goings on in the Dodge City diocese.

It was clear to anyone who listened to Dechant's acceptance speech in San Juan that he had given much thought and preparation to his primary initiatives as supreme knight. He began by dedicating his administration to the Blessed Mother. And he announced his intention to launch a program that would commit the Order to increasing voca-

New Supreme Knight Dechant returned to Kansas in April 1977 for a board meeting in Hays.

tions to religious life, similar to the program he had started as state deputy in Kansas.

Both initiatives would be tested, almost immediately, at the highest level. The following January, Dechant and his wife Ann took a trip to Rome for an audience with Pope Paul VI, Dechant's fourth such trip to Rome since his maiden visit in 1971. The frequent trips had strengthened the relationship between the K of C and the Holy See; in 1973, during a board meeting in Rome, the pope received the entire K of C board of directors in private audience and told them that they were "an immense force for good, a nation."

Escorted by Count Enrico Galeazzi, Dechant would now be received by Paul VI for the first time as supreme knight. Dechant explained to the pontiff that he had dedicated his administration to the Blessed Mother and that one of his major initiatives would be a program intended to promote vocations to the priesthood and religious life.

"Before we wade too far into it, I should ask you for your blessing," Dechant explained.

The pontiff, speaking in Italian and translated through Galeazzi, told Dechant, "What do you think you can do that the church isn't already doing?" He was speaking of vocations.

Dechant was stumped by the question and unsure how to respond. Before he could think of something to say, the pope came to his rescue.

"I'll tell you what you can do," the pope said. "You just told me that you had 1,250,000 members. Adding in wives and children, that's probably four million people or more. That's twice the size of Ireland.

"If Ireland has been able to provide all these priests to mission countries for so many years, so can you—if you set your mind to it. But the vocations must come from your own families. They've got to be your children, your nieces, your nephews."

Dechant was stunned. In one short conversation, the leader of the Catholic Church had weighed and measured his vocations idea. The verdict was clear—go for it.

"I took that to heart and never forgot it," Dechant later recalled. "Blessed Pope Paul was a man who probably understood the church as well as any pope. He'd been secretary of state and knew the far parts of the world. Once while visiting with him, he told me, 'The pope never sleeps. When they [Catholics] go to sleep in Rome, they rise in the Philippines.' He was saying that you're busy full time. He was the pope that gave us Humanae Vitae. He was *so* right, if you look back on what's happened since that time."

Beyond the vocations program, Dechant spent the first few months of his administration unveiling other changes, or tweaks, to the way the

Passing the torch: Past Supreme Knight McDevitt and Supreme Chaplain Archbishop Greco help install Dechant as supreme knight in 1977.

Order functioned. His many years working for the Order at the grassroots level (and as supreme secretary) gave him vast experience to draw from as he planned such changes.

One tweak was to make priests honorary life members, exempt from paying dues. This change put an end to some awkward situations that arose when priests were transferred to new parishes and chose to join new councils. Sometimes, a priest's home council would exempt their cleric from dues out of courtesy. Other councils didn't do things the same way, and, often a priest's former council would tire of paying per capita tax on his behalf and decide to suspend his membership, which only created a lot of unnecessary ill will.

Dechant also pledged that the Order would sponsor a daily Catholic Mass at St. Mary's Church in New Haven—where the Order had been founded—in honor of the Order's deceased members. Years later, a change was made to include deceased wives of members in the offering.

At the supreme convention that summer in Indianapolis, Indiana, (his first convention as supreme knight) Dechant announced that *Columbia* magazine, the Order's monthly publication, would continue to be offered to the widows of deceased Knights of Columbus, as long as these women wished to receive it. This was an initiative, no doubt, influenced by Dechant's experience as grand knight in Liebenthal, where he had received a phone call on the eve of the famed Liebenthal Columbus Day party from the widow of a member, asking if she was still welcome at the party. Dechant never forgot the incident, and, as he had promised himself, if given the opportunity, he would take any steps necessary to keep widows involved.

One change to the convention itself had Dechant's fingerprints all over it. During convention social gatherings and dinners, the wives of

Count Enrico Galeazzi, center, presented Dechant to Pope Paul VI during a 1973 audience for the board of directors.

Virgil and Ann Dechant, center, march through the streets of Detroit, Michigan, with K of C supreme officers, directors, and their wives.

the Order's officers and board members were seated on the dais with their husbands. No longer would they be forced to separate and sit with their jurisdictions.

In his Supreme Knight's report to the Indianapolis convention delegates, titled "Trust in Providence," Dechant graciously acknowledged his predecessor, McDevitt, for his 13 years of service as supreme knight. He also took the opportunity to affirm a strong pro-life position on behalf of the Order. He wrote, "Certainly one of the most important ways in which we can express our Catholic idealism today is to take a firm stand against the unabashed and wholesale destruction of human life through fetal infanticide."

It was clear in Dechant's report that the new supreme knight had an eye to the future, particularly 1982. Just five years away, 1982 would mark the centennial of the Knights of Columbus. To help chronicle all the Knights had accomplished in the previous century, Dechant solicited a writer and historian to begin work on producing the first definitive history of the Knights of Columbus. He filled both job descriptions with one man, Christopher J. Kauffman, Ph.D., who'd been recommended by "two prominent priest historians," Father Colman Barry, O.S.B., and Father Robert Trisco. Kauffman would take on the monumental task of researching and writing the history of the Order. He officially joined the home office staff in September 1977 with a tentative plan of five years to complete the work.

Dechant also eyed a brick-and-mortar museum to house the Order's many pieces of history. That project, in time, would also come to fruition.

Finally, Dechant found inspiration from his own father.

C.J. Dechant, an ardent believer in the power of prayer and the rosary, suggested to his son that the Order provide its new members with a complimentary rosary. Virgil was slow to heed his advice.

"I apparently gave him lip service," Virgil said, "so, finally, he bought the first 500 rosaries for the Order and shipped them to me with a note that said, 'Now let's start that program.'

"So the rosary program started as new, or readmitted members, came in. All the rosaries were blessed by the supreme chaplain. We sent them out a rosary in a little box. This became very popular. After Vatican II, many people, it seemed, had lost their rosaries in the rear of their dresser drawers. Or they had de-emphasized them. So we started the rosary program. This fell in with revamping our ceremonials. The post-Vatican II ceremonials that we had introduced in the late 1960s were not really getting the job done. So we brought back some of the old lessons that had been taught in the first, second, and third degrees. But the *new* thing was that we provided every new member with a rosary during the first degree. We asked them to commit themselves to praying it every day, or at least having it on their person at all times. And, I must say, that has received enormous support. Many of our meetings now are opened up with a decade of the rosary, and that emphasis is always there."

Dechant had set a fast pace for his administration. His agenda, ambitious. Now there was work to be done. And there was the reputation of his predecessors, Hart and McDevitt, to live up to.

CHAPTER SEVEN

Virgil Dechant sat in the back seat of a private car and watched in amazement. The car had a television and on it was being shown the worldwide broadcast of the funeral of Pope Paul VI.

It was August 1978, and Dechant had just arrived in New Orleans, Louisiana, where the Knights of Columbus supreme convention was being held. The convention hotel had sent a car to the airport to pick up the supreme knight, who in no small way was responsible for the broadcast he was watching on live TV.

Dechant was not watching alone, of course. Hundreds of millions of people around the world were tuning in to witness such a historic event, all through their television sets.

Virgil and Ann Dechant, above, second row, became frequent fliers, spanning the globe on Knights of Columbus business. Pictured in front of the Dechants are Supreme Advocate Harold J. Lamboley and his wife Genevieve.

That April, Dechant and the K of C board of directors had visited Rome for a meeting. While there, they had been received in private audience by the pontiff, whom Dechant noticed was ailing. His movements seemed slow, and he was being carried around on his silk-covered armchair—or, in Italian, his sedia gestatoria—everywhere he went. So it came as little surprise in August when Dechant received word of the pope's death at age 80.

Almost immediately after the death, Dechant was contacted from Rome by Polish Bishop Andrzej (Andrew) Maria Deskur, who headed the Pontifical Commission for Social Communications (renamed the Pontifical Council for Social Communications in 1989). Dechant was deeply immersed in his final preparations for the upcoming convention, but he took time to consider Deskur's request.

Supreme Knight Dechant speaks to a television reporter during the 1977 supreme convention in Indianapolis, Indiana.

It was actually three requests, Deskur told him: "When we established the Uplink program, we decided to cover Easter week services, Midnight Mass, and one other event. I don't know if you'd call this one event or three events, but I'd like to ask you to provide the Uplink of the funeral of Pope Paul VI, the opening of the conclave to elect the new pope, and then his installation Mass."

The Satellite Uplink program Deskur described, which was sponsored by the Knights of Columbus, allowed television signals to be broadcast throughout the world by satellite. Dechant had been heavily involved in consummating the agreement with Deskur in 1975 when he, Supreme Chaplain Bishop Charles Greco, and Elmer Von Feldt, editor of *Columbia*, had met in Rome to negotiate the terms of the deal. The agreement that was finalized, precisely as Deskur alluded to in his

Dechant, left, maintained close contact with his predecessor John McDevitt.

appeal to Dechant, called for the Knights to support the broadcast of three significant events of the Holy See each year—an Easter holy week ceremony, Christmas Midnight Mass, and another papal event, to be determined by the Vatican.

Now Deskur was asking the Knights of Columbus to do more, and fast, so the entire world could see the pope's funeral and the process by which his successor would be elected.

Dechant called an impromptu meeting of the executive and finance committee. The committee agreed. The Knights of Columbus would fund the broadcast of the pope's funeral to the world.

As Dechant sat in the back of the car and stared at the TV, he thought to himself, *What a wonderful program, to bring this to the entire world.*

Thus began a whirlwind two months for Dechant, the Vatican, and Catholics worldwide.

At the supreme convention in New Orleans, Dechant reported to convention delegates that the Order had instituted a survey by the National Opinion Research Center (NORC) at the University of Chicago to study the attitudes of young people, aged 14-30, toward the Catholic church and religious life. The survey came at the suggestion of then Archbishop of Cincinnati (and future Cardinal) Joseph Bernardin and was conducted by noted priest, author, and sociologist Fr. Andrew Greeley; its findings, which the Knights hoped would aid its vocations initiative, would be available in 1981.

Also in New Orleans, the order resolved to "unite with all other civic-minded citizens and agencies to stem the deluge of sex and violence," in response to the proliferation of sex, violence, and crime in popular culture.

On August 26, 1978, the papal conclave selected Albino Cardinal

From left: Count Enrico Galeazzi, Ann Dechant, Virgil Dechant, Bishop Charles Greco, and Pope John Paul I just three days prior to his installation as pope.

Luciani—an Italian archbishop, then known, as all archbishops of Venice, as the "Patriarch of Venice"—to become the new pope. He took the name John Paul I.

The K of C board of directors decided to send Virgil and Ann Dechant and Bishop Greco to Rome to attend the new pontiff's installation as representatives of the Order. The Dechants were greeted at the Rome airport by Count Enrico Galeazzi and his driver, Gianetti Bonaventura. Galeazzi told them the new pope was in retreat; that night the Dechants dined with Galeazzi at his home. The following day, sandwiched between the pope's appearances with the worldwide press, Galeazzi arranged for the Dechants to meet the new pontiff in private audience, three days

Pope John Paul I, left, was, according to Virgil Dechant, "very kind to Ann."

before his installation. It was the first such audience the new pope had granted.

"Of course that's very rare," Dechant later explained of his seven-minute meeting with the new pope. "I remember his zucchetto wouldn't even stay on his head; it kept falling off. They hadn't fitted him properly. But he was very kind, very smart, and very kind to Ann. If there's anything I can say about Pope John Paul I, it's that he was a great evangelizer. I was sure to read every one of his messages that were printed in *L'Osservatore Romano*."

As promised, the Knights of Columbus provided the uplink that helped introduce John Paul I to the world.

After the papal installation, the Dechants returned to the United States. Just 33 days later the world received shocking news. Pope John Paul I, 65, had died in his sleep, making his papacy among the shortest in modern times. The Fiat he had driven to attend the papal conclave a month before was still parked in the same spot on the street near the Vatican at the time of his death.

Soon after, Dechant, attending a board meeting in Canada, received a phone call from Bishop Deskur in Rome, and, he recalled, "it started all over."

"This time he [Deskur] wanted to broadcast the funeral Mass of John Paul I and then the first words of the new pope from the window of St. Peter's façade, where the pope, historically, makes his first appearance. Then the installation Mass.

"So we had a short meeting and agreed to provide for that. Again, the board voted to send Ann and me and Supreme Physician Dr. John and Mary Lou Griffin, and Bishop Greco, the supreme chaplain, to Rome. Our son Tom also went along."

The Dechants and their traveling party attended the installation

Mass of Cardinal Karol Jozef Wojtyla, from Poland, who was elected on the third day of the papal conclave. Wojtyla, who was a longtime friend of Bishop Deskur, took the name John Paul II.

When the Holy Father uttered his first words from the balcony of St. Peter's Basilica, Dechant thought to himself—just like he had from the car in New Orleans—*How fortunate we are to have arranged for the Uplink program that will bring these first words to the people of the world.*

"And we all know, when he came out of that window, he said, 'I come from a far country,'" Dechant recalled. "And then in the course of his speech he said, 'Be not afraid to welcome Christ and accept his power.' Another phrase he used throughout his papacy was, 'Open wide the doors to Christ.'"

There were more than 300,000 people in St. Peter's Square that day to see the new pope and more than one million people watching on television around the world, thanks, in part, to the generosity of the Knights of Columbus. The Dechants attended John Paul II's installation Mass and his first general audience, held in the Paul VI Audience Hall. Three days after the installation, the Dechants were granted a private audience with the new pontiff. It was a déjà vu experience, having greeted his predecessor little more than a month earlier. For Dechant, this audience with the pontiff would be the first of more than 70 personal encounters the two would share over the next two-and-a-half decades. They would also share much mutual respect and a strong friendship.

Dechant presented the new pope with a sculpture of the Madonna produced by Boleslaw Cybis, a Polish artist. At the suggestion of Knights of Columbus board member Julian Joseph and his wife Wanda, who were both of Polish descent, Dechant greeted John Paul II in Polish, uttering the phrase, "Praised be Jesus Christ."

The phrase in Polish ("Niech bedzie pochwalony Jezus Chrystus")

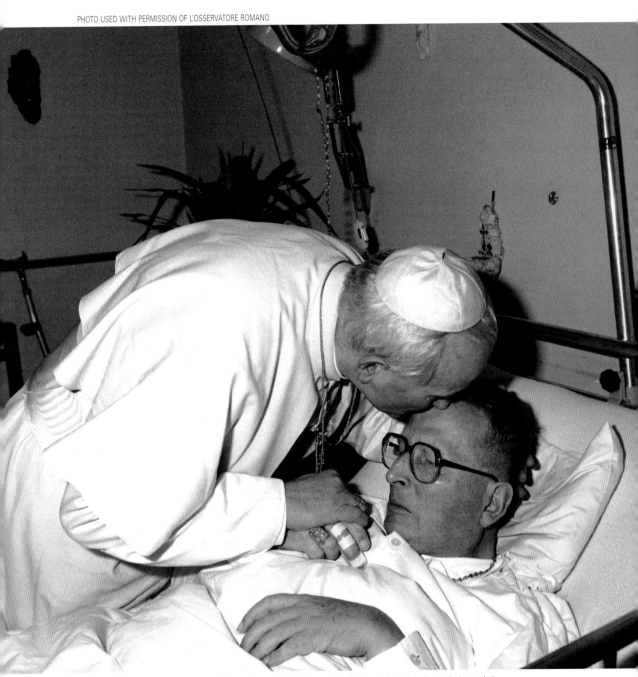

Pope John Paul II, almost immediately after becoming pope, visited his good friend Bishop Andrzej Maria Deskur in the hospital.

resembled the phrase in German ("Gelobt sei Jesus Christus") that Dechant had heard spoken around his house as a youth, and he delivered the greeting spot-on.

"You're Polish?" the Pope asked.

"No, Holy Father, I'm German," Dechant said.

The exchange confused the prefect of the papal household, Archbishop Jacques Martin, a Frenchman, who had always suspected Dechant was a French name. Martin was standing between Dechant and the Pope when Dechant mentioned his German heritage.

"I could see his chin drop," Dechant said.

Lost in the excitement of such a rapid papal transition, Archbishop Deskur, shortly after contacting Dechant about television coverage of the new pope's installation, suffered a stroke. He survived the episode but lived with its effects for the rest of his life, bound to a wheelchair, sometimes slurring his speech, making him hard to understand. His malady was not lost on his longtime friend, the new pontiff, who went to visit Deskur in the hospital shortly after being named pope; nor was it lost on Dechant, who would continue to pay Deskur visits for many years. Dechant said he took solace in the fact that the Polish cleric "was always praying for us." In 1985, Deskur would be named a cardinal.

The first few months of John Paul II's papacy were indicative of how this pontiff would cast his influence over Catholics across the world—he traveled. He would visit more than 100 countries during his years as pope, a style befitting the leader of the worldwide Church and a world that felt increasingly smaller thanks to modern technology and travel conveniences.

The pope's first trip in January 1979 was to Santo Domingo, the capital city of the Dominican Republic. Octavio Antonio Cardinal Beras

The Dechants and Bishop Greco were received by John Paul II in private audience just three days after his installation.

Rojas, the archbishop of Santo Domingo, invited the Dechants, Bishop Greco, and Supreme Treasurer Dan McCormick to Santo Domingo for the historic visit. The new pope's first visit to the Americas was packed with excitement, and the Dechants could feel the anticipation as they mixed with the people of Santo Domingo.

While in Santo Domingo, the Dechants, Bishop Greco, and McCormick met the Holy Father at the nunciature. They also met with Cardinal Beras Rojas to discuss establishing the Knights of Columbus in the Dominican Republic. Within a matter of months came a new council—Council #8000—and the Order has continued to grow in the Dominican Republic since that time.

From there, the pope continued on to Mexico. The Dechants, meanwhile, returned to New Haven.

The papal excursion to Mexico was preceded with controversy, rooted in the fallout from the persecution of Catholics and the suppression of organized religion that existed there until the middle of the 20th century. According to Dechant, "Everybody had a tongue-in-cheek take on how the Mexicans would accept the Holy Father. Since the persecution, priests weren't even allowed to dress up in priestly garments. But the pope went bravely into Mexico. As he said, 'Be not afraid.' And it was a tremendous success."

The success was both aided and captured through the assistance of the Knights of Columbus. The Mexican bank Banamex produced a professional-quality film documenting the pope's visit, and the Knights helped to distribute it.

Dechant called the film "a masterpiece of acceptance by the people of Mexico," and in little time the Knights parlayed that work into an effort to help break down the Iron Curtain in Europe. It came about, Dechant said, when, while attending the funeral of Cardinal John

Wright, he was contacted by Bishop Paul Marcinkus, president of the Institute for the Works of Religion (IOR) at the Vatican, commonly referred to as the Vatican Bank.

"Marcinkus, who traveled with the pope a lot, was a big, strong man, who sort of acted as his clerical bodyguard. He came to me and said, 'You know, the pope is getting ready to go to Poland. People are nervous over there.'

"The Iron Curtain was still in effect, and they were still under the domination of Russia. Marcinkus said, 'We'd like to show the reaction of the Mexican people to the people of Poland. Would the Knights of Columbus be willing to dub that film into Polish?'"

Dechant and the Order readily agreed to translate the film into Polish and English.

"We had to have those films smuggled into Poland by priests carrying them," Dechant said. "They were shown clandestinely in and around the country with the thought that this would give the Polish people courage and let them welcome home their native son with great enthusiasm in the face of opposition from the communist regime."

The pope made three major speeches in Poland, including one on the subject of the Common Christian Roots of the European Nations. The subject—the similar Christian backgrounds of all the European nations—was a cause that mattered deeply to the pontiff and one the Order would embrace on his behalf early in the next decade. The pope would later lament the fact that the Common Christian Roots were seemingly ignored in constitutional documents during the formation of the European Union.

The pope maintained his busy travel schedule into the fall. He visited the United States in October 1979, stopping in Boston, New York, and Washington, D.C. The Dechants attended the pope's Mass on the

John Paul II took time during his 1979 U.S. visit to meet with the K of C board of directors in Washington, D.C., at the papal nunciature.

Boston Common, where they sat next to Massachusetts Senator Edward "Ted" Kennedy and Henry Cabot Lodge Jr., onetime presidential representative to the Holy See, during a downpour that lasted throughout the 90-minute outdoor service. The Dechants followed the pope to New York, where he addressed the General Assembly of the United Nations and said Mass for 75,000 people at Yankee Stadium. Later, the Knights of Columbus helped erect a plaque to commemorate the papal visit beyond the outfield wall in the ballpark. The plaque was later moved to the "new" Yankee Stadium, which opened in 2009.

Then the Dechants followed the pope to Washington, D.C., where he celebrated Mass at the Basilica of the National Shrine of the Immaculate Conception and on the National Mall, the latter drawing 175,000 people. It was there that Virgil for the first time had the honor of receiving Holy Communion from the pope. It was a "thrill" beyond imagination, he said. While in Washington, Dechant also arranged for the pope to meet members of the Knights of Columbus board of directors at the house of the apostolic delegation.

For the new pontiff, the U.S. trip was a whirlwind. In addition to these east coast cities, he visited Philadelphia, Chicago, and Des Moines, Iowa. He gave an estimated 70 speeches during the weeklong trip, met crowds that routinely grew beyond 100,000 people, and affirmed the faith of countless American Catholics. The year 1979 also seemed like a whirlwind for the Dechants. In October, Virgil joined the leaders of five other fraternals in Glasgow, Scotland, to form the International Alliance of Catholic Knights (IACK).

At the K of C home office in New Haven, work on uncovering the history of the Order, one of the principal initiatives of Dechant's administration, was ongoing. At the helm was historian Christopher Kauffman, who had established a tiny writing space on the 17th floor at One Columbus Plaza. Kauffman was the consummate writer, the sort who worked in sudden flurries that others could only marvel at. If you opened up his desk drawer, you'd find a stash of cigars. He was an incessant smoker who frequently left trails of ashes on desks and files cabinets, much to the chagrin of other home office staffers.

"He was all over the place," remembered one former coworker.

Kauffman was also an expert researcher.

His task was monumental. Sherman Riley, the Order's historian at the home office, had been collecting pieces of history and records for some time, but these were a mixture of accuracies and inaccuracies. Kauffman's job was to sift through it all and separate fact from fiction. From time to time he would update the supreme knight on his progress, particularly if he had uncovered a noteworthy historical fact or evidence that ran contrary to long-held assumptions about the history of the Order.

Kauffman shared his small office with Mary Lou Cummings, who had been hired part-time to assist Kauffman and begin work on another major project, the creation of a Knights of Columbus Museum. Cummings was married to John Cummings, who was the art director for *Columbia* magazine, the Order's monthly publication. Throughout the history of the Knights of Columbus, it would have been difficult to find a husband-and-wife tandem who had contributed so much to the preservation of the Order's public image.

Cummings' greatest challenge was restoring aging pieces of K of C history that were sometimes not in the greatest condition.

"I had an area that was like someone's attic," she said. "It was a conglomeration of boxes and all sorts of artifacts and paintings and art-work. Things were either in great condition or horrible. The first year I spent a lot of time just finding restorers and conservators that could work with the collection we had and sort of make sense out of what we could group together. It was really an investigative process for every-thing that was there. We either didn't know where it came from or we had lost records of who the donors were.

"The biggest challenges were the restorations. Things in the McGivney gallery came from the old homestead site. When we first started, Virgil and some of the supreme officers went up to Waterbury because there was a man there who had cleared out the estate of the last niece, Anna McGivney. Everything was up in the attic, so the officers went up there and purchased it...that was the nucleus of the collection. But many of those pieces were in horrible condition. The drawings were torn; the paintings were in bad condition. Everything needed to go out for resto-ration. I was fortunate to find somebody in Waltham, Massachusetts, who was a paper restorer that was well known at the Fogg Museum in Boston. He did wonderful restoration work for me."

In light of her own expansive challenges, Cummings could only marvel at the work her colleague Kauffman did on the history book.

"He had some files that he could use and others that were erroneous, and he couldn't use them," she said. "He was always traveling, interviewing people. Interviews, interviews...I just don't know how he ever got it in chronological order. That was a feat in itself, to start from ground zero and get some idea of, not just the supreme knights, but how they worked with the church and the problems that each administration came up against."

Dechant's vision was to see the Knights of Columbus museum make its home on the fourth floor of One Columbus Plaza, a space previously occupied by the department of personnel. That floor would also be home to an office chapel, which was under construction during the same time.

The transformation from personnel office to museum allowed Dechant to showcase his own creativity, an often-overlooked aspect of his personality, Cummings explained. "He loved being involved in it," she said. "He had a vision of what it could be and the different areas that we could highlight or use as subject matter. He's visionary in that regard."

As soon as Cummings had made significant progress on the creation of exhibits, the Order invited state deputies from around the country to preview the collection during their annual trip to New Haven for the State Deputy Meeting. The artifacts were displayed on card tables on the fourth floor with simple labels in front of each exhibit. This exercise served two purposes: it showcased the work that had already been completed and it motivated the state deputies to return to their home states and call upon their state councils to submit historic artifacts for use in the museum.

The Basilica of the National Shrine of the Immaculate Conception in Washington, D.C. The Knights Tower is shown at left.

To transform the existing space on the fourth floor, the Knights hired architect Kevin Roche of the Roche-Dinkeloo firm in New Haven, well known for creating numerous designs, including the worldwide headquarters of John Deere in Moline, Illinois; the Ford Foundation in New York; and, of course, the home office of the Knights of Columbus at One Columbus Plaza, which he'd now be altering. For more than 40 years, Roche would serve as the chief architect of the Metropolitan Museum of Art. The chapel, which became known as the Holy Family Chapel, would get completed in 1980. The museum exhibits would officially be unveiled during the 1982 centennial year.

Dedicating the home office chapel to the family unit was symbolic of Dechant's belief that the Knights of Columbus should be a family organization. Indeed, that was part of his message to delegates at the 1979 supreme convention in San Diego, California. An effort was underway, Dechant told the delegates, to help transform the image of the Order from an "organization of Catholic men" to a "Catholic family, fraternal, service organization." This was Dechant's Kansas agenda, now being tested on a larger stage.

Also at the San Diego convention that year, the Knights of Columbus decided to honor former Supreme Knight Luke Hart for his many contributions to the Order. This was a cause especially close to Dechant's heart, since he had always fancied himself as a sort of Luke Hart protégé, dating back to his earliest years with the K of C. To honor Hart, the Knights established a fund in his name to provide for maintenance at the Basilica of the National Shrine of the Immaculate Conception in Washington, particularly the bell tower, which had been constructed in 1957 after the Knights pledged $1 million. Five years later, under Hart's leadership, the Knights donated an additional $150,000 to install a carillon of 56 bells.

Under Dechant, the Knights raised $500,000 for the Hart fund, and later that amount grew to $1 million. Within a few years, Dechant recalled, some repair work was needed on the tower's stone and bells, and the Knights covered the cost. In honoring traditions that dated back to medieval times, Shrine officials decided to name the tower's largest bells, and they did so after patrons of the Knights of Columbus. There was a "Christopher" bell, named after Christopher Columbus; a "Michael" bell, in honor of Father Michael McGivney; and, of course a "Luke" bell, in honor of Luke Hart, among others. In 1989, the Shrine honored Dechant with his own bell, dedicated in the name of Saint Virgil. Today, all past supreme knights have a bell named in their honor.

As a new decade dawned, Dechant and the Order focused intensely on the upcoming centennial. In 1980 at the supreme convention in Atlanta, Georgia, the supreme council passed a resolution inviting Pope John Paul II to the 1982 centennial convention in Hartford, Connecticut. The Order soon made plans to invite new U.S. President Ronald Reagan to the Hartford convention. Reagan's spirit, charm, and unique flavor of no-nonsense conservatism had taken the nation by storm, carrying him to a decisive victory in the November election—and into the collective conscience of the Knights of Columbus, who shared many of his values.

After sponsoring a series of regional seminars to reexamine the K of C

Brother Knights in Canada proudly welcomed Supreme Knight Dechant to their country in 1980.

ceremonials, Dechant appointed Samuel Dambrocia, past state deputy from Pennsylvania, as the director of ceremonials for the supreme council. The seminars had revealed widespread support for revisions, and Dechant assembled a team of Knights to work with Dambrocia on revamping the program. The revisions would get released to universal acclaim in 1981. Working with his brother Knights of Columbus on the project—namely Lou Mautino and Don Dreiling—Dechant was clearly in his element. As one former supreme director put it: "Mr. Dechant was a fraternalist."

Dechant invited his ceremonials team to his New Haven residence almost every evening while they reworked, rewrote, and rehearsed the program in his office at home. Discretion was a priority, given the secrecy that accompanies the Order's rituals. After they had finished their work for the evening, Ann Dechant would provide sandwiches and beverages for her husband and his colleagues.

In early 1980, at the suggestion of Bishop (and future cardinal) Bernard Law, the K of C provided a grant to the Pope John XXIII Medical Moral Research and Education Center to help study difficult scientific questions about issues related to birth control, reproductive rights, and so forth. The grant in part helped fund a workshop on these issues that year in Dallas, Texas, and provided additional funding for workshops in subsequent years.

In December 1980, at the urging of Count Galeazzi, Virgil and Ann decided to take their family to Rome for Christmas; they tied the trip in with a vacation to Germany. As usual, Galeazzi arranged for their every need in Rome. He telegrammed Dechant in November: "Papal audience probably twenty third...only dark suits for men...black veils for ladies available here...everything arranged for Midnight Mass."

The 1980 Rome trip was one of the few times Dechant visited the city for pleasure. However, he still found a way to mix in a significant amount of business. While Ann and the family toured the many land-marks in Rome, Virgil spent most of his days in meetings at the Vatican. One such meeting was with Cardinal Agostino Casaroli, the Vatican secretary of state, on the subject of inviting the pope to the 1982 centennial convention in Hartford. Casaroli advised Dechant that the protocol for such a request would be for Dechant to ask Archbishop John Whealon of Hartford to formally invite the Holy Father in writing; Dechant could then carry the letter and personally deliver it to the pope. Plans were set in motion to carry out this objective, but, as history would bear out, other forces would intervene.

The 1980 Rome trip was one of the most memorable for the Dechants. For one, they had their entire family in tow: Tom and his wife,

PHOTO USED WITH PERMISSION OF L'OSSERVATORE ROMANO.

1980 Rome trip, from left: Tom Dechant, Maggie Dechant, Ann Dechant, Pope John Paul II, Virgil Dechant, Karen Dechant, Dan Dechant, Bob Dechant.

the former Maggie Dunleavy; Dan, Karen, and Bobby. Visiting Rome at Christmas cemented the family's strong affinity for the city. The trip also furthered the relationship between the Dechants and the Galeazzis—a bond that remains strong to this day. Count Galeazzi insisted the Dechants join his family for multiple meals at his home during their stay, including Christmas dinner, where both families exchanged gifts.

On their second full day in Rome, the Dechants were granted a private audience with Pope John Paul II in the Throne Room. Virgil met alone with the Holy Father for 15 minutes before the rest of the family joined him. The pope presented everyone with a rosary, and he jokingly asked the women if they belonged to the Knights of Columbus.

From left: Count Enrico Galeazzi, Virgil Dechant, Bishop Charles Greco.

"We were all nervous," Ann wrote in her diary. "It certainly was a great privilege to have the whole family meet the Holy Father."

Maggie Dechant, Tom's wife—and the family's first in-law—was in awe of the Rome experience, she said. The same was true for the way her father-in-law was revered by the people in Rome.

"It was like, 'Oh, my God.' The way he [Virgil] was treated; he was so well respected. The immediate family had a private audience with John Paul II, and it was overwhelming. We had front-row seats at Midnight Mass, a private tour of the Sistine Chapel...the Galeazzis had us into their home for Christmas."

Dechant's profile in Rome was rising fast. Clearly, Galeazzi's influence had much to do with it. The former Vatican architect and Rome K of C ambassador was himself so well respected in Rome that any person he vouched for was treated in kind. Archbishop Deskur was another important advisor to Dechant on all matters in Rome, as was Archbishop Lino Zanini, from the Office of Administration of St. Peter's Basilica. Dechant described Zanini as "an industrious, brilliant bishop with an artistic appreciation." Together, these three helped Dechant navigate the sometimes-delicate diplomatic channels in Rome.

"They all assisted me in carrying out some of the programs that we were fortunate enough to participate in," Dechant said. "And they helped me understand the mentality that prevails on various issues in Rome."

The next two decades would provide Dechant and the Knights of Columbus with more opportunities for involvement with the Vatican—the sort of opportunities too important to pass up.

CHAPTER EIGHT

D uring the run-up to the 1982 centennial, the Knights of Columbus became heavily involved in numerous Vatican activities. Dechant and the Order, thanks in part to the strong relationships forged by Count Enrico Galeazzi, had captured significant momentum in working with the leadership of the worldwide church, and they didn't want to let it slip away.

Late in 1981, Rome was the host site for an international colloquium on the Common Christian Roots of the European Nations, a cause that mattered deeply to Pope John Paul II. A few hundred scholars attended the colloquium. The K of C supported the event financially, including paying for the expenses of many scholars who couldn't afford to travel to Rome, due in large part to the depleted value of eastern European currency. After the colloquium, the Knights were asked to provide for the printing and binding of the event's proceedings. The Knights complied with the request, printing two-volume sets of proceedings that totaled more than 1,000 pages; they took this assistance a step further by printing 1,500 special sets for the pope to personally distribute, at a cost of approximately $90,000. Dechant was given 10 sets, two of which were signed by the Holy Father; one for the Order and one for his family.

Dechant saw this involvement as something more than a simple print-and-bind job.

"In providing for this need, I thought that the Order was part of a very historic moment," Dechant said later. "Those documents contained the underlying theme that eastern Europe should be free from Russian domination. And that meant that they should bring down the wall and all the other pieces to that puzzle that happened in subsequent years."

Another important Vatican project took root that same year. Dechant was asked if the Knights of Columbus would finance the construction of a chapel in the grottoes beneath St. Peter's Basilica—near the tomb of St. Peter—in honor of Saints Benedict, Cyril, and Methodius, all patron saints of Europe (by a 1980 declaration of Pope John Paul II). Dechant took the matter to his board of directors, and they readily agreed to the project, with one provision. Dechant asked that a plaque be erected on the wall near the chapel's entrance to commemorate the Order's contribution to the project. The request was at first rebuffed, and Dechant was told that plaques aren't normally erected in St. Peter's to commemorate such events; eventually, the plaque would get approved.

Subsequently, the Order contributed to the enlargement of a nearby Polish-themed chapel dedicated in honor of Our Lady of Czestochowa. That work, too, would get a plaque.

The task of deciding how to parcel out the Order's charitable dollars, Dechant said, is one of the most difficult tasks on the plate of the supreme knight. On an almost daily basis, requests for funding came in from all parts of the world. Very few of the causes that reached the desk of the supreme knight were without merit, and most all of them were ongoing causes that required support year after year. The Holy See was just one area where the Knights of Columbus provided financial backing. The Order regularly assisted causes for vocations to religious life, family and pro-life programming, youth activities, Catholic education, support of bishops and other clergy, and various other cultural programs. Priority was typically given to charities located where the Order had formed existing councils.

Count Enrico Galeazzi, left, delivers newly printed copies of *The Common Christian Roots of the European Nations* to Pope John Paul II, right.

For causes with long-term sustainability that made appeals to the Order annually, Dechant believed in creating funds in a separate corporation. From this entity, money could be given to charities from the earnings of the fund while always leaving the corpus intact. Conceptually, the Order was creating endowments. As Dechant said, "adhering to this policy guarantees the financial support in perpetuity."

In 1974, the Order had established Knights of Columbus Charities, Inc., a 501 (c)(3) corporation, with an initial investment of $4.4 million, which came from the Order's general account. By the time Dechant took office as supreme knight, Charities, Inc. had grown to $5.2 million. At the time he retired, that amount had grown to $77 million, an increase of nearly 1,500 percent.

As Dechant's travels to Rome became more frequent, mostly as a result of the Order's continued support of the Holy See through causes such as the chapel construction in the grottoes of St. Peter's Basilica, he became aware that Pope John Paul II's access to funds for charities was surprisingly limited. Cardinal Agostino Casaroli, the Vatican secretary of state, in one such face-to-face encounter with Dechant, explained that since 1929 money for the pope's charities no longer came from the general patrimony of the Holy See. A program known as Peter's Pence had been started in France for the sole purpose of providing for the charitable concerns of the Holy Father. Casaroli pointed out that over the years those collections gradually became earmarked for the Holy See's general operating expenses, thus leaving the pope with small amounts to distribute occasionally.

Dechant had in mind an endowment similar to others the Order had created, which would provide funds annually for the pope's personal charities. As Dechant and others contemplated the idea, he asked for feedback from church leaders, including Casaroli, who told him during one visit in Rome that he thought the concept was wonderful. Archbishop Andrzej Maria Deskur thought the same. Apostolic Delegate Pio Laghi, who later became a cardinal, worked with the supreme knight and the supreme chaplain to set up the fund.

At the 1981 supreme convention in Louisville, Kentucky, where the weeklong theme was "First and Always Catholic," the 99th supreme council passed a resolution—the first act of the centennial—to establish an irrevocable endowment in the amount of $10 million with the express purpose of providing annually for the pope's personal charities. The endowment would be known as the Vicarius Christi Foundation (Fondazione).

"As with all our other gifts to the Holy Father, there will be 'no strings attached,'" the proposal read.

The K of C Board of Directors further specified their intention that the funds of the Vicarius Christi Foundation be invested "primarily in church loans, so that while we are assisting the Holy Father, we also, at the same time, shall continue to assist the ordinaries in their mission to serve God's people."

For Dechant, who placed complete trust in the pope's understanding of world affairs, creating the Vicarius Christi Foundation made perfect sense. As he said of the pontiff to a reporter from the *New Haven Register*, "He knows the needs of the world better than we do."

With the centennial celebration of the Order now underway and the centennial convention just a year away, the Knights of Columbus seemed poised to mark 100 years of fraternalism with grand style. Early in his administration, Dechant viewed the centennial preparations as a large-scale, four-year effort that would mark a once-in-a-generation opportunity to announce to the world what the Knights of Columbus was all about. Ready or not, that moment would soon arrive.

In May 1981, Dechant and Cardinal William Baum visited Rome

to attend a congress on vocations in conjunction with bishops from all over the world. Dechant recalls that just two laymen were invited to the congress, he and the head of Serra International, a lay organization dedicated to supporting and promoting vocations to religious life. Also in attendance was Father John McGuire, who then headed the Catholic Information Service and had been asked by Dechant to oversee the Order's vocation program.

On Wednesday, May 13, the congress held no meetings so attendees were free to see the pope's weekly audience in St. Peter's Square. That morning, Dechant and Galeazzi met with the substitute secretary of state, Archbishop Martinez Somalo and Archbishop Lino Zanini, to review progress on the construction of the chapel of the three saints beneath St. Peter's Basilica. There, Dechant and Galeazzi viewed a bronze model of the Carolingian crucifix that was going to be installed in the chapel, along with a bronze celebrant's chair, and a model of a triptych of the three saints—Benedict, Cyril, and Methodius—which would sit above the altar. All three pieces were the work of Tommaso Gismondi, a famed Italian sculptor. Archbishop Somalo informed Dechant that the pope was even considering the chapel for his eventual burial site.

After the meeting concluded, Dechant, Galeazzi, and Father McGuire headed to St. Peter's Square for the papal audience. It was there that a would-be assassin would make an attempt on the pope's life. The events that followed are best told from Dechant's own memories.

"I was so excited about the progress of the chapel, to be part of such history in the church, near the tomb of St. Peter. I was in awe. After that, Count Galeazzi and I went to the audience. We had seats, as usual when you went with the Count, in the front row in St. Peter's Square. While we were waiting for the pope to come, all of a sudden we heard gunshots.

Wounded in Vatican City: Papal aides rushed to the pope's side in the immediate aftermath of an attempt on his life in May 1981.

The pigeons flew overhead. And everybody knew immediately that there had been an attempt on the pope's life.

"The shooter, a Turk by the name of Mehmet Ali Agca, had wounded the pope with a bullet, very close to his heart. And I recall there was an auxiliary bishop of New York, who was of Italian heritage, Bishop Mestice, who grabbed the microphone and led everyone in saying the rosary in Italian. Then we watched as the ambulance and the jeep that the pope rode in went through the iron gates into St. Peter's. And they locked those gates and guarded them off so nobody else could enter there."

The large crowd in St. Peter's Square was left in stunned silence.

"Soon after, Archbishop Zanini came down from inside the Basilica and asked Count Galeazzi, Father McGuire, and me to go visit Archbishop Deskur, who was still recuperating from his stroke. So we went to see Deskur in his apartment, and there were all his nuns—and the pope's nuns—of Polish extraction. They took care of the pope, and they had all come over to pray with Deskur. We sat in his office. He was in a wheelchair, and he had a little pocket radio. We were listening to the news to hear how the pope was doing. They had taken him to Gemelli Hospital and were giving minute-by-minute progress reports. This was a serious thing. Everybody was very gloomy, very sad. I could see that those Polish sisters were taking it very solemnly. However, I could also sense that they were accustomed to difficult moments, coming from behind the Iron Curtain.

"We sat there and prayed and waited for what must have been an hour. Pretty soon, Archbishop Deskur looked up. Above his desk he had an icon of Our Lady of Czestochowa, to whom the pope was very devoted. Deskur looked at the icon and said, 'Today is the feast of Our Lady of Fatima. She will save him.'

"And as though a miracle happened, the nuns started to smile. They were relieved and had total trust in the Blessed Mother. We stood there for a while and contemplated that, then we decided to go say a prayer in the archbishop's chapel before we took our leave. So we went to that chapel, said our prayers, then we left.

"From there we went to Archbishop Zanini's apartment, which was in the other end of the building. So we went in, and he grabbed a bottle of Johnnie Walker Black and cracked it and said, 'I can't take it anymore.' So he poured himself a big belt.

"I said, 'Archbishop, I'll have one of those, too.' So we all had one."

While they lingered inside Archbishop Zanini's apartment, Zanini explained to Dechant, Galeazzi, and McGuire about the things that had happened inside the Vatican in the few hours since the shooting. Under normal circumstances, Cardinal Casaroli, the secretary of state, would be the person to assume the main leadership role, but Casaroli was traveling to the United States, where he was receiving an honorary degree from St. John's University in New York. In his absence, that duty fell on the shoulders of Italian Cardinal Carlo Confalonieri, dean of the College of Cardinals. On their walk to Archbishop Deskur's apartment, Dechant had spotted Confalonieri walking briskly toward Vatican offices, where, Dechant said, "he was now in command."

Zanini also shared with Dechant and others an eerie phenomenon. He showed his guests a pail full of coins—which, Dechant said, looked like medals—with likenesses of the devil imprinted on them. Amazingly, the coins were dated May 13, that very day, but of a different year. They had been scattered throughout St. Peter's Square on the morning of the shooting, and a group of Vatican employees had picked them up and turned them over to Zanini.

"Here, take one with you," Zanini told Dechant.

President Ronald Reagan, right, pictured with wife Nancy, left, became a close friend of Virgil Dechant and the Knights of Columbus during the 1980s. Here he is pictured at the celebration of the restoration of the Statue of Liberty on July 4, 1986—an event aided by the K of C Fourth Degree, which contributed $1 million.

Dechant, spooked, thought briefly about taking a coin, then told Zanini, "I don't want to travel with it—just ship it to me."

Dechant never heard another mention about the coins from Zanini or anyone. As far as he knows, he may be the only living witness to this historical oddity.

After Dechant and Galeazzi left Zanini's apartment, they found a seat on a cement bench in St. Peter's Square. They sat there for a few minutes, still in a state of shock, to contemplate all that had happened.

"It's strange what goes through your mind," Dechant said. "I was so eager to build that chapel. I thought to myself, 'If the pope dies, the next pope may have something totally different in mind, and that chapel may never even get built.'"

Fearing the worst, Dechant asked Vatican officials the following day if he could take the models of the bronze Gismondi sculptures back to the United States. He explained that the Order was in the process of assembling a collection of museum exhibits and the pieces would make for a great contribution, particularly with the upcoming centennial convention. They agreed, and Dechant traveled back to the U.S. the following day with the models of the crucifix and triptych in a Vatican valise that became part of his carry-on luggage.

"They were heavy as could be," he said. "But I thought that at the very least, I'd always be able to tell the story of the Order trying to build this chapel. But as it happened, the pope survived and we were able to finish building the chapel."

Indeed, the pontiff would survive the shooting. However, his condition was still unknown at the time of Dechant's departure from Rome, and the whole situation weighed heavily on his mind during his trip back to the United States.

The pope's recovery would last well into the fall. Suddenly, this placed Dechant's centennial convention plan in peril. It seemed impossible—at best, unlikely—that the Holy Father would fully recover in time to attend the events in Hartford the following summer. The same seemed true for U.S. President Ronald Reagan, whom Dechant had also invited to the centennial convention. Reagan was himself recovering

Father Michael J. McGivney.

from an assassination attempt at the hands of John Hinckley, Jr., that had occurred outside a Washington hotel in late March.

In October 1981, Dechant visited Rome on centennial business. Pertinent to these events was a plan to unearth Father McGivney's body from his family's burial plot in Waterbury, Connecticut, and relocate the remains to St. Mary's Church, where the Order had been founded. The church was in the midst of extensive K of C-sponsored renovations, so the timing seemed perfect. Moving McGivney's remains was just one part of a comprehensive plan to honor the founder of the Order. Part of the plan included establishing, without a doubt, that Father McGivney was the founder of the Knights of Columbus. Christopher Kauffman, during his work on writing the history of the Order, established this fact without dispute. The Order then requested that Kauffman continue his research on McGivney's life, partly in connection with an effort that was underway to explore the possibility of McGivney becoming a saint, which had been initiated in 1977 when

Bishop Ted McCarrick wrote to Supreme Physician Dr. John Griffin and instructed him to mention to Supreme Knight Dechant that the Order should explore the possibility of pursuing a cause for beatification. With the supreme knight's support, momentum for that cause would grow over time.

The Knights had received permission from the McGivney family to move the body; the next step was getting permission from the church, which came officially on January 21, 1981, when the Sacred Congregation for the Clergy granted the request. Dechant and Count Galeazzi met with church officials in Rome to discuss progress on the matter.

Dechant and Galeazzi also met with Archbishop Zanini to inspect the progress on the chapel of Saints Benedict, Cyril, and Methodius. The following day they met with the sculptor Tommaso Gismondi to inspect his work on the Carolingian Cross that he was making for the chapel. While there, Dechant placed a large order for small, replica crucifixes, which would be used as gifts at the supreme convention in Hartford. Dechant also ordered an exact duplicate of the original for St. Mary's Church in New Haven, with permission from the Vatican secretary of state.

Two days later, Dechant and Ann and Count Galeazzi visited Castel Gandolfo where the pope was recuperating from his gunshot wounds at his summer residence. Crowds of people stood outside, awaiting a public appearance from the Holy Father. The Dechants and Galeazzi were ushered into a small waiting room while the pope stepped out on the balcony to address the crowds. Then he met in private with the Dechants and Galeazzi. All three kissed the pope's ring and exchanged greetings. Dechant expressed the wishes of the Knights of Columbus that the pope continue his recovery. In her diary, Ann Dechant noted, "The Holy Father looked pale and drawn. Monsignor McGee had to keep

The Dechants and Count Galeazzi visited Pope John Paul II during his recovery at Castel Gandolfo in October 1981.

moving him along, as he wanted to stay. However, the pope was very much in command."

Galeazzi explained to the pope that the Knights had created the Vicarius Christi Fund for his personal charities. The pope flashed a wide smile and said, "Then I can use it as I like." He thanked the K of C for their generosity and presented Virgil, Ann, and Galeazzi each with a rosary.

It seemed obvious to Dechant after the October audience that Pope John Paul II would be unable to attend the centennial convention in Hartford. Dechant's plan was to ask the Holy Father to send a representative in his place, "someone important," Dechant recalled. The pope responded to this request with favor. That "someone important" would be just the person Dechant had hoped for, Cardinal Agostino Casaroli, the Vatican secretary of state and the second-highest-ranking official in the church.

Soon after, Dechant received word that President Ronald Reagan would be able to attend the supreme convention in Hartford and address the delegation. Now it seemed the grand plan was taking shape.

The centennial convention created an enormous public relations opportunity for the Knights of Columbus. With President Reagan and a personal delegate of the pope in attendance, the convention was certain to draw tremendous media interest. Although the convention wouldn't be held until the first week of August, by spring the K of C had a captive audience.

An article titled "100 Years of Changes in K of C" ran in the *Boston Sunday Globe* in late March; in it, Dechant described how the Order was in the midst of completing a transition from being a male-driven organization to a family oriented one. The same article also described the scope of the Order's charitable giving. On that subject, Dechant referenced a biblical theme, saying, "When you give, give quietly. And that's what we try to do."

Other stories aimed at general interest readers dispelled certain myths about the Order and offered a chance for readers to discover what the Knights of Columbus was truly about. In *The New York Times*, writer Charles Austin's piece "100th Year is Celebrated by Knights of Columbus" called the Order "a Catholic alternative to Freemasonry... that became a major force in American Catholicism." The same story pointed out the Order's longtime ties to conservative politics and progressive church programs.

And there were various laurels that accompanied the centennial. Supreme Knight Dechant was honored by Yale University at the annual Salute to New Haven, an honor that netted more publicity. Yale President Bartlett Giamatti, who in 1989 would become the commissioner of Major League Baseball, and Dechant were close friends and occasional dinner companions at New Haven's Quinnipiac Club. Dechant was quick to credit the K of C, not himself, for the Yale honor: "This is really for the Knights," he said publicly.

The General Assembly of the State of Connecticut resolved to praise the Knights of Columbus for a long history of public service to the state; similarly, a joint resolution by the U.S. Senate and House of Representatives did the same. This of course yielded more positive press.

Historian and author Christopher Kauffman had delivered his manuscript on the history of the Knights of Columbus on time, and it was well received. The book, which would be published by Harper and Row, was titled *Faith and Fraternalism: The History of the Knights of Columbus*. Father Theodore Hesburgh, president of the University of Notre Dame, called *Faith and Fraternalism* "a faithful chronicle of the organization's contributions to American culture." *Publishers Weekly*

The Pope sent Cardinal Agostino Casaroli, the Vatican secretary of state, as his delegate to the 1982 centennial convention of the Knights of Columbus in Hartford.

described the work as "a contribution to American history, both secular and religious." The book would sell for a retail price of $18.45, and advertisements for it began appearing in various publications, including *The New York Times*. The book and Dechant's commitment to memorializing the Order's many achievements would become an important piece of his legacy as supreme knight.

The theme of the 1982 supreme convention was "We Bear His Name; We Carry His Cross." In Dechant's report to convention delegates, he pointed out that Kauffman's *Faith and Fraternalism* had already sold nearly 12,500 copies to Knights of Columbus members and an additional 2,000 copies, which had been marketed by Harper and Row.

Christopher J. Kauffman Faith & Fraternalism: The History of the Knights of Columbus 1882-1982

Dechant also described the extensive renovations to St. Mary's Church, which were overseen by Supreme Treasurer William Van Tassell. Every pew in the church had been removed, stripped, and refinished; the basement was redone; a famous "tracker action" Hook's church organ, acquired from a parish in New York City through the generosity of Cardinal Terrance Cooke, was installed; the interior was completely repainted; a new rosewood floor, imported from Thailand, had been laid; new wiring was installed in the building; and the sanctuary was redesigned. The work had been supervised by architect Kevin Roche; G.P. Woodworking, a local firm run by Guido Petraiuolo, a member of the Knights of Columbus, provided much of the craftsmanship. The *Waterbury Republican* noted that the Order spent $650,000 to refurbish the church. Like other causes related to the centennial of the K of C, money, it seemed, was of little concern. Performing work of the highest quality took precedent.

Museum curator Mary Lou Cummings echoed that sentiment and said the same attitude prevailed in gathering and preparing museum exhibits. "We didn't have a budget," Cummings said. "Or at least we were never told; we were just supposed to do the job and get it done right and professionally. It was something that was going to be cared for permanently. It wasn't haphazard."

The first event held in the renovated church was the wedding of Dechant's daughter Karen to physician Bob Thompson, just two weeks before the supreme convention. Thompson joked that "the paint was still drying" in the church at the time of the ceremony.

The improvements to St. Mary's Church included the interment of Father McGivney's remains. In early 1981, the Knights of Columbus had engaged the Bergin Funeral Home in Waterbury, Connecticut, to begin the disinterment of McGivney's body. The first step in this process was determining where, exactly, in the McGivney family plot to start digging. Father McGivney had been buried among eight family members in Old St. Joseph's Cemetery; coincidentally, the grandfather of the Bergin Funeral Home's owner had conducted the McGivney funeral in 1890. A newspaper report of that service explained that McGivney's body had been buried in a casket and placed into a brick masonry vault and covered with two slabs of bluestone (each measuring 40 x 48 inches).

The Bergin staff probed for the bluestone slabs using a steel bar and eventually located the vault. In the process, they inadvertently cracked

The re-entombed remains of Father Michael J. McGivney, founder of the Knights of Columbus.

the stone, causing water to enter the vault. The bar also pierced the silver nameplate of McGivney's wooden casket and the glass that had been used to cover his body within the casket (a precaution due to the priest's cause of death, tuberculosis).

In December 1981—accompanied by Father Justin Cunningham, the pastor of St. Mary's, Supreme Knight Dechant, and the K of C supreme officers—the Bergin staff completed the disinterment. Every act of the process was documented by Dr. John Griffin and was notarized by Judge Patrick Donlin; film was shot of the event and *Columbia* magazine's John Cummings took photographs for posterity.

The Order had planned to re-entomb the remains of its founder in early 1982, but the Connecticut State Health Department impounded the remains so a culture could be performed to determine if the tuberculosis germ in McGivney's body was still active. The culture grew but died within a few weeks. That was enough to satisfy the Health Department, which determined there was no danger of exposure.

On March 29, 1982, the 100th anniversary of the Order, McGivney's remains were re-entombed in St. Mary's Church in a solid bronze casket and a copper inner casket that combined to weigh more than two tons. Architect Kevin Roche designed a granite sarcophagus to surround the casket, even incorporating the two slabs of bluestone and brick from the original vault into his design. Materials not re-entombed in the church or placed in the K of C Museum were vaulted and buried in St. Lawrence Cemetery in New Haven. McGivney's cassock, chasuble, scapulars, rabat, rosary, and various other personal burial items were kept for display in the museum. He was then buried in new vestments (made by Dominican nuns from North Guilford, CT), including the jewel of the K of C supreme chaplain and a K of C rosary.

The story of moving McGivney's remains was indeed a source of pride for Dechant, the K of C leadership, and convention delegates to Hartford in August 1982. A gala parade of more than 5,000 Knights was held through the streets of New Haven, and it culminated with the unveiling of a new statue of the Order's founder at the headquarters of the supreme council.

Another great source of pride at the convention came when Dechant presented the pope's legate, Cardinal Casaroli, with the first year's earnings ($1.2 million) of the Vicarius Christi Foundation for the Holy Father's personal charities.

The centennial convention also offered the opportunity for a rare political intersection. Dechant offered to vacate his suite at the convention hotel so President Reagan and Cardinal Casaroli could meet over

PHOTO USED WITH PERMISSION OF L'OSSERVATORE ROMANO.

Supreme Knight Dechant vacated his hotel suite to allow President Reagan to meet with Cardinal Casaroli at the 1982 supreme convention.

lunch and discuss various diplomatic matters, including the lack of an ambassadorial relationship between the two countries. The stage was set in Dechant's suite when a table was arranged, covered in a white tablecloth, with a jar of jellybeans in the center. Reagan and Casaroli met for lunch, shared greetings, and exchanged political ideologies. Later they sat side by side in front of the room's fireplace to continue their visit and allow for press photos.

"One of the things they discussed was the ambassadorial relationship between the Vatican and the United States," Dechant said. "Up until that time, the United States only had a personal representative of the president assigned to the Vatican, and the Vatican appointed the apostolic delegate to the United States. Other matters that were discussed at

Among many issues, Reagan and Casaroli discussed the ambassadorial relationship between the United States and Vatican City.

this meeting had much to do with the relationship with eastern Europe and the Iron Curtain."

Reagan's presidency, of course, would be marked by his efforts to end the Cold War, including his famous challenge to Soviet General Secretary Mikhail Gorbachev to "tear down this wall." The ambassadorial relationship between the U.S. and the Vatican came to fruition in 1984 when Reagan appointed American businessman William Wilson as the first U.S. Ambassador to the Holy See.

Reagan addressed convention delegates and others—a crowd of nearly 10,000—at the Hartford Civic Center on August 3. His speech, titled "Crucial Values," touched on a variety of topics, political and otherwise. He outlined his administration's agenda, which included jump-starting the economy by decreasing the size of government, supporting tuition tax credits, seeking worldwide peace through stronger arms controls, and campaigning across the globe for democracy. Reagan also affirmed a strong pro-life position and drew tremendous applause when he said, "The national tragedy of abortion on demand must end."

Later, he drew more applause when he uttered the following: "A Senate committee hearing was held recently to determine, if we can, when life actually begins. And there was exhaustive testimony of experts presenting both views. And, finally, the result was declared inconclusive. They could not arrive at an answer. Well, in my view alone, they did arrive at an answer, an answer that justifies the proposed legislation. If it is true we do not know when the unborn becomes a human life, then we have to opt in favor that it is a human life until someone proves it isn't."

Throughout his remarks, the president commended the good works of the Knights of Columbus and the values for which the Order stands. He surprised some in the crowd when he announced that his father had been a Knight. He acknowledged that the Knights in 1981 had made

President Reagan's address to convention delegates in Hartford won him many fans and lots of thunderous applause.

more than $41 million in charitable contributions and had donated more than 10 million hours of community service. Reagan said, "The Knights of Columbus is unrivaled in its dedication to family, community, country and church. And your corporal and spiritual works of mercy for those in need are both a legend and an example to your countrymen."

It was a proud moment for all convention goers and especially for Dechant, who had so tirelessly prepared for this moment since he took office as supreme knight.

During Reagan's speech, Dechant became fascinated by the president's expert use of a teleprompter, a display device that prompts a speaker on cue, thus eliminating the need for papers and cumbersome

Supreme Knight Dechant welcomes President Ronald Reagan to the 1982 Knights of Columbus supreme convention.

report covers. While teleprompter technology dates back to the 1950s, its use in the 1980s was just becoming commonplace for world leaders and frequent public speakers. Reagan's command of the device sparked in Dechant an idea for a post-centennial project: he thought the Knights of Columbus should purchase a teleprompter for the pope, who, in his duties as worldwide leader of the Catholic Church, gave countless speeches, often in multiple languages.

"I remember I was sitting in the front row with Count Galeazzi, and you couldn't tell that the president was using a teleprompter," Dechant recalled. "Everybody was amazed at his memory. He made just a few references to his notes. I was so impressed with that, the Order purchased a teleprompter for the pope, and I carried it with me to Rome on a trip there in 1983. The package consisted of eight large crates. But John Paul II used it just once. In accordance with Vatican tradition, he chose to speak from his papers, which were always in the hands of his secretary up until the moment he would give his remarks."

The papal teleprompter may have been the only "false start" while assisting the Holy See in Dechant's entire administration. But, nothing ventured, nothing gained. Ultimately, that teleprompter would get put to use by Vatican Radio.

Most everyone involved agreed the centennial convention of the Knights of Columbus came off as a great success. The event and its many activities served to further the public image of the Order, strengthen diplomatic ties to the presidency and the papacy, reinvigorate K of C members and their families, and re-establish a collective devotion to the Order's founder, Father Michael McGivney.

Amazingly, this had all been accomplished in just Dechant's fifth year as supreme knight.

In Dechant's convention report to delegates, he thanked Supreme Chaplain Charles P. Greco and Count Enrico Galeazzi, two mentors whose influence on the K of C and the supreme knight was instrumental in carrying out such a monumental affair.

Also in his report, Dechant permitted himself a moment of personal reflection. He concluded: "As a young man and as a young Knight, I could not have even guessed that I would be standing at this rostrum, in the centennial year of the Order, delivering the report of the supreme knight. Yet here I am."

CHAPTER NINE

No one questioned Virgil Dechant's religion. He was a Catholic; that was clear. But he also subscribed to another kind of credo: the religion of hard work.

This trait was no doubt bred into him through his hardworking parents, C.J. and Ursula. Others like the Dechants who toiled while making a life on the Kansas plains had no choice but to do the same. The world would have chewed them up and spit them out if they had tried to shortcut the inevitable struggle of rural life.

Dechant's colleagues, sometimes men half his age, had a hard time keeping up with his bustling, yet focused, pace. He wasted little time watching television or engaging in leisure activities.

Virgil C. Dechant: an extension of the Order.

He traveled the world, mostly for business and rarely for pleasure. He was the sort that would change his own flat tire in a suit and tie if necessary (or for a family member, as he once did for daughter Karen after a long day at the office). For Dechant, the job of supreme knight had no days off, and that included holidays. Dechant was known to call state deputies and their families to offer his greetings on Christmas Day, even before he spent time with his own family. It was the kind of gesture certain to leave a positive impression, which it did on at least one state deputy, Lou Mautino, from Missouri.

"I thought, 'Why in the hell is the supreme knight taking the time to call me?'" Mautino recalled. "Looking back on it, that's pretty good business. It really impressed me. I hung up the phone and said to my wife, 'That was the supreme knight.' It was a great honor."

In 1973 Dechant moved his family from their North Haven residence to a house on Hartford Turnpike, adjacent to the entrance to the New Haven Country Club. Dechant belonged to the club, but he didn't play golf or tennis. Rather, he used the club to entertain Knights of Columbus staff for holiday parties and other gatherings. As for the house, he had bought it because it was well suited to his family's needs. It was close to St. Stephen's Catholic School where he sent his children, and it reduced his daily commute to One Columbus Plaza. And, of course, the secluded neighborhood with easy country club access was a prime piece of real estate. And Dechant could always spot a desirable piece of property.

It's easy to speculate that being a child of the Great Depression sparked Dechant's drive to succeed. Despite his youth, the memories of those difficult times had been permanently etched in his mind. But his love of hard work carried with it another quality—enjoyment. The man worked hard because, well, he liked what he was doing.

Dechant's hobby, if you'd call it that, was the Knights of Columbus. His next favorite hobby was managing his Kansas farming and business interests. Both pastimes were also his life's work.

"I always thought of my father's career as a vocation, a little bit like a priest with a family," said his daughter Karen. "He was able to work in a career that was more like a vocation than a job. Other people got up to go to work, and for them it was just a job."

Indeed, for Supreme Knight Dechant, the Knights of Columbus was more than a job. It was a calling. He would sometimes remind others that he had once been a seminarian pursuing another calling, the priesthood. But that path was not meant to be.

"I'd have liked to have been a priest, if I'd had a second life," Dechant told writer Priscilla Hart as part of a 1983 profile titled "A Day in the Life of the Supreme Knight" that was published in *Columbia* magazine. "It would have been very, very rewarding. I wasn't cut out to do that, that's all. I hope I'm more effective as supreme knight. That way I can help a lot of men who are thinking of entering the priesthood. I might not have been able to do that as a single priest, a single man."

That paradigm—the seminarian turned businessman turned fraternal executive—helps illustrate the qualities that Dechant brought to the job which made him so well qualified. Indeed, in her profile of the supreme knight, Hart described "the tension between the business of insurance and the vocation of being a Christian; between the secular and the sacred." It was a tension that took a careful hand to navigate, and Dechant seemed to own a magic touch.

Tom Smith, who in 2012 became an executive vice president and chief insurance officer of the Knights of Columbus, started working for the Order in 1974 as an entry-level employee in the mailroom. Shortly after Dechant became supreme knight, he invited every home office employee to meet him and pose for a photograph. Dechant knew who Smith was thanks to Bill Piedmont, who ran the Fraternal Services Department. Smith delivered Piedmont's mail every day, and they got to know each other well enough for Piedmont to tell Dechant that the young kid in the mailroom had real potential. As he shook Smith's hand and posed for the photograph, Dechant told him there was a job coming open in the Fraternal Services Department.

Smith accepted the job. It was the beginning of a long, successful ascent through the Knights of Columbus for Smith, and it may have been Dechant's first promotion as supreme knight. Two things about the exchange impressed Smith: Dechant cared enough to take the time to meet every employee at the home office, and, rather surprisingly, he already knew much about many of them—including Smith. Such intimate knowledge of people demonstrated much about the leader of the Order.

"What he brought to the office that's unique, I think even to this day, is a business acumen that is spot-on," Smith said. "He knows how to make a dollar, how to turn a profit. He knows how to look at balance sheets because he ran his own businesses. He also brought tremendous broad fraternal understanding, having been a state deputy, a member of the board of directors, on the road 50 weeks a year doing degrees. He knew both aspects of the Order perfectly. The Knights of Columbus needed that at that particular time. In 1977 we needed to really take a quantum leap forward.

"There are several occasions in your business life when you have choices: you can either move forward aggressively or accept the status quo and pray that the best comes from that. When you're green, you're growing; when you're ripe, you rot. That's how it goes. He came to us at a time when we really needed to take that quantum leap forward, or we would have been like many other fraternals that you see in the world today, which are making money and staying in business, but they're not dynamic, they're not growing, and they're not making a difference.

"You could be up in Virgil's waiting room on the 20th floor, and in that hallway there would be a guy from fraternal services waiting to talk to him about membership; his ceremonial director would be there waiting to talk to him about the first, second, and third degrees; the vocations director, who was a priest, was waiting to talk to him about spiritual issues; and the head of insurance would be waiting to talk to him about how the insurance business could grow. When you think about the typical role of a chief executive officer in the world today in a Fortune 1,000 company, they're generally single-focused. You can diversify, but it's still product, marketing, distribution. Here you have a guy who, in the morning, would be talking about how we're going to get more priests in the United States, and, in the afternoon, would be talk-

Count Enrico Galeazzi was frequently Dechant's guide through Rome and Vatican City, including this visit to one of the Order's playgrounds for youth.

ing about where we're going to put the next $10 million that comes in. That's a very unique skill set that very, very few people have. The Order was blessed to get him."

A typical day in the life of the supreme knight—according to writer Priscilla Hart and others who worked alongside Dechant—was anything but typical. Each day brought with it its own new set of challenges. There were department heads that needed to meet with the supreme knight, high-ranking Catholic officials who wanted a few minutes on the phone with Dechant, and lots of complicated decision-making that wound up on his desk. It amounted to a job full of pressure, both internal and external.

Yet, Dechant kept a steady hand.

"I never saw him blink, I can tell you that," Smith said.

There was also the job of serving as the public face of the Knights of Columbus, and that came with its own unique set of responsibilities, including maintaining a likeable persona and being ready to answer any question on behalf of the Order at a moment's notice. That included an appearance on a CBS documentary about the K of C that aired as part of the network's "For Our Times" series. Regarding the CBS interview, Hart wrote of Dechant, "He seems poised, alert, thoughtful, ready to take on any question, as if his knowledge of the Knights' organization is so intimate and profound that the Order has become an extension of himself…it is a masterful performance."

"The culture he built at the Knights of Columbus—and this was amazing—but when people went to meet with my dad, they'd put their suit jacket on," said Virgil's son Bob Dechant. "They wouldn't just come in. They would be sitting at their own desk, and they would stand up and put on their jacket. It was a business meeting."

That attention to detail, even for simple things such as appearance and dress, was something Dechant's children had observed in their father all their lives, even back to their days in Kansas.

His son Dan Dechant called it "the attitude of dressing for the job you want to have."

Paula Forni began working for Dechant as his personal secretary in 1990. Forni began her employment at the K of C in 1967 and for many years had worked for Joe Mauro in the insurance department. She recalled the manner of doing business that Dechant brought to bear at One Columbus Plaza.

"He was great at dealing with people," Forni said. "One thing I admired about him was if there was something that had to be done, good or bad, he did it. He didn't delegate it. He delegated to departments and things like that, but when it came to someone at the management level, he was the one that did that. And for all the years I worked for him, I don't remember where he had someone fired. If there were people that were not getting along in departments, I remember that he would find someplace for them. He'd move them into a department that would suit them better. To me, that always seemed to work out. He let people manage their own departments, but he was always hands-on. If there were important decisions to be made, these people would run them by him first.

"There were a lot of people in that building, but he could go onto an elevator, and he actually knew a lot of people by their first name. He'd say 'hi' to them. Naturally, he didn't know everyone. But by knowing most of them, if there were people coming up for promotions, he knew who to suggest because he had a sense of whether they were cut out for certain jobs."

Ron Tracz, another home office staffer, suggested Dechant's command of the Order's business practices started with his grassroots knowledge of the Knights of Columbus.

"He had a definite philosophy," Tracz said. "I think he liked the idea that we were a lean and mean organization, so we didn't have a lot of overhead. He didn't like being on the cutting edge of IT initiatives and things like that because there were always drawbacks with it. His decisions were always based on what's good for the member, what's good for the Order, what's good for the insurance programs, and how we continue to increase membership."

Dechant delighted in meeting members of the Order all over the world. The members enjoyed meeting him, too, and they could tell his enthusiasm was not just a polite pretense. He once ran into a young district deputy from Pennsylvania in the lobby of a Washington, D.C. hotel, just down the street from the Capitol. The district deputy, who was in Washington to be sworn into practice before the United States Supreme Court, recognized Dechant from his picture in *Columbia* magazine and said to his wife, "That's Virgil Dechant." He approached Dechant and introduced himself.

Dechant asked him, "Would you like to go to lunch?"

The man was taken aback but had to decline the invitation because he had already made plans with his wife and kids. He was Michael O'Connor, who in 2006 would become state deputy of Pennsylvania and in 2007 would join the Knights of Columbus board of directors. In 2016, O'Connor was named supreme secretary.

"That was very gracious of him, asking a guy he'd just met in a hotel lobby out to lunch," O'Connor recalled. "But I guess that's what a fraternalist would do, right?"

The job of the supreme knight demanded long hours. Most days in the office started before 9 a.m. and usually lasted until long after every other home office employee had left the building. Priscilla Hart described Dechant's 20th-floor office as "big as a living room, fitting a man who

Top photo: Dechant met with Puerto Rico Governor Rafael Hernández Colón and Cardinal Aponte of San Juan.

Above: Dechant and his assistant Paul McGlinchey and their wives met with Filipino President Ferdinand Marcos.

practically lives at his job." While it seemed Dechant did live at his job, he was often living that job far away from the home office in New Haven. Between his travels to Rome, Mexico, Canada, Guam, the Philippines, and countless stops in the continental United States, it seemed Dechant was always on the go. Ann Dechant accompanied her husband on most of these trips, often keeping detailed journals of their travels. In Hart's magazine interview, Dechant estimated he made between 40 and 50 trips per year.

In 1980, Dechant visited the Philippines to help celebrate the 75th anniversary of the founding of the Knights of Columbus there. His visit marked just the third visit by a supreme knight to the Philippines; the convention's keynote address was delivered by Philippine President Ferdinand E. Marcos. Dechant returned to the Philippines again in 1984 for a 12-day stay, during which he visited numerous councils and oversaw their many projects, including a communal vegetable and fruit farm that assisted malnutrition relief in the country. The growth of the Order in the Philippines was due in a large part to the work of Rev. George Willmann, SJ., who served as the liaison between the supreme knight and the Order's councils in the Philippines. Other vitals links in the Philippines were Oscar Ledesma, the former Ambassador to the United States, who served as the first territorial deputy and was subsequently named an honorary member of the Supreme Council board of directors; and Mardonio Santos, who served as the second territorial deputy of the Philippines and later on the K of C board of directors.

So extensive were his travel demands that Dechant created an in-house travel department for home office employees of the Knights of Columbus. He handpicked someone for that position, too: Kathy Cogan, from the purchasing department. Dechant chose Cogan because it seemed whenever he called purchasing with a question, she was the person who always had the answer. That sort of efficiency, at least in Dechant's eyes, was enough to earn a promotion. He didn't overthink the hire.

"I started that job before there were really computers," Cogan recalled. "I would look through a book and see what airlines offered flights, then call the airline, and then I would hand-write the ticket."

Cogan estimated that Dechant's travel schedule encompassed 35 to 40 percent of his time, yet, she says, he never seemed out of touch with matters at the home office.

"He always had a good grasp on what was going on there. He was a hands-on person."

When Dechant traveled to the Knights' Rome office, located within earshot of the Vatican, he set to work immediately. It was typical behavior for Dechant, and at first it surprised members of the Rome office staff. Enrico Demajo, Count Galeazzi's grandson, who today manages the Rome office, said it was the sort of trait that set Dechant apart from other executives.

"He was always a tremendous worker," Demajo said. "He used to land in Rome after a very long flight and go straight to work. He had a little apartment in the office. Why? Because it was a way to save money, by going straight to the office. Then he could rest whenever he wanted. We were there, ready to help him. He always hated to waste time by checking in and checking out of hotels. This was straight, fast, convenient."

The most-regular trip Dechant made took place every summer. The destination was La Crosse, Kansas, to oversee the harvesting of his wheat crop. Nothing got between Dechant and his wheat harvest. The June trip also gave him a chance to check up on Dechant Motors, which maintained steady business, despite the lean years of the 1980s that devastated so many farmers and others who made their living in agriculture.

By the 1980s, the New Haven team that surrounded Dechant and made his extensive workload possible was looking younger than ever before in Dechant's tenure. When Dechant first came to New Haven to work for the Knights of Columbus full time, he was, by a fairly wide margin, the new kid on the block. But by his second decade, Dechant was the one looking older than those around him. As a man who possessed an eye for identifying capable talent, this fact did little to bother him.

Among the young talent, there was Charles Walden, director of investments, whom Priscilla Hart described by his clean-cut appearance: "wearing, suitably, the pinstripes of a banker and projecting the *savoir-faire* of a Wall Street stock broker." Dechant and Walden shared a close working relationship, meeting regularly to discuss the ebb and flow of the stock market and the many investment opportunities the K of C chose to pursue.

"Very simply stated," Walden said, "it was a very typical life insurance portfolio in the sense that there were a lot of corporate bonds and government bonds that probably comprised about 80 percent of the portfolio, which, at that time, was probably $500 million or $550 million. And then there was the real estate that was either directly owned or in some form of a lease-back arrangement. These were the things that Luke Hart had done; that element was two or three percent. Then five percent was in common stocks. And then the rest was in church loans and other assets."

Dechant's most reliable everyday aide was Paul McGlinchey, assistant to the supreme knight. McGlinchey was a New Jersey native, a veteran of the U.S. Army, and a former seminarian (having studied at the

American College of the Immaculate Conception in Louvain, Belgium).
He began his employment with the K of C in 1971, working as associate
editor of *Columbia*. McGlinchey was described by colleagues as a sort of
renaissance man, the kind of guy who got just as much enjoyment out of
reading a French novel as he did from watching a football game or edit-
ing one of the supreme knight's speeches. Every obstacle, he met with
vigor. In little time, McGlinchey got to know Dechant, perhaps better
than anybody in the home office. He knew Dechant's feelings on most
matters and how to best craft his public remarks.

"Paul was a great asset," said Walden. "His capabilities as a word-
smith were fantastic. When I was writing difficult stuff, even if it
had business terminology, I would often take it to him and say, 'Take a
whack at it, you're not going to upset me.' He had an incredible gift
for that."

And there was Harvey Bacque, who ran the Fraternal Service department. Bacque was a whirl of perpetual motion who tackled any task,
large or small, with the same level of enthusiasm—the sort who could
rattle off the answer to any question before it had even been completely
asked. A native of Louisiana, where he had served as grand knight of his
college council, Bacque got his start at the Order's home office working
under Bill Piedmont in Fraternal Services. Bacque was instrumental in
revamping the Surge with Service program, "the first and most important step of which," remembered Virgil Dechant, "was that we describe
the Order as a Catholic family fraternal service organization."

"Harvey had a very close relationship with Virgil," said one former
Fraternal Services staffer. "Virgil leaned on him a lot for our fraternal
activities and our service program activities and, particularly, with college councils. They made a pretty good team."

Dechant also brought a touch of Kansas to New Haven in the person of Don Dreiling, from Hays, who in 1969-1970 had served as Kansas state deputy (and had previously served as Dechant's membership director in Kansas). Dreiling was an Air Force veteran and a former business owner, having operated a hardware store in western Kansas. After serving the supreme council as a program consultant and administrator

Dechant, right, and supreme officers such as Supreme Advocate Pat Donlin, left, became White House regulars and close friends with U.S. President Ronald Reagan, center.

to its New Council division, in 1980, Dechant named Dreiling assistant to the supreme knight for fraternal affairs.

Dreiling and Dechant were old friends, and the supreme knight knew exactly the sorts of duties he could place under Dreiling's direction. One such effort was the roundtable program, designed so the works of a council composed of members from multiple parishes could benefit each of those parishes. In many instances, after a few years of roundtable existence, these councils evolve into parish councils. Under Dreiling's direction, the emphasis on new councils in the late 1970s and early 1980s led to tremendous growth for the Order. Another Kansan who came to New Haven was Jack Dowd, who was tabbed to run the Order's Catholic Information Service.

By 1984, with the supreme knight's duties continuing to expand and the introduction of new regulatory insurance controls, Dechant recommended that the board of directors hire Ellis D. Flinn, a consulting actuary for 16 years, as deputy supreme knight. Flinn was designated the chief operating officer of the insurance program, while Dechant retained overall control of policy. In this role, Flinn would serve the K of C ably until his retirement in 1997 due to health reasons.

There was little time for the Dechants to bask in the glory of the tremendous success that was the centennial supreme convention. If anything, the added free time allowed the couple to take on certain challenges they had put on hold during the busy centennial planning.

In 1982, Pope John Paul II appointed Virgil and Ann Dechant as members of the Pontifical Council for the Family; they were one couple of just 20 worldwide chosen for the honor. They would be reappointed to the council for five-year terms in 1988, 1993, and 1998.

In 1983, the K of C board of directors met in Rome in conjunction with the fifth anniversary of Pope John Paul II's election to the papacy.

A dinner was held one night in Rome to honor Cardinal Agostino Casaroli, the Vatican secretary of state, and at that event Casaroli—on behalf of the Holy Father—invested Dechant as a Knight Grand Cross in the Order of Pius IX, the highest honor granted by the Holy See to a Catholic layman who is not a head of state.

That July, back in the United States, the Dechants were invited by U.S. President Ronald Reagan to a state dinner at the White House in honor of his highness Shaikh Isa Bin Salmon Al-Khalifa, Amir of the State of Bahrain. Virgil sat at the same table as the president and other luminaries, including basketball star Moses Malone and astronaut Sally Ride. Ann was seated at a table with Nancy Reagan and others. The state dinner was more than just a token invitation from the president. Reagan and Dechant found they shared common ground on numerous political matters that furthered both their conservative agendas, including the advancement of private education, curbing drug use, ending abortion, and pushing the president's tax plan.

On the subject of education, the Knights of Columbus as an organization strongly favored two key initiatives: voluntary prayer in public schools and tuition tax credits for families who paid to send their children to private schools. Dechant was once quoted as calling private education "the greatest philanthropy in America today because it saves government about $15 billion a year."

Reagan's affinity for the Knights of Columbus became obvious. Each year, the president sent a letter to delegates at the supreme convention. He took that greeting a step further when he sent a videotaped message—six or seven times, Dechant recalled—to be shown to convention delegates; he even spoke live through satellite on at least one occasion.

On August 6, 1985, Reagan invited the entire executive committee of the board of the Knights of Columbus to Washington for a meeting

Dechant and Reagan: a friendship built on mutual respect and trust that would ultimately help society, the country, and the Order.

in his cabinet room, the subject of which was his upcoming tax reform proposal. One subject discussed was the Knights' tax-exempt status, an issue the Order's leaders would continue to monitor as they fought to conduct their good works within the framework of the law.

"This established a good relationship with President

THE WHITE HOUSE
WASHINGTON

November 7, 1983

Dear Virgil:

I was pleased to learn that you have been honored with the prestigious Knight of the Grand Cross in the Order of Pope Pius IX. Nancy joins me in sending our warm congratulations.

This is well-deserved recognition of your hard work in support of the many cherished values which we share. You can take great pride and satisfaction in your accomplishment.

Once again, our congratulations and our best wishes to you and Mrs. Dechant.

Sincerely,

Ronald Reagan

Mr. Virgil C. Dechant
Supreme Knight
Knights of Columbus
1 Columbus Plaza
New Haven, Connecticut 06507

Reagan," Dechant said. "I had many meetings in the White House during those years, oftentimes in his cabinet room, where I often had the privilege of sitting next to the president. Those meetings were about Catholic or private education. They were sometimes about the use of narcotics. Reagan had appointed a drug czar, Bill Bennett, and so we worked with him on that. There were different efforts where we could assist the White House in carrying out its functions."

On April 5, 1984, Dechant was asked by Reagan to accompany him from Washington to New York where the president that night would present the Presidential Medal of Freedom posthumously to Cardinal Terence James Cooke, archbishop of New York. Dechant met the president at Andrews Air Force Base outside Washington and joined him on Air Force One for the short flight into Newark. Throughout the day he accompanied the president on various visits around the city, culminating that evening at the Waldorf Astoria for the Cooke honors, sponsored by the New York State Federation of Catholic School Parents.

The Order's assistance to the private education battle dated back to 1980 when Monsignor John F. Meyers, president of the National Catholic Educational Association (NCEA), asked the K of C for its assistance in confronting the many problems facing Catholic education. Coincidentally, Meyers had once been a classmate of Virgil Dechant's at the Josephinum seminary in Worthington, Ohio. The Knights' assistance with Catholic education led to the formation of the Father Michael J. McGivney Memorial Fund for New Initiatives in Catholic Education, which started when a fund was created within Knights of Columbus Charities, Inc. in the amount of $1 million (raised through a $1.00 per-capita levy on K of C members).

"Because of Virgil Dechant's business expertise and knowledge of managing money, he was able to put things like this together," Monsignor Meyers said of the McGivney fund. "Catholic schools were closing rapidly and people were unaware of the true cost of schools because lay faculty were starting to replace priests and nuns. Lay faculty needed to be paid more, and this caught everyone by surprise. Our reputation was also beginning to wane because of public school standards in modern times.

ABOARD

Air Force One

OUR DESTINATION IS NEWARK, NJ

THE EXPECTED ARRIVAL TIME IS 11:15 AM

TIME CHANGE ON THIS LEG: NO CHANGE

OUR FLIGHT ALTITUDE WILL BE 15,000 FEET,

AND OUR SPEED WILL AVERAGE 400 M.P.H.

WE WILL FLY OVER WILMINGTON, DEL

DESTINATION WEATHER FORECAST

CONDITIONS: CLOUDY WITH RAIN SHOWERS AND

STRONG GUSTY WINDS

TEMPERATURE: 57

"Virgil was the right man at the right time for the Knights of Columbus: very clever, very astute."

The joy and progress of these events was offset by sadness. On June 12, 1984, C.J. Dechant, Virgil's father, died at age 83. Funeral services were held in Hays at Immaculate Heart of Mary Church.

The last seven months of C.J.'s life had been a struggle due to the effects of a stroke he had suffered shortly before Thanksgiving the prior year. Following his father's death, Virgil's brother Emerald shared with family members in writing some anecdotes about C.J. the grocer and businessman, which demonstrated his gentle understanding of the plight of his fellow man. Emerald wrote, "When farmers paid on their bill (especially when it was a large one), they never went away empty-handed. Dad offered the men a beer, a pop for the women, and candy (from a large glass case or glass jar) to the children. Dad had one motto: treat every customer like a guest; offer old-fashioned service."

The *Wichita Eagle* published a tribute to the life of C.J. Dechant and the generosity he showed his friends. In that article it was revealed that during the Depression years, Dechant was known to tear up accounts of people he knew couldn't pay so as not to "pester anybody." And when oil was discovered beneath his Ellis County land, C.J. pledged to give a percentage of his earnings to charity—a promise he kept the rest of his life.

While his son Virgil had preceded C.J. in joining the Knights of Columbus, C.J. himself left a strong legacy with the Order. That legacy, of course, was his suggestion to Virgil that the Order offer a rosary to its newest inducted members as a symbol of their devotion to the Blessed Mother. The program, instituted shortly after the younger Dechant became supreme knight, continues today.

By 1985, the Knights of Columbus boasted $10 billion of insurance

A young Count Enrico Galeazzi, the K of C's man in Rome, wearing the regalia of a papal chamberlain.

In April 1985, work began on a seven-phase restoration of the façade of St. Peter's Basilica that was underwritten by the Knights of Columbus. Roughly the size of two football fields, the façade hadn't been touched in nearly 400 years and decades of air pollution and weather had left their mark.

Dechant presented Pope John Paul II with a gilded bronze replica of the façade to commemorate the restoration.

in force and assets of $1.7 billion. Between his dealings with the president, the pope, and other church and world leaders, all on behalf of the Order, it seemed in the 1980s that Dechant could do no wrong. Then in 1985, the Knights of Columbus undertook perhaps the Order's most ambitious project to date with the Vatican, the restoration of the façade of St. Peter's Basilica in Rome.

The relationship between the K of C and the Vatican, at least in modern times, began in 1920, during the term of Supreme Knight James A. Flaherty, when a K of C delegation visited Pope Benedict XV in the Vatican Gardens. Pope Benedict requested that the Knights establish playgrounds for the youth of Rome, partially in response to Protestant efforts to proselytize the youth of the city. The Holy Father aided the Order by providing a piece of land near St. Peter's Basilica, which four years later would become the site of the Order's first playground in Rome, St. Peter's Oratory. The Knights later bought an adjacent tract of land, which had once been the site of a foundry, to expand the playground. More playgrounds would soon follow, strengthening the Order's presence in Rome and demonstrating a reverent obedience to almost any request that came out of Vatican City. During World War II, the K of C sports facilities were used to help feed the poor and hungry of Rome.

The relationship stayed strong over the decades, thanks in part to the smooth diplomacy of Count Enrico Galeazzi. Then in the late 1960s, during the papacy of Paul VI, the Knights of Columbus, under the direction of John McDevitt, donated the entire oratory to the Holy See for the construction of a modern, indoor audience hall, which would be named in honor of Paul VI (sometimes called Nervi Hall in honor of its Italian architect). During Dechant's tenure as supreme knight, there had been numerous interactions between the K of C and the Holy See which continued to advance the relationship; these included providing for

Dechant, right, served as lector during the opening Mass of the 1985 Extraordinary Synod to commemorate the 25th anniversary of the close of the Second Vatican Council.

the satellite feed which broadcast papal events to the world, providing seed money to kickstart the Vatican Film Library that had been created by Saint John XXIII, and the creation of the Vicarius Christi Foundation for the pope's personal charities. These efforts were all part of progress toward something bigger, and that opportunity came along when the Order decided to underwrite the façade restoration.

"The façade of the Basilica hadn't been touched in almost 400 years," Virgil Dechant said. "It's the size of two football fields. And it was in bad shape. Stones were cracked and broken. Marble, too. The statuary was not in good shape. So we undertook the project of underwriting the cost to completely rehabilitate and refurbish it, including the monumental statues of St. Peter and St. Paul, which are out in the square."

The 1985 Synod celebrated the changes of Vatican II while also calling for deeper introspection on the part of the church.

Decades of extreme weather conditions and urban pollution had taken their toll on the façade of the Basilica, a massive structure measuring 116 meters long, 53 meters high, and covering a total area of 10,500 square meters. There were large vertical cracks in stone columns, pieces missing from the statues, and significant growth of trees and bushes in large crevices that developed mature root structures, posing a significant threat to the health of the Basilica. The statue of John the Baptist provided a typical example of the damage. Before the restoration, an iron cable formed a brace and supported the statue; this makeshift remedy was replaced by a more solid stainless steel brace and three brass rings to support John's right arm. And there was the high-relief marble depiction of "Christ giving the keys to St. Peter," which, when one looked closely, revealed extensive damage. The depiction included numerous sculptures of apostles with broken or missing marble fingers and a large volume of atmospheric dust. Clearly, the restoration was long overdue.

The seven-phase restoration began in April 1985. Work was completed 20 months later, involving 70 people and three architects—totaling 79,274 working hours. An average of 21 square meters were completed daily throughout the course of the project.

Dechant spent considerable time in Rome throughout the restoration, including nearly three continuous weeks in late October and early November 1985 when he was appointed as an auditor to the Extraordinary Synod to commemorate the 25th anniversary of the close of the Second Vatican Council. This was no small opportunity, and Dechant was sure to make the most of it. He had the privilege of serving as a lector during the Synod's opening Mass, and at that same Mass he and Ann received Holy Communion from Pope John Paul II.

A typical day of meetings at the Synod lasted from 9 a.m. until 12:30, then resumed for a few hours in the early evening. When the delegation broke into separate committees, Dechant found himself paired with Cardinal Bernard Law and Cardinal William Wakefield Baum, both from the United States. The Dechants spent considerable time during their stay with Count Galeazzi and his family. One evening they were the invited guests of U.S. Ambassador William Wilson to a reception at the American Embassy.

During the Synod, Dechant made the acquaintance of another

Top photo: Dechant and other lay auditors were invited to a private Mass in the pope's chapel...so was Mother Teresa of Calcutta.

Above: The pope's private Mass was followed by breakfast, making Dechant witness to an incredible conversation between John Paul II and Mother Teresa.

attendee, Mother Teresa, of Calcutta, India, known the world over for her incredible works of charity. Ann Dechant had already met the future Saint Teresa in 1980 when the famous nun served as the principal speaker at a natural family planning seminar—sponsored by the Knights of Columbus—that Ann had attended in Guatemala, along with Dr. John and Mary Lou Griffin. At the Synod in Rome, Virgil sat just a few seats away from Mother Teresa during the main proceedings. Her unyielding persistence made an instant impression.

"Mother Teresa had a habit of handing out prayer cards, so the first few days of the meetings at the audience hall in Rome, she asked the bishops in attendance to help hand out some of her cards. They did that for a few days, then she asked members of the staff to hand them out. When they got tired of doing that, she asked me to help her hand out the prayer cards. So there I was, handing out Mother Teresa's prayer cards to bishops and others. And in that process I got to know her pretty well. She had something on her mind. A film had just been made about her life and all her good works, and she wanted to show it to all the bishops. She also wanted the pope to be there for it. It was very difficult to get that on the agenda, but she kept working on it. Finally, one afternoon, we broke early, and the pope came over and we watched the film.

"Later, the Holy Father invited the laypeople in attendance and Mother Teresa to his private Mass one morning, which was at 6 a.m., to be followed immediately by breakfast. Because of the size of the chapel, we were told to come by ourselves, without spouses or family members. Mother Teresa showed up with about six or seven of her nuns, but everybody just smiled at her, and her sisters sat on the floor.

"At breakfast, Mother Teresa sat opposite the pope, and I sat two seats to her left. She really dominated the conversation. The pope was getting ready to go to India, and she insisted that he stop at her Mother-

From left: Virgil Dechant, Count Enrico Galeazzi, Ann Dechant, and Marissa Galeazzi Demajo at the count's country villa.

house first. If I recall, the pope said, 'Well, the bishops of India want me to come that first day to the office of the national conference of bishops.' Then Mother said, 'Well—I'll talk to the bishops.' And it wasn't long after that when the pope went to India, the first place he stopped was Motherhouse.

"The other thing she had on her mind was getting the pope to canonize Father Damien, the priest famously known for caring for victims of leprosy. She worked the Holy Father over on that one. Finally, the pope looked over at his secretary, Monsignor Stanislaw Dziwisz, now Cardinal Dziwisz, and nodded his head as if to say, 'put that on my agenda.' Not too long after that, he announced the canonization of Father Damien. She traveled to Belgium for that event.

Dechant and other K of C supreme officers visiting the grottoes of St. Peter's Basilica.

"I learned quickly that she was a lady of strong will."

The final report of the 1985 Synod essentially affirmed the changes in church procedures brought on by Vatican II. It read in part, "Unanimously we celebrate the Second Vatican Council as a grace of God and a gift of the Holy Spirit from which many spiritual fruits in the universal churches, in the particular church and also in all people of our day have gone forth. Unanimously and with joy we also verify the Second Vatican Council as a legitimate and solid expression and interpretation of the deposit of faith, as it is contained in scripture and in the lived tradition of the Church."

The Synod's report also allowed for further introspection in light of "the defects and difficulties in the reception of the Council." In the two decades since the close of Vatican II, society as a whole—and organized religion—had undergone a transformation that required a new attentiveness, a more permanent cohesion. Cardinal Bernard Law suggested a commission of cardinals prepare a universal catechism as one way of combatting societal transformations. In 1986, the pope commissioned a group of cardinals and bishops—led by Cardinal Joseph Ratzinger, who would later become Pope Benedict XVI—to prepare the universal catechism.

Restoration of the façade of St. Peter's Basilica carried on through 1985 and well into 1986. In July 1985, the pope—accompanied by Archbishop Lino Zanini, Count Galeazzi, and others—visited the terrace atop the Basilica to personally inspect the progress. In late November 1986, after 20 months of intense work, the project reached completion. The pope celebrated this landmark event with a reception for the Knights of Columbus executive and finance committee. There, the Knights of Columbus presented him with a gilded bronze model of the façade atop a marble-inscribed base made by Tommaso Gismondi to commemorate the restoration. That special gift was topped by the Holy Father, who gave to the Order the copper-clad cross from the statue of Christ the Redeemer, which had been constructed in 1613 by Ambrogio Buonvicino to sit atop the façade of St. Peter's Basilica. A new cross was created to replace the Buonvicino cross, by then nearly 400 years old.

"That cross is now the centerpiece of the Knights of Columbus Museum in New Haven," Dechant said. "And this was done rather quietly. After he got permission from the pope, Archbishop Zanini didn't ask too many questions before sending that cross over to us. We once had a Vatican archivist visit our museum who was shocked that we had that cross in our possession. It's a documented gift, and it ties the Knights of Columbus to the Holy See, particularly to St. Peter's Basilica.

"A lot of things came our way then in Rome. Our relationship with the Vatican kept growing and growing. It boosted our image and our respect throughout the church. I must say that the reason we were so successful in doing this is that the Vatican trusted us, and still trusts us, 100 percent. When you get to that level, it's a game of trust. You can't pull a surprise on the Curia. We've got to keep doing what's expected of us. The Vatican must have full confidence in our willingness to do what's right. I think it's paid us dividends."

The Holy Father in his address said of the project's benefactors: "For more than a hundred years, the Knights of Columbus have distinguished themselves by their love for Christ and loyalty to the Church, by their service to the poor and needy, by their defense of the handicapped and unborn and by their strong support of family life. You stand forth as a shining example of the role of the laity in the life and mission of the church."

Once the façade restoration was complete, the Knights of Columbus agreed to support interior work on the Basilica. There were two large interior rooms that had been workrooms for the Basilica's original architects, including Michelangelo and Carlo Maderno, which Vatican officials desired for other uses. The rooms had open windows, which needed to be winterized. During the process of this restoration, these rooms were converted into six separate rooms, some of which were used to store paintings of all the popes going back to St. Peter and the Basilica's archives. One of the new rooms was dedicated to Count Enrico Galeazzi in honor of his many years of service to the Holy See.

Indeed, Galeazzi had given most of his life to the Holy See and to the Knights of Columbus. He had spent that life on a first-name basis with heads of state, church leaders, popes, presidents, and supreme knights. In September 1986, Count Enrico Galeazzi died at age 90.

At the time of his death, Galeazzi's close friends were in the process of compiling a book of tributes from the Holy Father, church leaders, and other important dignitaries. Sadly, Galeazzi never saw the finished product.

Accompanied by John McDevitt and Paul McGlinchey, the Dechants traveled to Rome for Galeazzi's funeral. They arrived at the Galeazzi home on the morning of the funeral and viewed his body before it was placed into a casket, which was soldered shut, in accordance with Roman custom. The funeral Mass was held at the Pontifical North American College in Rome (which Galeazzi had designed in the 1950s), and Galeazzi was buried in the chapel of the lower crypts.

To commemorate Galeazzi's love for the seminary where he was buried, the Knights of Columbus in 1982 had established a $2 million fund within Knights of Columbus Charities Inc., the earnings of which are paid to the college annually and in perpetuity. Subsequently, the corpus of that fund was increased to $4 million.

The loss of Galeazzi, Dechant's mentor in Rome and of all things inside the Vatican, was much to bear. Yet, he chose to reflect on the good times they had spent together, as co-workers and as friends. It was Galeazzi, Dechant always said, who instructed him on how to be a diplomat.

"It is my sincere belief that without the many contributions of Count Galeazzi, the Order of the Knights of Columbus would never have achieved such prestigious status in Rome and with the Holy See," Dechant said. "To him, much credit is due."

Galeazzi's secretary Cecilia Gospodinoff filled the position on an interim basis until Galeazzi's grandson Enrico Demajo chose to follow in his grandfather's footsteps early the next decade by assuming control over the daily operations of the Rome office. Demajo recounted Galeazzi's bullish take on Dechant as follows: "Virgil became supreme knight very, very young, and here, in Rome, the diplomacy is very difficult. To play the right diplomacy, in terms of Vatican diplomacy, you have to pay attention to what you do continuously. At the beginning, Virgil wasn't as refined in it. So grandfather, I think, helped him a lot.

"I used to remember him telling me that Virgil was the best supreme knight he ever met in his life. I'm absolutely certain about that. I remember his sentence very clearly. So I think for him it was something he really felt he should do, helping this young man to grow and become more polished in knowing how the Vatican works.

"Most people think the Vatican is a little state. It's a little state, but with 1.2 billion people that are related as Catholics, it's a gigantic state. Things change continuously. Somebody retires. Somebody has been promoted. You have to be up-to-date on what's going on. In that sense, it was a sort of challenge that my grandfather took on with Virgil. He always talked about how he was an extremely brilliant young man who could be the greatest supreme knight as it was. I think the relation-

SYNODUS EPISCOPORUM

His Holiness

Pope John Paul II

has appointed

Mr. and Mrs.

VIRGIL AND ANN DECHANT

AUDITOR et AUDITRIX

to

the Seventh Ordinary General Assembly of the Synod of Bishops

The Vatican, 13 August 1987

+ Jan P. Schotte

+ Jan P. Schotte, C.I.C.M.
Titular Archbishop of Silli
General Secretary

Numerous noteworthy appointments came the Dechants' way in the 1980s, including a chance to serve as auditors at the Seventh General Assembly of the Synod of Bishops.

SECRETARIA STATUS

His Holiness

John Paul II

has chosen

Mr. Virgil C. Dechant,

of the Archdiocese of Hartford to be among his Gentlemen of Honor.

M. Dechant is hereby duly informed of this appointment.

From the Apostolic Palace, April, 20, 1987.

L. + S.

Traduzione dal testo originale

+ Lino Zanini
Archbishop

Signed

+ E. Martinez
Subst.

ship between the two—Virgil and my grandfather—was so good, it produced a great affect for the Knights of Columbus. Grandfather was already a little old when he met Virgil, so he knew he could not last forever. He knew that Virgil would have to go it alone someday, and that's what happened. Grandfather's idea was to prepare him to be alone and manage the Order's interests in Rome without his help."

Indeed, Galeazzi had prepared his protégé to go it alone.

Dechant and other members of the Knights of Columbus greeted Pope John Paul II in San Francisco during his 1987 visit to the United States.

CHAPTER TEN

Virgil and Ann Dechant stood in the warm, sunny Florida sunshine and waited.

And waited.

And waited.

The steamy tarmac at Miami International Airport made the air seem twice as warm as the actual temperature. The large crowd stifled any air movement. It was September 10, 1987, and they were awaiting the arrival of two of the decade's most prominent world leaders: U.S. President Ronald Reagan and Pope John Paul II.

The pope was about to begin a 10-day pilgrimage through the United States in Miami, and President Reagan—having formally established diplomatic relations with the Holy See—was set to welcome the pope for the first time since consummating the ambassadorial relationship. The Dechants were among the crowd of thousands at the Miami airport that day to see the historic greeting. Air Force One arrived first, and the president and first lady waited on the plane for the pope's flight to arrive. On board the pontiff's airplane, John Paul II had spent some of his long flight answering questions from the press in five languages. The sometimes-hostile nature of the questions (concerning church positions on issues such as priestly celibacy, birth control, divorce, and homosexuality) and the pope's controlled, compassionate answers demonstrated much about the growing divide between the public perception of the Catholic Church and the true feelings of its faithful.

When the pope touched down in Miami, he told the crowd that he was visiting the U.S. as a pilgrim. The president assured the pope that the reception he could expect from Americans would exceed the warmth of the late-summer sunshine that made Florida so famous. In the crowd, the Dechants took special note when the president referenced the Knights of Columbus and the great work they were doing assisting those less fortunate across the country.

There's no greater example of this work than the Order's involvement in the International Special Olympics Games. Founded by Eunice Kennedy Shriver in 1968, the Special Olympics grew steadily over the years. The Knights of Columbus became involved, slowly at first, and then on a much larger scale in 1987 when they provided $250,000 in support and thousands of volunteers to help carry out the International Games in South Bend, Indiana. Dechant and Bishop Thomas Daily attended the event that year and escorted the Italian delegation into the opening ceremonies. There Dechant met the queen of Jordan.

"Very few families are not touched by someone who has special needs," Dechant said. "A lot of emotion goes along with this sort of involvement. This program is a winner, and it's a great fit for the Knights of Columbus."

With this level of in-

1350 New York Ave. N.W., Suite 500,
Washington, D.C. USA 20005

(202) 628-3630
telex 440730 ITS

June 9, 1987

Mr. Virgil Dechant
Supreme Knight
Knights of Columbus
Columbus Plaza
New Haven, Connecticut 06507

Dear Mr. Dechant:

Our visit to the Knights of Columbus headquarters was a special treat for John Chromy and me. We enjoyed your hospitality and appreciate your great generosity to Special Olympics, and for printing John Terelak's especially beautiful poster you will distribute at the International Games.

Thank you so much for the magnificent cross, which is an inspiring work of art I will treasure.

My thanks also to your wife. I enjoyed our conversations about our work, homes, and the future of Special Olympics. We are very pleased to have you on the Special Olympics team. See you in South Bend.

Sincerely,

Eunice Kennedy Shriver
Eunice Kennedy Shriver

EKS/jnr

Created by The Joseph P. Kennedy, Jr. Foundation for the Benefit of Citizens with Mental Retardation.

During their travels the Dechants had the opportunity to meet King Juan Carlos I, left, of Spain.

volvement, it's easy to understand Reagan's admiration for the Knights of Columbus, and vice versa. It's hard to imagine a more comfortable relationship between a U.S. president and the K of C. In June 1985, Reagan had appointed Dechant and 21 other people, including New York Governor Mario Cuomo and Greek businessman Alexander "Alecko" Papamarkou, to the Christopher Columbus Quincentenary Jubilee Commission.

"This afforded us more numerous occasions to meet in the White House and make plans for the celebrations of 1992," Dechant said. "We also had the opportunity to meet in Rome; Genoa, Italy; Madrid, and various other cities in Spain. While in Spain, we had the privilege of

Bishop Thomas V. Daily, whose father had once been a state deputy in Maine, succeeded Bishop Charles P. Greco as supreme chaplain of the Knights of Columbus.

meeting the King and Queen at a reception that he held in our honor, and later Alecko, Ann, and I were invited to a dinner in the home of the King's sister. He also took us to the palace of the Duchess D'Alba, who held more aristocratic titles than any other living person."

Dechant's presence on the Quincentenary Commission also spawned new opportunities for the Knights of Columbus, such as an evangelization program where K of C state councils shared crosses modeled after the pope's "Cross of the New World," which he presented during a 1984 visit to Santo Domingo, Dominican Republic, to celebrate 500 years of Christianity in the Americas. The Knights funded the production of replica crosses to visit diocesan cathedrals and parishes; one such cross was even placed in the central nave of St. Peter's Basilica in Rome. And the Order funded the construction of Holy Savior Church in the Bahamas near the site believed to be where Christopher Columbus made landfall in 1492.

During his 1987 U.S. visit, the pope heard "several forceful pleas that lay people be given a greater voice in church affairs," according to *The New York Times*. There were also pleas to re-examine the role of women in the church. So it was perhaps good timing a month later when the pope convened a Synod of Bishops in Rome to examine the role of the laity in church affairs. Virgil and Ann Dechant, appointed by the pope as auditors, were among the 232 Synod participants. They left for Rome on September 30. But on October 19, 1987, a day that became known as "Black Monday," the stock market crashed. The Dow Jones Industrial Average that day fell 508 points. As Dechant recalled, "this caused a great paper loss for the Order, so I decided I was needed in New Haven. I thought it wise to go home."

Dechant explained his predicament to the secretary of state and arranged to leave the Synod early. Fortunately, the Federal Re-

Political allies: Dechant became just as close with President George H.W. Bush as he had been with President Ronald Reagan.

serve's efforts to encourage banks to continue lending money, even sometimes at a loss, would help restore consumer confidence, and the American economy soon returned to a more favorable state.

For Dechant and the Order, 1987 was tinged with sadness. On January 20, Supreme Chaplain Bishop Charles P. Greco died at age 92. Greco, the longtime bishop of Alexandria in Louisiana, had served as supreme chaplain of the Knights of Columbus since January 14, 1961.

Greco's successor as supreme chaplain was Bishop Thomas V. Daily, then of the diocese of Palm Beach, Florida, and later bishop of the diocese of Brooklyn. His father, John Daily, had been state deputy of Maine in the early 1900s. Dechant and Daily were good friends who shared much mutual respect, and their relationship would help the Order prosper over the next two decades. Whenever possible, Dechant invited the supreme chaplain to K of C meetings in Rome, particularly when there was an opportunity to interact with the Holy Father.

In November 1988, President Ronald Reagan's vice president, George H.W. Bush, was elected president, resoundingly defeating Democrat Michael Dukakis after having campaigned on a platform that included support for prayer in schools and pro-life activities. Reagan's

From left: Ann Dechant, Virgil Dechant, and President George Bush—friends and supporters.

eight years as president had provided the Knights of Columbus with a once-in-a-generation ally in the White House, and the Bush years would offer much of the same.

The Dechants had spent time with the Bushes over Labor Day weekend 1988, dining together at the vice president's home in Washington. During that visit they were introduced to their son, George W. Bush, and his wife Laura, who would later become president and first lady. Then in 1991, President Bush invited the Dechants to a state dinner honoring Brazilian President Fernando Collor de Mello. Later that decade, the Dechants were again guests of the president; this time the location was Camp David, where the president had invited them to attend the dedication of the chapel. The Knights of Columbus played an important role in the dedication ceremony, having funded the purchase of the chapel's pipe organ at the suggestion of Cardinal James Hickey.

The elder Bush's administration and the Order would collaborate, as Dechant recalled, "in many areas," but one key initiative stood out. During a speech at the Republican National Convention and later at his inauguration, Bush mentioned the phrase "a thousand points of light." This helped spark the Points of Light Awards, which Bush handed out daily during his presidency to recognize outstanding individuals (or entities) who contributed volunteer work in communities across the country. The Knights of Columbus agreed to support the program at a cost of $250,000 per year; this support would continue through the presidencies of Bill Clinton and George W. Bush. The Order itself was once honored with the award in recognition of its wide-ranging volunteerism around the country and the world.

Bush and Dechant shared enough trust to discuss closely guarded matters, even involving personnel. While making small talk before

Virgil Dechant, pictured at the Christopher Columbus monument in Santo Domingo: a conservative man "with a very large supply of creativity and imagination."

lunch at Camp David in 1991, Dechant recommended that the president nominate Bill Barr for his attorney general's post. Barr, a Columbia-educated litigator, had worked in the Reagan White House and had earned Dechant's confidence. Indeed, Barr would get his chance, first stepping in for his predecessor as acting attorney general and later, following a nomination from Bush, full-time. Barr later served the Knights of Columbus as a member of the board of directors.

Beyond Dechant's relationship with Reagan and Bush, the Order kept itself relevant in Washington, D.C., by opening an office there in the late 1980s where it could promote its good works and interact with lawmakers to generate interest in its key political initiatives, such as tuition tax credits and pro-life causes. To help staff the new Washington office, Dechant hired Russell Shaw, who lived in Washington, as a public relations official to help tell the Order's story. Shaw had spent the previous 18 years working as the director of information for the

Dechant's honors extended around the world, including becoming a knight commander in the Order of Christopher Columbus, which he received from President Joaquin Balaguer during a trip to the Dominican Republic.

Carl Anderson, seated to Dechant's left, became vice president and dean of the Pontifical John Paul II Institute.

U.S. Conference of Catholic Bishops. He was interested in a new challenge, and Archbishop John Foley—a mutual friend of Shaw and Dechant—suggested to Shaw that he'd be a perfect fit for the Knights of Columbus. Shaw visited New Haven to interview with Dechant, but the position Dechant had in mind for Shaw was editor of *Columbia*, a job that would require Shaw to move his family to New Haven.

During a follow-up meeting with Dechant and Supreme Treasurer Bill Van Tassell in Washington, Shaw reluctantly told Dechant that, while he was flattered by the offer, he simply couldn't move his family to New Haven. But Shaw had another idea.

"What the Knights of Columbus really needs is an experienced public relations man to get the word around about the program," Shaw told Dechant. "And the best place to have such a person is situated right here in Washington, D.C."

Shaw's idea was an even better fit for the Knights of Columbus than he realized at the time of his pitch.

"You don't know this yet, but we're planning to open a Washington office anyway," Dechant explained. "Carl Anderson is coming on to serve as the director of that office, and you could work there."

And thus Shaw was hired. He officially began his public relations job with the Knights of Columbus in late 1987.

Shaw found out immediately that there was more to Virgil Dechant than he had first suspected.

"What I learned is that he was and is a man with a very large supply of creativity and imagination, which surprised me when I began to realize it," Shaw said. "Virgil is a very conservative man. He dresses conservatively. You meet him and you get the feeling that this is a conservative Midwestern businessman. Well, all that is true and part of the reality of Virgil Dechant. But he's also a man with a lot of creativity and a very inventive imagination. And he brought to bear his creativity on the Knights of Columbus. He was always coming up with new initiatives, new things for the Order to do. And he was interested in other people's ideas and suggestions. If there was some potential in advancing the interests of the Knights of Columbus, he wanted to hear about it."

Carl Anderson, who ran the Knights' Washington office, was familiar with how things ran in the nation's capital. Since 1983, Anderson had served in the Executive Office of the President of the United States, including a stint as special assistant to President Reagan. Anderson also taught family law as a visiting professor at the Pontifical John Paul II Institute for Studies on Marriage and Family at the Pontifical Lateran University in Rome.

Around the time that the Knights were establishing their Washington office, Dechant, Anderson, and the Order began discussions to

Tom Dechant, Virgil's oldest son, followed in his father's footsteps and became state deputy of the Kansas State Council of the Knights of Columbus in 1988. Later, he became vice supreme master of the Fourth Degree.

open a North American campus of the John Paul II Institute for Studies on Marriage and Family. "We agreed that this would be a wonderful undertaking because what the church really needed was family life experts," Dechant said. "And the goal of this institute would be to train these teachers and administrators of family life programs for the various dioceses."

Dechant and Anderson had to first get approval from the office of the Vatican secretary of state. They met in Rome with Cardinal William Wakefield Baum, prefect of the Sacred Congregation for Catholic Education, and Monsignor Justin Francis Rigali, to explain their plan. Whether or not the concept of a U.S. campus was a tough sell, Dechant—and, as an extension, Anderson—was the perfect man to make such a pitch, said Rigali, now a cardinal and the archbishop emeritus of Philadelphia.

"I view his contribution to the church as being solidly in agreement with the Second Vatican Council's description of the vocation of the laity: following Christ and giving witness to him in the world," said Cardinal Rigali.

Having satisfied the Holy See, the U.S. campus of the Pontifical John Paul II Institute for Studies on Marriage and Family opened in 1988, with the Knights of Columbus serving as its benefactor. Carl Anderson, with his unique expertise on family life matters, was named vice president and dean of the institute.

Dechant credited Anderson, saying, "Carl has given much of himself to make that school work. And I have to give him total credit for that. It's produced countless experts in family life."

On September 8 of that year, Cardinal Baum served as celebrant for a Mass to commemorate the opening of the North American campus.

In 1988, Tom Dechant, Virgil's oldest son, became state deputy of the Kansas State Council. Tom had joined the Knights of Columbus as a

The K of C funded the construction of Holy Savior Church in San Salvador, where Columbus is believed to have made landfall.

college student at the University of Notre Dame in the 1970s (Council #1477, the Order's first college council) and eventually became grand knight of that council. After college he returned to Kansas to hang out his own shingle as a certified public accountant in La Crosse. He became grand knight of Council #2970 in 1981 and worked his way through the state council chairs before becoming state deputy.

Tom Dechant proved to be a chip off the old block. His two-year term as Kansas state deputy was highlighted by tremendous growth. Sixteen new councils were added in Kansas during that time, the most ever by a Kansas state deputy. For Virgil Dechant, who so strongly valued council and membership growth as a means of expanding the Order, his son's success made him proud.

Supreme Knight Dechant: always in touch with K of C affairs worldwide.

One might conclude that Tom's term as state deputy gave Virgil Dechant an opportunity to reconnect with his colleagues from the Kansas State Council, but the truth is that no such reconnection was needed. Despite his ascent to the Order's highest office and the busy schedule that accompanied the job of supreme knight, Dechant had never lost touch with K of C affairs in Kansas. Nor did he ever lose touch with the business scene in La Crosse. The Kansas State Council's annual convention was a fixture on his calendar; so was the early summer wheat harvest.

Dechant's affinity for his home state was not lost on his brother Knights in Kansas.

"Regardless of where he was at, at least whenever I was there, Virgil would always mention his Kansas roots," said Tom Zarda, who preceded Tom Dechant as Kansas state deputy. "He would give Kansas credit for a lot of things. He'd say, 'In Kansas, this is how they do things.' We always held receptions for Virgil at the supreme conventions, and we wanted to make sure those were done right. There wasn't any pressure to do it that way, but it was an honor.

"Just a little side story to help explain this man. I was elected state deputy in Dodge City. Virgil and I—we were friends—and we were sitting on a bench out in front on the sidewalk after the election of officers. We were talking about how things were going to go and who was going to get this or that appointment. I think we were coming down to activities director, and we went through a bunch of names. I had this book, and I was trying to throw it to Tom [Dechant] so he could look through it. I said, 'Here's the book—tell me who's good for the position.' I threw it and it accidentally hit Virgil right in the face. It just slipped out of my hands. And Virgil jokingly said, 'Tom, you threw the book at me.' I was embarrassed about that, but we all laughed about it. Patience, fortitude, and piety—they are all embodied in this person, Virgil Dechant."

While it's true that nothing ever kept Virgil Dechant from visiting Kansas every June for wheat harvest, one episode in 1988 certainly gave him second thoughts. Dechant was at the Hartford airport on June 16, about to board a flight that would take him to Kansas, when he received word that Mother Teresa had called the New Haven office, asking to speak with him. She wanted to come see him in New Haven to discuss the status of her congregation's constitution, which had just been approved by the Holy See and which the Knights of Columbus had agreed to print and bind for her Missionaries of Charity. Dechant made arrangements for his assistant Paul McGlinchey and Father John McGuire, who ran the Order's Catholic Information Service, to go to New York by car to pick up Mother Teresa and a few of her sisters and bring them to New Haven.

McGlinchey was glad he went. At one point during the car ride, Mother Teresa began to lead everyone in the car in praying the rosary. McGlinchey later told Dechant the whole experience was "pretty powerful."

When Mother Teresa arrived in New Haven, she agreed to address the entire home office staff at One Columbus Plaza. Dechant, of course, was on a plane en route to Kansas. Years later, Mother Teresa brought up the visit with Dechant.

"That time I came to New Haven," she said, "you couldn't have cancelled your trip?"

There was little Dechant could say in response that he felt would be a satisfactory excuse.

"I never cancelled my wheat harvest," he recalled years later. "I never scheduled any appointments around that time. That was the one thing I reserved for myself, that private time, to go out and oversee my harvest. But I got her message loud and clear. Her memory was fantastic.

"I would never stand up Mother Teresa again."

When the printing was finished, the Knights of Columbus bound the Missionaries of Charity constitution in a light blue leather cover. When Mother Teresa saw the finished work, she was at first unhappy, telling Dechant that such high-end binding was "too elaborate for her sisters." Dechant convinced her to accept the constitution by explaining that each of her sisters could treasure it for life, knowing it was so carefully bound.

The Knights of Columbus continued to help Mother Teresa and her nuns in various ways. The board of directors voted to provide her

RECEIVED
NOV 29 1990
Supreme Knight

CARDINAL'S OFFICE
1011 FIRST AVENUE
NEW YORK, NY 10022

November 21, 1990

Dear Virgil,

Words cannot express my gratitude to you for your willingness to answer our Holy Father's request for your help. All of us who are so deeply concerned for the financial well-being of the Holy See look forward to benefits that your expertise and experience will bring.

Having worked closely with Professor Caloia for the past several years, I trust that you will find him dedicated to the Church and possessed of remarkable talent. Though the task before you seems insurmountable, you will find it richly rewarding. Like myself, you will find Rome not only a source of a broader vision of the Church but the opportunity to deepen your appreciation of the real gift that is the Church.

As we celebrate Thanksgiving, I am grateful to God for the gift which you are to the Church. Please give Ann my love.

With warm personal regards, and

Faithfully in Christ,

John Cardinal O'Connor
Archbishop of New York

Mr. Virgil C. Dechant
Supreme Knight
Knights of Columbus
Columbus Plaza
New Haven, CT 06507

Archdiocese of Newark   31 Mulberry Street Newark, New Jersey 07102   201159614000

Office of the Archbishop

December 6, 1990

Mr. Virgil C. Dechant
Supreme Knight
Knights of Columbus
Columbus Plaza
New Haven, Connecticut   06507

RECEIVED
DEC 11 1990
Supreme Knight

Dear Virgil:

The Lord is surely using you every minute of the day, and now He wants to use you even more.

My congratulations to you on being named to the lay Board of Directors of the Institute for the Works of Religion. I can appreciate that this will be another demanding responsibility, but your own background -- both as a Catholic leader and as an extraordinary businessman -- will certainly be a great blessing to the Church and to this important work.

Once again I promise you my prayers for this new challenge. You have my prayers for so many other things, but I'll fit this one in too.

Give my love to Ann and all the family. I hope to see you soon.

With every good wish, I am, as always,

Fraternally,

fr. Ted

Most Reverend Theodore E. McCarrick
Archbishop of Newark

csw

with a monthly stipend of $10,000 to feed the poor for as long as she lived. Once during a meeting in Rome, Dechant personally carried one of the monthly stipend checks to present to Mother Teresa in person. He was shocked when she refused the money.

"Mother, why do that?" he asked. "You've got so many needs."

She told Dechant, "Our charism is to go out and beg and depend on divine providence. If we start taking money from the Knights of Columbus, we'll lose that. I can't let that happen."

"Well, how else can we help you?" Dechant asked.

Mother Teresa explained that her sisters needed help accessing telephones. Sending and receiving facsimiles was another need. So was printing—prayer cards, leaflets, and other spiritual directives. And her chapels needed to be outfitted with statuary. The Knights of Columbus agreed to cover the cost of all these things. They also promised to help staff her soup kitchens and collect food for her homes for the poor, all part of a collaborative program called Operation Share. In later years they would underwrite video productions that showcased the impact of her charity around the world.

During this same visit, Dechant also presented Mother Teresa with a silver medal. On one side of the medal was a likeness of the pope, and on the other side was a likeness of Father Michael McGivney. She accepted the medal, provided Dechant would help her place it at the foot of the Blessed Mother in her chapel. While they were walking toward the chapel, Mother Teresa leaned in and whispered to Dechant, "When I was in Russia last year, I was given a *gold* medal." Dechant never forgot the remark.

The Knights of Columbus also provided assistance to Mother Angelica of the Annunciation, the Franciscan nun who became a popular television personality, best known for founding the cable network

From left: Pope John Paul II, Virgil Dechant, Ann Dechant, Supreme Treasurer Bill Van Tassell.

President George Bush addressed the Knights of Columbus in person at the 1992 supreme convention in New York City.

EWTN. Mother visited the home office in New Haven to ask the Knights of Columbus for financial assistance. Over the years, her efforts to start and maintain a television network were always on the verge of failing because of taking on too much debt. Dechant sent Charles Walden, Harvey Bacque, and Paul McGlinchey to Birmingham, Alabama, to see her operation in person and better assess her needs. The trio spent two days there and returned to New Haven to report their findings to Dechant.

In 1988 the Order began providing an annual grant (what Dechant called "a nominal sum") for EWTN to broadcast live Masses from the Basilica of the National Shrine of the Immaculate Conception in Washington. It may have been a nominal sum, but the Knights of Columbus became key supporters of EWTN at a time when the network was most in need. The K of C continued supporting Mother Angelica and EWTN long after the network launched. When Mother Angelica passed away in 2016 at age 92, Dechant was invited to attend her funeral—he made the trip to Irondale.

In 1989, as part of the bicentennial celebration of the Catholic hierarchy in the United States, the Knights of Columbus gave $2 million in honor of Bishop Charles Greco to fund the construction of a chapel at the headquarters of the National Conference of Catholic Bishops (NCCB) in Washington, D.C.

For Virgil Dechant, the new decade dawned with two noteworthy appointments. One came care of the pope: a consulting position with the Pontifical Council for Social Communications, where he would serve until 2006. And, in December 1990, Dechant was appointed by the commission of cardinals to the board of directors for the Vatican's Institute for the Works of Religion, or IOR, more commonly known as the Vatican Bank. In 2001, Dechant would be appointed vice president of this prestigious council of five laypersons.

During his years on the board of the Vatican Bank, Dechant assisted in bringing in auditors from Price Waterhouse to audit the

THE WHITE HOUSE
WASHINGTON

August 17, 1992

Dear Virgil:

I was pleased to be with you and to address your membership at the Knights of Columbus Supreme Council Convention. You already know how deeply I appreciate your dedicated work, which is so essential to the moral fiber of our Nation.

Your gift of the crystal flag is an outstanding example of American craftsmanship and a beautiful expression of your commitment to our country. Thank you for your thoughtful remembrance, and most of all, for the friendship that prompted it.

Best wishes.

Sincerely,

G Bush

Mr. Virgil Dechant
Supreme Knight
Knights of Columbus
Suite 501
1275 Pennsylvania Avenue, N.W.
Washington, D.C. 20004

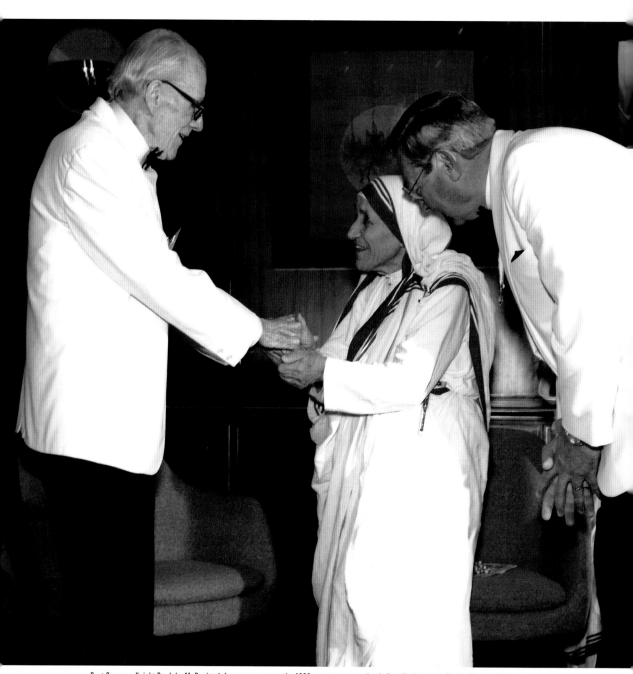

Past Supreme Knight Dr. John McDevitt, left, was present at the 1992 supreme convention in New York to meet Mother Teresa of Calcutta.

bank's books. By Dechant's recollection, it was the first such audit for the IOR. He also played a significant role in negotiating the sales of two of the bank's key United States holdings, a bank in New Jersey and a shopping center in Scottsdale, Arizona. Dechant helped negotiate a desirable sales price on both properties, which, up to that point, had delivered the bank very little return on its investment.

The timing of Dechant's appointment to the board was noteworthy. In the early 1980s, the bank went through a widely publicized scandal following the $1 billion collapse of Italy's Banco Ambrosiano. The Vatican paid creditors $250 million as part of a goodwill settlement.

While it's true the Vatican Bank has endured its fair share of controversy and eye-catching newspaper headlines over the years, Dechant says much of these claims are rooted in very little substance.

"All these wild stories you read, they're not always true," Dechant said. "I can't speak to what happened after I left, but we had no significant problems while I was there."

The year 1992 promised big things for the Knights of Columbus. Historian Christopher Kauffman was asked to produce a revised edition of *Faith and Fraternalism*, mostly to provide an update on the progress the Order had made in the decade since its release. Kauffman also wrote *Columbianism and the Knights of Columbus: A Quincentenary History*, described on the book's jacket as "a popular history of the Knights of Columbus, the world's largest Catholic fraternal society," written to commemorate the 500th anniversary of Columbus's first voyage of discovery. His work didn't stop there: he later authored a book on the history of the Order's Fourth Degree, *Patriotism and Fraternalism in the Knights of Columbus*.

The 1992 supreme convention would be held in New York City.

From left: Virgil Dechant, Bernard Cardinal Law, Ann Dechant, Mother Teresa, John Cardinal O'Connor, Cardinal James Hickey, Bishop Thomas V. Daily.

As part of the festivities, His Grace Cristobal Colon, Duke of Veragua, Marquis of Jamaica, a twentieth direct descendant of Christopher Columbus, and his wife, attended the convention as honored guests. So did Cardinal John O'Connor, archbishop of New York, who challenged the Knights and their families to build at least one "Tomb of the Unborn" in every diocese nationwide to honor the victims of abortion. Dechant, speaking on behalf of his brothers knights and their families, accepted O'Connor's challenge. Today, more than 10,000 such "tombs" have been erected across the country.

Mother Teresa was another honored guest in New York. Her presence, Dechant explained, was especially noteworthy.

"The Knights of Columbus had never honored anybody on a national or international level," he said. "We had been talking about that for years, and the time came and we decided that we should be honoring somebody that really merits it. With her concern for the poor and needy of the world, she was our first choice. We designed an award around the constitution of Vatican II, Gaudium Et Spes. The joy and hope."

Dechant phoned Mother Teresa in India and explained that the Knights of Columbus wished to honor her with an award. At first she refused, telling Dechant

Dechant charmed Mother Teresa by announcing the K of C would make a contribution equivalent to the cost of the 1992 States' Dinner.

that she didn't receive awards. Dechant had prepared himself for such a reaction, so he told her he'd been advised to call by Cardinal O'Connor, someone she admired and respected.

"She said she would take it under advisement and call me back," Dechant said. "So I called her back after some time, and she said, 'I will accept, but I will not accept a dinner.'"

The Knights of Columbus created the Gaudium Et Spes award as the organization's highest honor, given to individuals for their contributions to the faith and society, "only in special circumstances and only to individuals of exceptional merit." The award came with an honorarium of $100,000.

For the award itself, the Order struck a medal. Dechant joked that he "made darn sure it would be in gold." On one side of the medal was a likeness of Father Michael McGivney comforting the widow and children of a deceased member of the Order, and on the other side was a depiction of the crucifix of Pope John Paul II's crosier, which made reference to the Gaudium Et Spes encyclical.

The week of the convention arrived, and the award ceremony was scheduled on the day of the States' Dinner. Dechant arranged to carry out the program on Mother Teresa's terms: the award would be presented prior to the dinner. First there would be a small reception with the bishops in attendance, then a larger presentation in the banquet hall. The plan allowed Mother Teresa time to leave after receiving the award, before the guests were served dinner. She explained to Dechant that when she received the Nobel Peace Prize, she told the event's organizers that she would not accept the award with a dinner, so they scrapped the dinner and provided her with the honorarium and an additional amount equivalent to the cost of the dinner. Dechant took note of this story.

"The reception went beautifully," Dechant said. "A lot of bishops showed up to greet Mother Teresa. She carried a big purse, and I know it got pretty full because many in attendance were slipping envelopes with checks into it. Cameras were flickering constantly. She told Ann, 'I used to refuse to take pictures because I felt I was committing a sin of pride, but I made a deal with the Lord that every time I agreed to have a picture taken, He would let a soul out of purgatory. So now I don't mind taking a lot of pictures.' Once she had finished with all the photos, Mother leaned over and said to Ann, 'Tonight, many souls got out of purgatory. Maybe it's already empty.'"

After photos with the bishops, Dechant told Mother Teresa it was

The Dechants were present at World Youth Day in Denver, Colorado, in 1993 to greet Pope John Paul II.

time for the presentation. She was puzzled. They walked out into the hall where the States' Dinner guests had assembled—a crowd of more than 2,000 people—and she was shocked.

""You said there would be no dinner," she told Dechant.

Virgil Dechant served as the best man for Enrico's Demajo's wedding. From left: Enrico Demajo, Anabella Demajo, Ann Dechant, and Virgil Dechant.

"Mother," he explained to her, "the dinner is afterwards." This satisfied her.

Mother Teresa spoke to the large delegation on various subjects, but the majority of her speech was spent making the case for the pro-life position. After the speech, Dechant and Bishop Daily presented her the award and the honorarium. Then Dechant announced to the crowd and to Mother Teresa that the Knights of Columbus board of directors had agreed to provide her an additional contribution of $135,000, equivalent to the cost of the dinner that night.

The joyful smile that Mother Teresa gave after hearing Dechant's pledge melted the hearts of everyone in the room.

After her speech, Dechant helped escort Mother Teresa to the car that would take her back to the Bronx. She asked Dechant, "This gold medal, it's mine now?"

"Yes, Mother, that's yours," he said.

"You know what I'd like to do with it," she said. "I'm going to melt it down and make wedding rings out of it for the young girls I pick up off the streets in India. That would be my dowry to them."

Dechant encouraged her to keep the gold medal intact and promised that the Knights of Columbus would provide for the cost of the wedding rings.

"Then that would be a dowry from the Knights of Columbus," she said. "I want it to be my dowry."

Realizing there would be no winning on this topic, Dechant said, "Mother, you do whatever you wish with it."

Dechant later learned that some of the sisters who assisted Mother Teresa in her works of charity put the Gaudium Et Spes medal aside in a collection of items they were saving to commemorate her amazing life. This came to his attention when Mother Teresa called him one day, nearly a year after the convention, looking for the medal. She suspected she had accidentally left it in the car that drove her home that night. In fact, her sisters had set it aside for safekeeping before Mother Teresa had a chance to melt it down.

The relationship between the Knights of Columbus and Mother Teresa stayed strong long after she received the Gaudium Et Spes award. On numerous occasions, the Dechants and Bishop Daily and other members of the board of directors visited her and her sisters in the Bronx. When she was trying to make her way to China, she contacted Dechant to see if there was anything he could do to help her enter the country. And he once had the privilege of visiting her homes for the needy in the Philippines, where, as he said, "she took care of the poorest of the poor."

"Mother Teresa was streetwise," Dechant said. "She knew everything that was going on in the world. What a great comfort it was to know her."

In 1993, Denver, Colorado hosted World Youth Day, a Catholic Church-sponsored gathering of young people from around the world. The Denver meeting marked the first time a North American city had been chosen to host the event. The guest of honor was Pope John Paul II, who decided the gathering of thousands of young people merited a trip to the U.S.

In preparation for World Youth Day, the Knights of Columbus assisted the Archdiocese of Denver in various upgrades to their cathedral. The Order made plans to distribute rosaries and prayer cards to the youth who had traveled to Denver. Unsure of how many rosaries they would need, the Knights brought 100,000 to Denver and set up a booth where they could hand them out, one by one.

"It takes an awful lot of handing out to give away 100,000 rosaries," Dechant recalled. "But the kids got their rosaries. Then they came back and asked for some for their brothers and sisters, mothers and fathers. It was a joy to provide those to them."

In the weeks leading up to World Youth Day, Dechant noticed a disappointing trend among major media outlets: a sense of apprehension over the Holy Father's upcoming visit. Just as the pope had encountered during his visit to the United States six years earlier, skepticism over the church and its teachings had enveloped the mass media. John Paul II overcame these criticisms mostly through sheer charisma, especially in his dealings with the youth of the world.

"The press was eagerly hoping that he would strike out at that event, but he won the hearts and souls of not only the youth, but all of America. Much to their dismay," Dechant said.

Two years later, the Dechants would again attend World Youth Day, this time in Manila, Philippines, where they were the invited guests of Cardinal Jaime Sin, archbishop of Manila. Pope John Paul II attended that rendition of World Youth Day, too, and the crowds of people waiting to see him for the event's closing Mass were so congested, traffic was held up and the start of Mass was delayed for hours, prompting the Holy Father to fly into the venue by helicopter. Crowds that day were estimated at 5 million, making it the largest papal gathering in history. Dechant described the scene in Manila "like walking in a can of sardines." However, Dechant and Ann were escorted to meet the pope and Cardinal Sodano before the start of Mass. The delayed start of Mass affected satellite television coverage of the event—which was underwritten by the Knights of Columbus—and Dechant made the decision to extend the coverage by an additional two-and-a-half hours so the world could see the enthusiasm of the Catholic youth and the people of the Philippines for their faith.

A month after World Youth Day 1993, Virgil Dechant celebrated his

63rd birthday. It seemed he was a young 63. By most accounts, Dechant was at the height of his career. The Order was growing. The insurance business was steady. And the public image of the Knights of Columbus was arguably at an all-time high.

Having observed for years that K of C state councils were spending nearly every dollar they raised each year—leaving them with little in the way of reserves—Dechant undertook the development of the Christopher Fund, which provides that the supreme council sets aside matching funds for every dollar a state council saves in new money through K of C Charities, Inc. Annually, each state then receives the earnings of the joint amount to give to a charitable cause of their designation. By the year 2000, that fund would grow to nearly $11 million.

In 1994, at the request of the Holy See, the Knights of Columbus made a loan for the purchase of property to serve as the Holy See's United Nations headquarters in New York City. The Vatican returned the favor a few years later by assisting the K of C to obtain non-governmental organization (NGO) status at the U.N. That same year, the Order purchased a new portable organ for the Sistine Chapel, specially crafted in Germany.

Looking ahead on the calendar, the 1995 supreme convention was scheduled to be held in Kansas City and hosted by the Kansas State Council. Dechant would be 65 years old that year, and some wondered if it was more than just a coincidence that the convention was headed back to his home state. Was retirement imminent?

While this speculation wasn't entirely unfounded, the 1995 supreme convention in Kansas City would not be his last hurrah.

Shortly into his tenure as supreme knight, Dechant had suggested to convention delegates that the mandatory retirement age in the K of C be lowered from 70 to 65, but as Dechant was approaching that age, people were living and working longer than ever before. Mandatory retirement at 65 limited the breadth of talented, experienced people the Order could attract as employees and board members. A resolution emerged from the State Council of Hawaii providing that the retirement age for board members and officers be restored to 70. It passed unanimously. Dechant had no plans of slowing down anytime soon, so the change seemed to come at the perfect time. He could now continue the job of supreme knight through the end of the century.

However, the final years of Dechant's tenure as supreme knight would pose some of the greatest challenges, both professionally and personally, that he had ever faced.

A series of events in the mid-1990s tested Virgil and Ann Dechant, pictured here in Rome on their way to the Synod on the Laity, like they never had been tested before.

CHAPTER ELEVEN

He didn't see it coming, but adversity was closing in on Virgil Dechant. As a French novelist once warned, if you stay in one place long enough, things and people will go to pot on you. No, the Knights of Columbus wasn't about to crumble. And no, there was no mutiny onboard the titanic fraternal ship that Dechant was captaining. But the second half of the 1990s would test Dechant like no other era had since he assumed leadership of the Knights of Columbus in 1977.

After all, if you stay in one place long enough, you're bound to get tested.

In early 1995, Dechant and members of his staff became aware of an impending article in the *Boston Sunday Globe* that purported to expose the supreme knight and other executives of the Knights of Columbus on a variety of fronts, including their supposedly high salaries and the lengths they went to in protecting the Order's tax-exempt status. What should have been a celebrated year for the K of C—it marked the launch of a new fraternal benefit to compensate for the death of a child in infancy and the accidental death of a member or spouse, and it marked the start of a campaign to raise $5 million for a cultural center in Washington, D.C., to honor Pope John Paul II—1995 now threatened to be forgettable.

From the beginning, Dechant sensed the article was a hatchet job. When the *Globe* requested an interview, he chose to respond to written questions through the Washington office of a Chicago-based law firm, Kirkland and Ellis. He and his staff were unsure exactly when the article would be published, so he spent the weekends leading up to its release bunkered down in his office at One Columbus Plaza, trying to focus on his work, preparing for whatever was soon to come out in print.

"Everybody was real uptight about the whole thing," said Dechant's secretary Paula Forni.

She could sense the collective unease.

"I remember finally going into his office, and he said, 'You know, this is tough on all of us.'"

"They were very upset. We didn't know—nobody knew—until it came out what exactly was going to be in the story, and that's why everybody felt worried. I remember going out early one morning to buy the paper, but, of course, the story didn't run that day. We didn't know when it was going to appear."

The two-part *Boston Globe* story on Dechant and the Knights of Columbus was published in early April 1995. Its attack was two-pronged. It labeled Dechant as "a tall imposing man from the farmlands of Kansas" equipped with "an unusual blend of religious fervor and business acumen" who was obsessed by his public image and a need for control. One Columbus Plaza was dramatized as Dechant's "personal fiefdom" and "a factory-style environment without clocks on office walls, in which many workers must report to work, leave and return from breaks at the sound of a bell." Dechant was portrayed as a controlling autocrat. In an era of corporate scandal and soulless executives, the article's writers were holding his feet to the fire for his insistence on being accountable for all aspects of his business, large or small.

Then came attacks on the Order's works. The article depicted the Knights of Columbus's work to end abortion and pornography as a "crusade." The Knights' investment strategy was also called into question. And it called the Knights "sophisticated political players" capable of mobilizing their base to strong-arm Washington lawmakers in order to maintain their tax-exempt status.

A few weeks later, the *National Catholic Reporter* ran its own article on the supposed scandal at the K of C, mostly parroting the *Globe's* story. Dechant's salary—and those of other supreme officers—was described as exorbitant; so was his company car, country club membership, and use of an apartment in Rome, where he traveled monthly. Somehow lost in the reporting was the fact that the Rome apartment, located down the hallway from the Knights' frugal Rome office, was intended to save the Order money and offer Dechant the best opportunity to operate at high efficiency on his trips to the Vatican.

"The *Boston Globe* somehow got onto a story, for which they'd been given a version of reality by a disaffected former insurance agent, I believe," said Russell Shaw, then the public relations voice of the Knights of Columbus. "The complaint was that Virgil and others were living high on the hog and treating themselves very well at the expense of the K of C and there was a real scandal here that was just crying out to be exposed by the *Boston Globe*.

"Well, they tried hard, and they ultimately put a lot of stuff into print. But it didn't add up to anything. I think anybody reading would conclude that there wasn't any scandal there. They would conclude that these men were hard-working people running a very successful organization. They're paid relatively well by church standards, but by the standards of a very successful insurance company, their pay was quite modest, actually.

"I think the editors, after they published all this stuff, figured there wasn't any story here. They had been sold a bill of goods."

Still, even a bill of goods, especially one sold by a widely read newspaper, threatened to harm the Order's reputation.

Shaw cited the *Boston Globe* story as an extreme example of a problem he began noticing in dealing with the media on behalf of the Knights of Columbus: the Order's good works, generally, are not the sort that garner attention-grabbing headlines.

"I felt then and, as time went by, I felt more and more, that the Knights of Columbus were then and are now extremely underappreciated by the media," Shaw said. "The extremely important role played by the Knights of Columbus in American Catholicism and in the United States generally is not grasped and appreciated by most people."

Shaw's theory applied even in Kansas, Dechant's home state. During Paul Lenherr's tenure as state deputy in the early 1990s, Lenherr had been contacted by a reporter from the *Wichita Eagle*, interested in writing a piece on Dechant's salary.

"Somebody said an insurance agent who wanted to become a general agent wasn't appointed, so he started a story that we're collecting Tootsie Roll money to pay Virgil's salary," Lenherr recalled. "I was kind of giving it to them over the phone when they called for an interview. I said, 'You know, if Virgil Dechant was the CEO of Boeing, what sort of salary would he be making? Or any other comparable insurance agency? Come on.' That paper didn't get from me what they wanted to hear."

Lenherr wasn't the only one

GEORGE BUSH

May 3, 1995

Dear Virgil,

Thanks for your very nice letter.

All I did was to tell the truth to the *Boston Globe*. You are a good man. The Knights of Columbus is a fine organization, and it was a pleasure to share my high regard for you with all who read that article.

There are a lot of things I don't miss about my previous job. One of them is dealing with the national press. If they took a shot at you in the article, which I have not seen, don't worry about it.

My warm best wishes,

G. Bush

Mr. Virgil C. Dechant
Supreme Knight
Knights of Columbus
Columbus Plaza
New Haven, Connecticut 06507-0901

10000 MEMORIAL DRIVE · HOUSTON, TEXAS 77024

who voiced his support for Dechant publicly. One courtesy the *Boston Globe* did extend was to contact former President George H.W. Bush, who had been rumored to place Dechant on a shortlist for the position of ambassador to the Vatican. Bush wasn't buying what the *Globe* was trying to sell.

"You can put me down as having a high personal regard for Virgil Dechant," Bush told the *Globe*. The quote was included in the story.

To be fair, not all of the press Dechant and the Knights of Columbus received during his time as supreme knight was hostile. In 1994, the *New Haven Register* published a three-part series on Dechant and the Knights titled "Tower of Power." For that story, home office employees went on the record by name. The result was a more comprehensive, balanced assessment of the Knights of Columbus and its involvement in world affairs.

The issue of the Order's tax-exempt status was something Dechant had monitored very closely. For instance, Don Kehoe, a former state deputy from Virginia, was hired to work for the supreme council in New Haven. Kehoe was a longtime employee of the Internal Revenue Service (IRS) who had worked in the Exempt Organizations and Charities area and knew well the tax concerns of the Knights of Columbus. In January 2000, after Kehoe's retirement from the federal government, Dechant offered him a job as administrator of tax compliance and charities to, as Kehoe put it, "make sure the Knights worked specifically within the framework of the law and the regulations so they didn't overstep or do something that would jeopardize that tax-exempt status—especially when trying to do good and do things for people."

Kehoe would one day become supreme secretary under the administration of Dechant's successor.

With criticisms being leveled his way, Dechant made little in the way of a public response to the *Globe* story. Instead, his objective was to bear down and work even harder. He was never the sort to back down, said Tom Smith, who by then had moved from Fraternal Services into the Insurance Department, positioning himself to one day take over the Order's insurance operations.

"There were some very difficult times in the nineties when there were some very personal criticisms—very personal yet public criticisms—of him," Smith said. "He was leading the Order when a lot of these social issues began to nip at our heels.

"There were some situations when he had a very clear choice of withdrawing a little bit and saying, 'Let's think about this and let me figure out what I'm going to have to do.' Instinctually, he would act first to protect the interests of the Order, and then he would act to make sure that the information that was being disseminated, by whatever party was disseminating it, was accurate. And he never backed down. He never hesitated. You had to know, if you were going to cross him, there was no compromise and there was no retreat. You were going to finish. When you started something, it was going to get to a conclusion. And I never saw him lose."

Smith described a situation when a small but unhappy group of disgruntled K of C members decided to launch a public campaign opposing Dechant's leadership style. Smith recalled that a few newspapers even picked up on the story. Dechant's response was to meet them head on.

"He had this phrase that I saw both Virgil and Tom Dechant use, so it probably comes from someplace out in western Kansas," Smith recalled. "The phrase was: 'We're going to give 'em a lesson in Kansas politics.' So rather than staying silent for awhile, he would say, 'I'll give them a lesson in Kansas politics. We'll show them how this is all going

Dechant, right, during a meeting of multi-faith leaders involved in private education, found a close ally in U.S. President George Bush, who was always bullish about his feelings for Dechant.

to work out.' When adversity came calling at the office of Virgil Dechant, it generally left with its head down."

"He took some direct shots on a lot of things," said Ron Tracz. "I could see where it was somewhat discouraging to Virgil. To his credit, he was a Catholic gentleman during the whole thing, but the fact of the matter is that it's always easy to point fingers at other people when you don't have to make those decisions yourself. Even today, there are individuals who want the Knights of Columbus to be more Catholic than the church, and that's a difficult thing. The two or three different circumstances that I can recall revolved around pro-life issues and taking shots at the Knights of Columbus or the supreme officers or the supreme knight directly for not doing enough to support the pro-life cause. That's probably the biggest joke out there, because we were the most staunch defenders of the pro-life position for the Catholic Church since the mid-1970s. But those individuals failed to admit that."

Indeed, the Knights of Columbus were on the front lines of the battle to end abortion. In the early 1990s, as chair of the NCCB pro-life committee, Cardinal John O'Connor, on behalf of the nation's Catholic bishops, began what Dechant called an "all-out offensive" on the pro-life issue. The bishops engaged Hill & Knowlton, one of the country's leading public relations firms, and the Wirthlin Group, a polling concern, to help transform public opinion. The K of C provided $4 million of funding during the first year of this effort and $750,000 annually since that time.

In July 1995, New Haven, Connecticut, hosted the Special Olympics World Games. More than 6,000 athletes from 120 countries and half-a-million spectators descended upon New Haven, providing a tremendous boost for the local economy. The Knights of Columbus elevated their level of support, donating $1 million and providing 6,000 volunteers to help with operations.

A month later, the 113th supreme convention was held in Kansas City under the theme, "Proclaim the Gospel of Life." The host hotels may have been on the Missouri side of the state border, but the Kansas State Council was chiefly responsible for hosting the convention activities. And, true to form, the Kansas Knights put on a great show.

Kansas touches were everywhere: sunflower displays adorned the hotel lobbies; characters from *The Wizard of Oz* such as Dorothy Gale and the Scarecrow greeted guests as they checked in; and delegates received miniature stone post bookends carved out of Kansas limestone at convention registration. The Kansas State Council was pulling out all the stops to hail their native son as he returned to his home state.

"Hosting the convention was quite a responsibility when you think about it," said Tom Zarda, who was chief among the Kansas organizers.

Dechant's visits to Rome frequently included stops to pay his respects at the tomb of Count Enrico Galeazzi in the lower crypts of the North American College.

"How do you organize all that? Well, we planned for a long time. We worked on that for five years or more because we had to put our invitation in for it in advance. We had a great group of Knights and wives."

At the opening meeting, Dechant spoke of his own descendants, Volga German wheat farmers who emigrated from Germany through Russia and eventually settled in western Kansas. He also recalled some of his fondest memories from his early days with the Order in Kansas.

"Having grown up with the Order in Kansas, I have many warm and wonderful memories of mentors and close friends—some here present but many others who have gone to their rewards," Dechant said. "We Kansans will know who they are. Some of my happiest memories revolved around weekends spent on the side roads of Kansas with these dedicated Knights exemplifying the Third Degree; in my second year as state deputy, we conducted 73 major degrees."

The 1995 supreme convention was a tremendous feather in the cap for the Kansas Knights. Visiting guests hailed the friendly hospitality and personal touches. For the Dechants, the most nostalgic moment came during an invitation-only reception the Kansas delegation held in

SARGENT SHRIVER
1325 G STREET, N.W., SUITE 500
WASHINGTON, D.C. 20005

June 18, 1997

RECEIVED
JUN 23 1997
Supreme Knight

Virgil C. Dechant
Supreme Knight
Knights of Columbus
Columbus Plaza
New Haven, Connecticut 06507-0901

Dear Virgil:

I was delighted to read in the recent issue of "Columbia" that we Knights are continuing our "National Apostolate" for People With Mental Retardation.

The Knights have been a tremendous financial support for Special Olympics; but even more important, in my opinion, has been their wide-spread individual commitment to the work with persons with mental retardation carried and symbolized by the Special Olympics Movement. It's great to have the Knights with us. Surely we would not have more than a million registered athletes now participating in Special Olympics were it not for the generous support of organizations like yours.

I am glad I am a Knight and have been one for 47 years or more.

All the best,

Sargent Shriver

P.S. Thanks, too, for that marvelous TV spot which talks about the Knights' work with Special Olympics. It aired last evening on one of our local stations.

their honor. The presentation included a short video tribute that lauded their years of service to the Knights of Columbus and the Catholic Church. Indeed, the Kansas City convention helped ease the pain from the personal attacks that had dogged Dechant for most of the year.

A few months later, thousands of Knights of Columbus and their families traveled to New York City to witness a papal visit by John Paul II. It was a trip that had actually been planned for the previous year, but a hip ailment prevented the pope from traveling, so the visit was rescheduled for October 1995. The Knights of Columbus were called on to play an important role during the pope's visit. Through the assistance of the National Conference of Catholic Bishops (NCCB), the Holy See asked the Knights of Columbus to host a Mass for family life during the pope's U.S. visit. Shea Stadium was supposed to be the venue for a prayer service in 1994, but that facility was unavailable the following year, so organizers had to look elsewhere. Madison Square Garden was one possibility, but the Vatican and the NCCB, in partnership with the Diocese of Brooklyn and the K of C, settled on the Aqueduct Racetrack in Queens. With the existing grandstand and additional seating on the track's infield, the K of C expected the facility to hold close to 80,000 people for the Mass, much more than they could have fit into Madison Square Garden.

Dechant and his supreme officers wanted nothing more than to execute a first-class event that every member of the Knights of Columbus could be proud of. Dechant called the opportunity "the greatest singular honor that has come our way."

"What a compliment it was for us to be recognized as the premier family organization that the Vatican felt comfortable enough with to host the Holy Father."

To manage the colossal task of orchestrating such a large-scale event, Dechant leaned heavily on Deputy Supreme Knight Bob Wade and Dechant's assistant, former Director of Fraternal Services, Harvey Bacque.

A former state deputy from New Jersey and a longtime labor relations manager at Exxon, Wade had become a human Swiss army knife for Dechant, capable of handling complicated projects with calm and poise. Wade had first impressed Dechant during the 1980s when he negotiated with the National Football League's NFL Properties about sponsoring the league's Punt, Pass, and Kick youth football contest. Disagreements on insurance liability ultimately doomed the partnership, but Wade had displayed his negotiating savvy and Dechant liked what he saw.

Wade was again helpful when Dechant made the difficult decision to outsource the printing of *Columbia* magazine and other materials, which eliminated most of the Order's union printing jobs at its New Haven printing plant. Wade crafted a generous separation package, and together he and Dechant faced the printers to deliver the news. Wade said the deal was done "without a lot of weeping and gnashing of teeth," a testament to Dechant's willingness to tackle the problem straight on.

Wade's most delicate maneuvering took place in the early 1990s when Dechant asked him to peacefully help resolve a brewing conflict of interest between the Knights of Columbus and several well-known politicians who were members of the Order, including Massachusetts Senator Ted Kennedy, New Jersey Governor James Florio, and Connecticut Senator Chris Dodd. These men and others had publicly affirmed pro-choice positions on the abortion issue, which stood in direct opposition to the pro-life tenets of the Catholic Church. The Knights of Columbus, standing in solidarity with the church and its teachings, came under criticism from a small but boisterous faction of pro-lifers who felt the K of C should dismiss these politicians from the Order. They wanted the K of C to voice their pro-life stance more fervently through the

A massive crowd swarmed Aqueduct Racetrack in Queens, NY, in the fall of 1995 to see Pope John Paul II.

Virgil and Ann Dechant played key roles in the pope's 1995 Mass for family life at Aqueduct.

media. The Catholic Church hadn't thrown them out for not being practical Catholics, so how could the K of C do so? In substance, these detractors wanted the Knights of Columbus to be more restrictive than the magisterium of the church. The whole situation was a potential firestorm that could lead to unwanted publicity for all parties involved. Wade carefully arranged for these politicians, some who were delinquent in paying their dues, to quietly withdraw from the Knights of Columbus with the possibility of reinstatement should their public positions on abortion ever change.

Wade had proven himself to be a close ally of Dechant's in difficult times.

One of the more challenging aspects of preparing Aqueduct for the papal Mass was seating. The Knights once again engaged Kevin Roche—the architect who designed the supreme council building in New Haven—to design a seating plan for the infield. There were specific guidelines for aisle widths and seat dimensions that Roche had to follow to satisfy security and handicap accessibility requirements. Roche would also design the altar and the papal chair used during the Mass; the chair was later used by Pope Benedict XVI during a U.S. visit and is now part of the permanent collection at the K of C Museum.

Security was a major concern. The United States Secret Service took the lead, but numerous other public safety agencies became involved, including the New York City Police Department, the New York State Police, the Federal Bureau of Investigation (FBI), its SWAT team and so on. It seemed any safety agency whose employees could carry a gun had some involvement in security for the pope's Mass.

In the days leading up to Mass at Aqueduct, the Secret Service surveyed every rooftop within a 10-mile radius as possible locations to place armed snipers. Even members of the clergy had to wear proper

The executive and finance committee of the Knights of Columbus funded specially-outfitted vans (such as the one in the background) to assist the Vatican with its television communications.

identification to get into Aqueduct and participate in the liturgy on the day of the service. And as the pope approached the racetrack by helicopter on Mass day, scuba rescue teams were waiting along the East River and the Hudson Bay, just in case.

The night before the Mass, Wade and Bacque were still prepping at the racetrack well past midnight. At 2:30 a.m., the Secret Service evacuated everyone from the facility to conduct one last inspection using bomb-sniffing dogs. Wade and Bacque shared a thermos of coffee outside the gates before finishing their setup, then they returned to their hotels to change into tuxedos for the long day ahead.

When daybreak came, visitors to Aqueduct were greeted with blue skies, ample sunshine, unseasonably warm temperatures, and lots of wind. The wind caused various problems during the liturgy but nothing substantial enough to distract from the celebration. As representatives of the Knights of Columbus, Virgil and Ann Dechant had preferred seats on the specially constructed, 300-foot-wide papal platform designed by architect Roche. Virgil would serve as a lector during Mass that day, and all of the members of the K of C board of directors would receive Holy Communion from the pope. K of C Supreme Chaplain Bishop Thomas V. Daily concelebrated the Mass with the Holy Father.

"We were privileged to be on that altar," Dechant joked, "but, I must say, we almost blew away."

Even the pope couldn't resist making a subtle joke about the force of the wind, as he likened it to the power of the Holy Spirit.

The crowd that day at Aqueduct was estimated between 75,000 and 80,000. Ten cardinals, 23 bishops, and 3 archbishops assisted the pope during Mass. So did countless priests in white robes who distributed Holy Communion to the large crowd.

The pontiff used this platform to speak to the crowd on the importance of restoring traditional family values. He was quoted as saying, "There can be no life worthy of the human person without a culture and a legal system that honors and defends marriage and the family."

Dechant summarized the incredible effort of the Knights of Columbus that day succinctly: "It was a great success and a great honor for us. I say it was our finest hour."

Virgil and Ann Dechant spent Christmas 1995 at their home in Hamden, surrounded by their children and grandchildren—the latter then numbering 9. With their busy travel schedule and geographical separation, opportunities to get the their whole family together were becoming more rare.

The new year began with optimism, but those feelings soon gave way to more heartache. On February 3, Dechant and his fellow supreme officers were shocked when they received word that Pat Donlin, the supreme advocate (or chief counsel), had died suddenly. Donlin, a Wisconsin native and an active member of St. Mary's Church in New Haven, was just 58. He was survived by his wife Nancy, two daughters, and two sons.

Donlin's death was not the only event to rock the supreme office to its core. In early December, on the night of the supreme council's annual Christmas party, Dechant's trusted assistant Harvey Bacque, 53, died suddenly.

Both deaths saddened Dechant and his colleagues and left tremendous holes to fill in the Knights of Columbus operation. Ron Tracz was appointed to Bacque's post; Supreme Director Judge Ricardo Garcia, from Texas, was tabbed to replace Donlin. Garcia would continue to reside in Texas, so the Order selected Pat Cipollone to handle the New Haven part of the workload. Cipollone would later become a board member and supreme advocate. His efforts were largely responsible for maintaining the Order's tax-exempt status in Canada.

The following spring, after a visit to Kansas where she complained to family members about a strange mix of symptoms, Ann Dechant underwent an operation to remove what doctors thought was a benign tumor. They ultimately discovered that the tumor was stage-4 cancer. After the operation they determined there was nothing more they could do. Ann was given a limited amount of time before the cancer would take over her body. It was a grim report.

The Dechants were devastated. Mother Teresa heard about Ann Dechant's illness and called to offer support.

"Ann, I'm going to send you a medal of Our Lady," Mother Teresa told her. "Wear it near the cancer, and it will go away."

When the medal arrived, Ann wore it as instructed and hasn't taken it off since.

Top photo: First-class medical care and the prayers of Mother Teresa, pictured, helped Ann Dechant survive cancer.

Above: The Dechants and other supreme officers visited Mother Teresa's satellite operations in Harlem, Brooklyn, and the South Bronx.

Then, as Virgil Dechant described, "a doctor in New Haven came out of nowhere." In fact, Dechant had rallied from the devastating news and had begun searching for a surgeon that would consider operating on his wife. The doctor that emerged, from Yale New Haven Hospital, told Dechant he had performed similar surgeries on other patients and was willing to give it a try with Ann. And he agreed to come to the Hospital of Saint Raphael, where the Order had been a longtime supporter (and had funded the Fr. McGivney Cancer Center), and where Ann had been in care since the initial operation.

Ann went into surgery with Mother Teresa's medal pinned to her hospital gown. Five hours later, the surgery was deemed a success. There were some complications following the operation: a lengthy bout of radiation treatment and hip replacement surgery the following year. But for Ann Dechant, Mother Teresa's intercession and her husband's persistence— plus her own dogged pursuit of recovery—of-

Ann L. Dechant
196 HARTFORD TURNPIKE
HAMDEN, CONNECTICUT 06517

Copy of letter sent to Mother Teresa

June 3, 1997

Mother Teresa
Missionaries of Charity
335 East 145th Street
Bronx NY 10451

Dear Mother Teresa:

During the time of my recuperation from surgery here in the hospital of St. Raphael I cannot tell you how much my spirits were uplifted by your very special phone call and especially to know that my intentions would be kept in your prayers and in the prayers of your Sisters. I know that your prayers, Mother, are powerful, and, when joined with the prayers of so many others, will surely be heard by Our Lord and His Blessed Mother.

I am especially grateful for your gift of a Miraculous Medal which you told me should be placed on the area of my operation. Now that I have this medal, it surely will serve to petition Our Lady's intercession to whom Jesus can refuse nothing, and I am truly grateful to you for this.

As an aside, I also am wearing a relic of St. Theresa, the Little Flower which, when joined to the medal given to me by you, Mother Teresa, will give me great hope for a complete and speedy recovery.

I hope someday, in the not too distant future, I can personally thank you for your many kindnesses, blessings and prayers.

Respectfully,

Ann Dechant

Ann Dechant

JMJ.
Dear Mr. Dechant, 13/5/91
God love you for the love you share with each one of us through your beautiful gift of printing our Constitutions and new our directory my gratitude to you, your family & all the lights thy prayer for you. God bless you M. Teresa

RECEIVED

OCT 23 1992

MISSIONARIES OF CHARITY
54A ACHARYA J CHANDRA BOSE ROAD
CALCUTTA 700016, INDIA

VCD. Supreme Knight

24-9-92.

Dear Mr. V.C. Dechant
and all the Knights
of Columbus.
May God's blessing be
with each one of you,
your families and with
those who work with
you and for you.
My gratitude to you
for the award and
the sacrifice of the
meal is my prayer for
you that you may
grow in holiness through
this love for each other
with the sacrifice of the
meal money, besides the

the Christmas meal to hun
dreds of our Poor we will
build and repair their
little houses. So our Poor
will be very closely conne
cted with you.
You will be very happy
to know our M.C. Fathers
have come to Rome and
7 of their Seminarians
were admitted into the
Angelicum College – so
please pray for them
that they become Holy
M.C. Priest.
Please pray for our Society
Our Poor and for me.
God bless you
Ac Teresa mc

fered her a new lease on life.
Check-up after check-up came
and went for Ann Dechant in the years following her surgery, but the
cancer never returned.

Speaking of Ann's unlikely recovery, Virgil said, "We can't help but
believe that Mother Teresa brought that about."

Just a few short months after consoling Ann Dechant in her time of
need, Mother Teresa of Calcutta, 87, died after years of declining health.
She was given a state funeral by the Indian government—an event Virgil Dechant had hoped to attend but elected to miss to stay home with
Ann during her recovery from hip surgery.

Supreme Knight Dechant issued a statement on behalf of the Knights of Columbus on Mother Teresa's passing. In part, it read: "We are deeply saddened by the news of Mother Teresa's death. It is clear that this marks the passing of one of the truly great human beings of our day. The world is poorer without her luminous presence."

Shortly after her death, the Holy See opened her cause for canonization, ultimately clearing a path to sainthood. In 2003 she was beatified and given the distinction of "Blessed." Her canonization would follow on September 4, 2016, an event Dechant was unable to attend due to health reasons.

Following Ann's illness and the death of Mother Teresa, life returned to normal for Virgil and Ann Dechant. For more than two years they had been tested by one dramatic event after another, and still they had persevered.

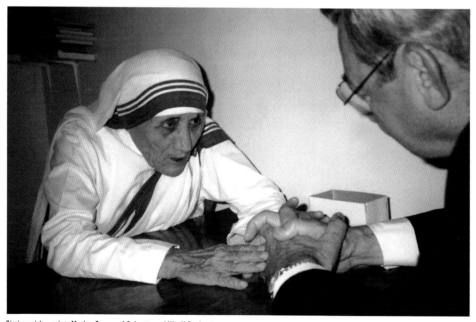

Sitting with a saint: Mother Teresa of Calcutta and Virgil Dechant.

In 1997, the Knights of Columbus launched the Order's first website, joining the globally connected computer network that took the world by storm in 1995. At the time, Dechant said, launching a website seemed like an act of little consequence. He had no way of knowing how critical a step this would be in the future course of the Order. Dechant simply called the decision a way of "getting our feet wet."

Since that initial launch, the Knights' website has continued to change and grow. "They've done very well with it," Dechant said. "But websites don't recruit members. You've still got to go out and do that one on one, face to face."

That same year, the Order established a scholarship fund in honor of Supreme Chaplain Bishop Thomas V. Daily for men studying for the priesthood.

The year 1997 also marked a memorable development in the Order's desire for Father Michael McGivney to become a saint. That year the Archdiocese of Hartford, with full support of the Knights of Columbus, officially opened the cause for canonization of Father McGivney. The development is a testament to the perseverance of so many who believed in the sanctity of the Order's founder.

By Dechant's memory, the efforts to canonize McGivney began shortly after he became supreme knight. It started with a simple note, a letter from then-Bishop Ted McCarrick, to Supreme Physician Dr. John Griffin, suggesting that the Order consider initiating an investigation into McGivney's life. In April 1978, at the April board meeting in Rome, Dechant, his wife Ann, Count Enrico Galeazzi, and Bishop Charles P. Greco, met with Cardinal John Wright, prefect of the Congregation for the Clergy. Wright suggested the Knights of Columbus pursue McGivney's cause. Wright even mentioned to the group that his archives in Pittsburgh contained a file on McGivney's life. Cardinal Wright would

Dechant's meetings with the Holy Father sometimes placed him front and center (and behind a microphone) in the papal palace.

die a year later, and his secretary, Father Donald Wuerl, later made cardinal, offered to visit Pittsburgh and search for Wright's McGivney file. Unfortunately, no such file ever surfaced.

Wuerl was subsequently appointed by Dechant to conduct preliminary research on McGivney and the cause.

"I had the opportunity to visit a number of sites significant in the life of Father McGivney to begin to determine the impact of his life and mission, the recognition of his sanctity, and the possibility of ongoing cult reflective of the great admiration in which he was held," Wuerl recounted.

When historian Christopher Kauffman began researching the history of the Order, an early task was establishing that McGivney was the true founder of the Knights of Columbus. In 1980, Dechant received a letter from Archbishop John Whealon (archbishop of the Hartford, CT Archdiocese), advising to continue the Order's investigation into McGivney's life and their search for substantial evidence of heroic sanctity. Kauffman subsequently sent a copy of his biographical study to Whealon for review. The archbishop wrote to Dechant after studying Kauffman's materials that he found "no evidence of heroic sanctity." However, Whealon advised Dechant to continue to search, especially by looking through McGivney's writings.

The problem, Dechant explained, was that no such writings existed.

"After he left St. Mary's Church in New Haven, the church he was at, St. Thomas in Thomaston, Connecticut, sustained a fire in the rectory, and all of his writings were destroyed," Dechant said. "Archbishop Whealon, and rightly so, wanted us to find writings that were concrete evidence of his heroic sanctity. They were just not in existence."

The next step in pursuing the cause was establishing the moral miracle of the Knights of Columbus, or, simply, the fact that the Order had survived for more than 100 years and had initiated significant charity throughout the world.

On November 12, 1981, the home office of the Knights of Columbus issued a questionnaire concerning the Order's founder to past and present state officers, inquiring about their devotion to McGivney. Responses indicated that many of these individuals prayed regularly to McGivney, and some received favors. In Dechant's 1983 annual report, he noted that "the presence of Father McGivney's tomb in St. Mary's will prompt members and other visitors to focus on his saintly life, to pray to him, and to implore blessings on the Order and many activities it carries on."

In 1983, Archbishop Whealon again communicated with Dechant

The Dechants, meeting with Pope John Paul II in his private office at the Vatican.

by letter, explaining to him some recent changes in the criteria for determining sainthood. He also stressed the need to demonstrate McGivney's heroic virtue. Shortly after, the Order produced a prayer card for the cause, authored by Bishop Greco.

In 1992, Archbishop Daniel Cronin was installed as ordinary of the Hartford Archdiocese. Cronin, having worked in the secretary of state's office in Rome, was well versed in the procedures for determining sainthood. He wrote to Dechant in September of that year, explaining that "it will be a joy and privilege for me to discuss with you the next steps to be taken in the hope of instituting a cause for the beatification of Father Michael J. McGivney."

"The first step was to secure the agreement and support of the bishops of the United States," Cronin recalled. "At an annual meeting

Dechant and other K of C board members, pictured during a meeting in Vatican City.

of the Conference of Bishops, I presented the request to all the bishops for their endorsement, which they gave unanimously. Virgil was delighted."

On August 4, 1993, at the supreme convention of the Knights of Columbus in Washington, D.C., Regis Sheehan, a past state deputy from Pittsburgh, Pennsylvania, delivered remarks to convention delegates, inviting them to Pittsburgh for the supreme convention the following year. After he returned to his seat he collapsed from an apparent heart attack. A few doctors that were part of the convention delegation declared him dead, yet Sheehan was transported to a nearby medical facility in the company of his wife, Bishop Wuerl, and Bishop Daily. The convention delegation, 1,500 members strong, asked for McGivney's intercession and immediately began praying the rosary, led by Cardinal Edouard Gagnon, a member of the Congregation for the Causes of Saints. Amazingly, Sheehan was brought back to life.

When Bishop Wuerl returned from the hospital, he told Dechant, "We now have our miracle."

"To me, that's still a strong case," Dechant said.

Recalling that event, Wuerl said, "It was the supreme knight who called upon the members to begin to say the rosary as we waited for the arrival of paramedics."

In 1996, Father Gabriel O'Donnell, O.P., was named postulator for the McGivney cause. A year later, the Order founded the Father McGivney Guild to promote the cause; Cronin and Bishop Daily were named co-chairmen.

In July 1997, Cronin wrote a letter in which he advised that nothing was hindering the cause from proceeding. Finally, in December of that year, the cause was officially opened.

"For some time the cause for beatification and canonization of

Father McGivney had been a desired goal of the Knights of Columbus because they recognized that their founder was a saintly man," Cronin said. "His holiness shone through in the works of charity and social service that he founded and encouraged among the Catholic faithful of his day. The organization which he founded—the Knights of Columbus—continues the work in even greater measure to the present day. In fact, it contributes mightily to the work of the New Evangelization which the church called for in this *our* day."

As the new century approached, Virgil Dechant began to turn his attention to the future of the Knights of Columbus after his retirement. Others in the supreme council began to do the same. In 2000, Dechant would turn 70, thus ending his run as supreme knight. The change in bylaws that had occurred in 1995 had given Dechant five more years on the job, and, just as importantly, five more years to consider and groom a successor.

As Dechant fulfilled his remaining years as supreme knight, he weighed the many factors involved in recommending a successor. He knew there might be hurt feelings and bruised egos, but, ultimately, his job was to do what was in the best interest of the Knights of Columbus. During that discernment process, one candidate emerged above all others.

He was Supreme Secretary Carl Anderson.

Supreme Knight Dechant was often accompanied by his wife Ann and Supreme Chaplain Bishop Thomas V. Daily on his trips to the Vatican to see the pope and other Holy See officials. On some occasions, such as the one pictured from October 1998, Dechant would bring the entire K of C board of directors and their families to Rome for a meeting and audience with the pope. Many times those same invitations were extended to top-performing K of C insurance agents and other members of the Order. These demonstrations of support made it clear to Pope John Paul II that the Knights and their families were always ready to serve as the right arm of the church.

nside a jam-packed hotel ballroom in Boston, the man at the microphone held the audience in the palm of his large hand. In a sense, this was *his* night. For decades he had sat and listened to other speakers—some of them prominent world leaders—hold court at the same dinner. But on this night, the crowd of thousands was listening to him.

The man at the microphone was Supreme Knight Virgil Dechant.

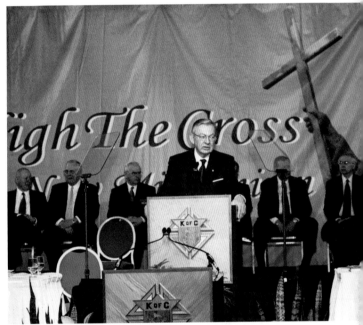

In front of a large sign depicting the theme "Lift High the Cross," Dechant addresses supreme convention delegates in August 2000.

It was August 2000, and Dechant was the principal speaker at the annual States' Dinner, the formal gala for thousands of delegates thrown at each supreme convention. The supreme knight, entering his final months at the helm of the Knights of Columbus, decided on this night to speak from the heart. There were some scripted moments that packed plenty of punch, certainly, but for the most part, Dechant told stories in an off-the-cuff manner. His timing was spot on. So was his blend of history, context, and frankness.

He shared his memories of Mother Teresa of Calcutta and tales from his many audiences with Pope John Paul II. He even recounted the day he was in St. Peter's Square when the pope was shot. The audience hung on his every word. The fact that most people in the hotel ballroom that night were aware this would be Dechant's last convention as supreme knight only added to the moment. They were counting on a great speech, and Dechant delivered.

The supreme convention might have been a formal last hurrah, but there was still much work to be done before Dechant left office. Chief among his remaining tasks was making sure everything was in place to pass the torch to his successor, Supreme Secretary Carl Anderson.

Anderson had big shoes to fill. Anecdotally, Dechant's size-14 feet, which were unusually large for a man of his generation, left a large imprint everywhere he went. But figuratively, Dechant's impact on the Order was colossal.

From 1976 to 1999, the annual financial contributions to charity made by the Knights of Columbus grew by 633 percent, from $14 million to $109 million. In that time the Order's annual hours of documented community service rose 724 percent (to 55.3 million by 1999). More than 5,600 new councils were added, membership grew by nearly 400,000, and the Order's insurance in force grew by more than 1,000 percent (from $3 billion in 1975 to $40.4 billion in 2000). In 1969,

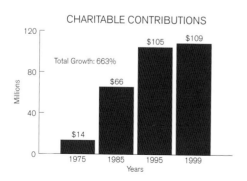

CHARITABLE CONTRIBUTIONS

Total Growth: 663%

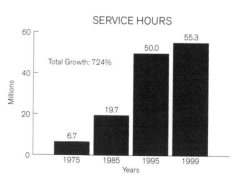

SERVICE HOURS

Total Growth: 724%

the Order had assets of $4.5 million spread throughout its various charitable entities; by year-end 2000, those assets had grown to $77 million.

The Order's operational gain—a benchmark that Dechant believes to be the most important statistic of an insurance organization—rose from $26.3 million in 1976 to $363.3 million in 2000, an increase of 1,279 percent. For any insurance organization, the margin of safety it provides for its members, called its surplus, is also important. The Knights of Columbus in 2000 had $1.3 billion of surplus funds and a solvency ratio of 17.8 percent, among the highest in the industry. Finally, the Order's net investment income rose from $40.2 million in 1976 to $544 million in 2000, an increase of 1,252 percent.

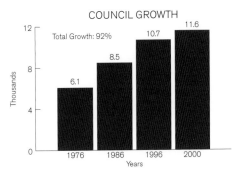

COUNCIL GROWTH

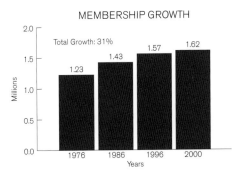

MEMBERSHIP GROWTH

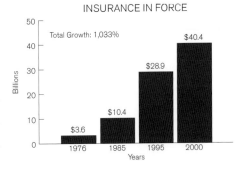

INSURANCE IN FORCE

The themes of Dechant's tenure—Marian devotion, vocations, Catholic education, pro-life, family life and evangelization—had left Anderson and the Knights of Columbus a clear road map to follow. Many of those initiatives have been maintained over the years.

Dechant's term as supreme knight had done much to help the church evangelize, "quietly," as Dechant was often quoted saying. At the

CHARTING
THE GROWTH
OF AN ORGANIZATION

In 1976, the K of C's net investment income was $40.2 million. By 2000, that amount had grown to $544 million. Delinquencies in the Order's securities were practically zero. Dechant is quick to credit Charles Walden, senior vice president of investments, for this level of success.

Under Dechant's leadership, the Knights of Columbus was both generous and aggressive in allocating dividends to its insurance members. Those dividends amounted to $17.5 million in 1976 and grew nearly 1,500 percent to $275.2 million by 2000. During that same time, the Order's operational gain grew from $26.3 million to $363.3 million.

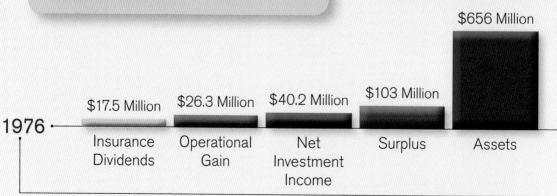

$656 Million

$17.5 Million — $26.3 Million — $40.2 Million — $103 Million

1976

Insurance Dividends | Operational Gain | Net Investment Income | Surplus | Assets

For an insurance organization like the K of C, the surplus, or margin of safety it provides to its members, is an important benchmark. By year-end 2000, the K of C had $1.3 billion of surplus funds for a solvency ratio of 17.8 percent, among the highest in the industry.

Perhaps no growth was more spectacular under Dechant's leadership than the Order's assets, which rose from $656 million in 1976 to $8.6 billion in 2000, a gain of more than 1,000 percent.

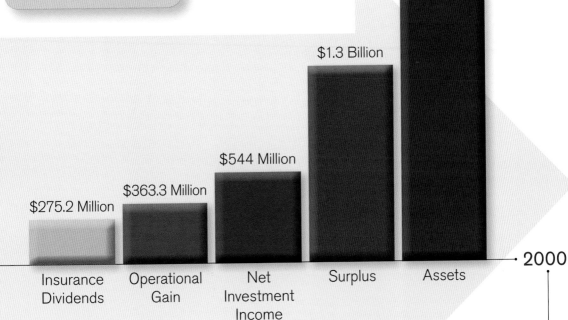

$8.6 Billion

$1.3 Billion

$544 Million

$363.3 Million

$275.2 Million

Insurance Dividends

Operational Gain

Net Investment Income

Surplus

Assets

2000

Knights of Columbus Charitable Funds (at year-end 2000)

EDUCATION

	U.S. & Other	Canada
• Albertus Magnus College Fund	$250,000	
• Arthur F. and Anna Batista Scholarship Fund		$1,561,495
• Bicentennial of the United States Hierarchy (Catholic Univ., D.C.)	$2,000,000	
• Bishop Charles Greco Fellowship Trust	$125,000	
• The Catholic University of America Fellowship Trust	$500,000	
• Estate of Anthony LaBella Scholarship Fund	$190,598	
• Estate of Percy Johnson Scholarship Fund	$353,200	
• Fr. McGivney Fund for New Initiatives in Catholic Education (NCEA)	$1,000,000	
• Fourth Degree Pro Deo et Pro Patria Scholarship Fund	$4,000,000	$1,000,000
• Francis Matthews and John Swift Educational Trust Fund	$1,282,769	
• Frank F. Goularte Scholarship Fund	$100,182	
• John W. McDevitt Fourth Degree Scholarship Fund	$3,255,325	
• Mexico Scholarships (16 annually)		
• New Haven Catholic High Schools Fund	$500,000	
• Pontifical Institute of Medieval Studies Fund		$250,000
• Puerto Rico Scholarships (16 annually)		
• Saint John Paul II Institute for Marriage and Family Fellowship Fund	$211,214	
• Sister Theo Bowman Foundation Scholarships (5 annually)		
• Virgil C. and Ann L. Dechant Scholarship Fund	$427,143	
TOTAL EDUCATION FUNDS	$14,195,431	$2,811,495

VOCATIONS	U.S. & Other	Canada
• Bishop Charles Greco American College Fund	$400,000	
• Bishop Thomas V. Daily Vocations Scholarship Fund	$1,500,000	$250,000
• Count Enrico Galeazzi Fund for Pontifical North American College	$2,000,000	
• Fr. McGivney Fund for Advanced Studies for Priests in Puerto Rico	$240,000	
• Fr. McGivney Fund for Advanced Studies for Priests in Philippines	$200,000	
• Our Lady of Guadalupe Fund for Advanced Studies for Priests in Mexico	$350,000	
• Fr. McGivney Fund for Advanced Studies for Priests in Canada		$600,000
• Fr. McGivney Vocations Scholarship Fund	$5,000,000	$800,000
• K of C Vocations Scholarship Fund (RSVP)	$4,000,000	$625,000
TOTAL VOCATIONS FUNDS	$13,690,000	$2,275,000

ADDITIONAL FUNDS	U.S. & Other	Canada
• Saint Francois de Laval Fund		$1,000,000
• Catholic Initiatives in Canada Fund		$319,054
• Christopher Fund	$10,858,409	$2,831,044
• Fourth Degree Fund for Religious Liberties	$1,000,000	
• General Charities Fund	$376,440	
• Historic Sites Fund	$47,231	
• Italian Welfare Fund	$2,002,374	
• Luke E. Hart Memorial Fund for Shrine of the Immaculate Conception	$1,000,000	
• Military Vicariate Fund	$1,654,000	
• Pope John Paul II Cultural Center (in addition to $2.5 million grant)	$2,000,000	$500,000
• Vicarius Christi Fund	$20,000,000	
TOTAL ADDITIONAL FUNDS	$38,938,454	$4,650,098

TOTAL FUNDS RESERVED	$76.5 million

time he left the office of supreme knight, the Knights of Columbus had given away more than 3 million rosaries. The back cover of *Columbia* magazine was reserved every issue for a testimonial promoting religious vocations. And there was RSVP, which stands for Refund Support Vocations Program, an initiative whereby the supreme council of the Knights of Columbus refunds local councils, Fourth Degree assemblies, or Columbian Squires circles that contribute at least $500 to a seminarian or individual in religious formation. This program annually benefits more than 4,000 seminarians and postulates. RSVP perfectly complemented "In Solidarity With Our Priests," an initiative developed to publicly affirm the Order's support of Catholic priests, many of whom had been dealt harsh criticisms during Dechant's time as supreme knight.

Dechant's personal honors were just as impressive as the Order's growth. He received honorary doctoral degrees from 16 colleges and universities. He had been named a Knight Grand Cross of St. Gregory the Great, a Knight Grand Cross in the Order of Pius IX (the highest honor granted to a Catholic layman who is not a head of state), a Knight Grand Cross in the Equestrian Order of the Holy Sepulchre, a Gentiluomo (or, a "gentleman of His Holiness," which makes him a member of the papal household), and a Knight of the Sovereign Military Order of Malta, among numerous other distinctions. Enrico Demajo joked: "The Vatican cannot honor or thank him more than what they did, because anything he could be, he is." Peter Bander van Duren, author of *Orders of Knighthood and of Merit*, referred to Dechant as the "most distinguished and decorated layman in the Catholic Church, the Curia, and the Vatican City State."

By any measure, the two-and-a-half decades of Virgil Dechant's leadership (to date, the longest tenure of any supreme knight) had set a high bar for any future supreme knight to aim at.

Anderson was Dechant's choice. He had proven himself most capable, and Dechant sensed that he was the right man at the right time. It was Dechant, in fact, who had signed up Anderson in the Knights of Columbus.

"Carl had proven himself, both to me and to other members of the Order. And while reaching a decision on who to recommend to the board of directors as my successor was a difficult one, ultimately I felt that Carl possessed all the qualities needed in a supreme knight. There are many variables one has to weigh when making such a decision: ability, experience, age, tenure, and so forth. I had always aspired to leave the Order better off than I found it, and I know that Carl will try and do the same."

In April 2000, months before the supreme convention in Boston, the Knights of Columbus hosted a pilgrimage to the Basilica of the Shrine of the Immaculate Conception in Washington, D.C., to commemorate the millennium and to help open the pope's program of the new evangelization. If ever there was a public display of the tremendous strength of Catholic fraternalism, this was it. More than 12,000 Knights and their families participated in the event, including more than 1,200 Fourth Degree members. Through the magic of satellite television, Pope John Paul II was able to lead the gathering during the praying of the rosary. Dechant noted in his 2000 annual report that "many priests commented later that this had been a tremendous faith experience for them."

"The first thing I did when I was elected supreme knight was to go to the Shrine with the board of directors and dedicate my administration to the Blessed Mother," Dechant said. "That produced great fruits, so in arranging for this event for the Knights in 2000 I asked Supreme Secretary Anderson to organize this beautiful Mass. And what a magnificent display of Christianity it was."

The year 2000 was another landmark in the growth of the relationship between the Knights of Columbus and the Holy See. The Vatican's Holy Year Door at St. Peter's Basilica was overdue for a cleaning, and the Knights of Columbus sponsored its restoration, along with the cleaning and restoration of the Maderno Atrium. At more than 200 feet long, 40 feet wide and 60 feet high, the Atrium, considered "the front porch" of the Basilica, had been mostly untouched since the 1600s. In Dechant's annual report he described for his fellow Knights the elaborate cleaning and repair process of the magnificent stucco work that depicts the life of St. Peter.

In preparation for the jubilee year, the Knights of Columbus tied many of the pope's favorite themes into their programming. They began a recruitment campaign known as "Jubilee 2000" and instituted

PHOTO USED WITH PERMISSION OF L'OSSERVATORE ROMANO.

Dechant, accompanied by Cardinal Donald Wuerl, center, greets Pope John Paul II for the final time during a 2004 visit to Rome.

a Holy Year Door program for K of C families. That Christmas Eve, the Dechants visited Rome for the opening of the Holy Door and the subsequent celebration of Midnight Mass at the Vatican. During a private audience on December 23, Dechant presented the pope with a $1.6 million check for earnings from the Vicarius Christi fund. To date, more than $50 million in earnings has been given to the pope from this fund.

A year later, in December 2000, the Dechants and the Andersons visited Rome for another private audience with Pope John Paul II. The pontiff and Anderson were already acquainted; however, Dechant wished to formally introduce his successor as supreme knight to the pope. In Dechant's mind, this marked the moment when he bowed out as the leader of the Knights of Columbus. A new supreme knight was now in command.

Dechant arranged with Anderson to maintain an office at One Columbus Plaza temporarily.

Over Labor Day weekend 2001, the Dechants invited friends and family to New Haven to help celebrate their 50th wedding anniversary. A Mass in their honor was held at St. Stephen's Church, followed by a reception at the New Haven Country Club. Guests toasted the couple and recounted their favorite Virgil and Ann stories.

Just a week later, the United States was devastated by the worst terrorist attack in the country's history on September 11. In response, the Knights of Columbus established the Heroes Fund, which provided assistance to the nearly 400 families of lost rescue workers. President George W. Bush, in his video message to the Knights at the supreme convention the following August, thanked them for the role they played in helping the nation recover from the horrific attacks. Bush credited the Knights as being "among the first to step up after September 11."

The Dechants kept a low profile during their final months in New Haven. This was no accident. Dechant wanted to close the book on his business affairs and cause as little interference as possible for Anderson and his regime. Yet, he was nearby if Anderson needed to call on his vast institutional memory.

"I think that transition went well because Carl and Virgil worked real well together," said Don Kehoe. "Both had a similar outlook and a similar understanding of the relationship with the church, which is key for the Knights, to be involved with the church."

Dechant's plan was to stay around just long enough to ease a smooth transition, then he and Ann would move back to Kansas.

"Leaving quickly was probably a smart thing on Virgil's part," said Ron Tracz. "When a transition takes place, regardless of how good the relationship is between the two, the incoming leader wants to do his own thing. The last thing you want is to have somebody looking over your shoulder."

Virgil focused his attention on the opening of a new Knights of Columbus Museum on State Street, near the home office at One Columbus Plaza. The Order had purchased the property in 1994 with the goal of one day moving its museum there. It was a modern-looking, trapezoidal building that had been designed by New Haven architect Edwin W. DeCossy. Previously it had served as a community services building, home to various non-profit organizations.

Dechant delegated much of the day-to-day supervision of the reno-

In Solidarity with the Holy See

Through the years, the Order has supported the Vatican in many ways, from the construction of Roman playgrounds in the 1920s to the microfilming of manuscripts from the Vatican Library in the 1950s to the uplink of satellite transmissions for TV broadcasts in the 1970s to today. In the 1980s, the Knights established the Vicarius Christi Fund to support the pope's charities and financed a project to restore the facade of St. Peter's Basilica. In 1988, the Order approved financial and administrative support of the Lateran University's North American campus of the Pontifical John Paul II Institute for Studies on Marriage and Family. Along the way, the Order supported several of Pope John Paul II's pastoral travels, most notably co-sponsoring with the Brooklyn Diocese his 1995 Mass at Aqueduct Race Track in New York. In 1999, the Order funded the restoration of the Maderno Atrium and the Holy Door in St. Peter's Basilica for Jubilee 2000.

In 1961, the board of directors conducted a meeting in the Vatican—an unprecedented privilege. In September 1978, Supreme Knight Virgil C. Dechant and Mrs. Ann Dechant, accompanied by Supreme Chaplain Bishop Charles P. Greco, met with Pope John Paul I in his first audience with laypersons. Similarly, three days after his installation, Pope John Paul II received Dechant in a private audience, the beginning of the [...] relationship that any supreme knight has had with [...]

Facing page: The copper cross from the statue "Christ the Redeemer," which sat above St. Peter's Basilica for hundreds of years, is now "the centerpiece" of the K of C Museum.

Above: The Father McGivney reliquary inside the K of C Museum.

vation of the new museum property to Supreme Master Charlie Foos and assigned Biagio "Gino" Gulino to assist him. But make no mistake, Foos said, the museum was still Dechant's baby.

"It was a big challenge, and he was there tooth and nail. We had to deal with designers, builders, government people. It was a huge job, and he was tenacious. Previously, there were 400 people working in that building. We said, 'Take out all the glass from one end of the building, drop in a small bulldozer, and just drive it from one end to the other, pushing everything out.' We cleared everything out. You could walk in there and all you saw were the supporting posts.

"That museum was one of his crowning glories, and he made sure it was ready for the opening in September 2000."

Indeed, the three-story, 77,000-square-foot museum was a crowning glory. Its completion was one of Dechant's last major accomplishments as supreme knight and certainly his most visible. Architect Kevin Roche oversaw the design inside the museum, and Tony Spagnola—well known for his work in museum and exhibition design—managed the construction of individual exhibits. Dechant himself called the new museum "a masterpiece" and "one of the finest museums in the country." In 2003 it was ranked by *USA Today* as one of "the 10 great places to explore religion in artistic detail." In 2007 it was a winner of the American Association of Museums design competition in the category of "institutions with budgets greater than $750,000." Guests can visit special galleries, including the McGivney Gallery—devoted to the K of C founder—and the Papal Gallery—which provides a history of the longtime association between the Order and the Holy See. Admission is free of charge and parking is available, also for free, beneath the building. In addition to the permanent exhibits, each year the Order brings in at least one or two traveling exhibits, sometimes from the Vatican.

Exhibits such as this inside the K of C Museum help tell the history of the Order.

Longtime Knights of Columbus Archivist Sue Brosnan said of the new museum: "While the old museum told the history of the Order, it was not readily available to the public because of its location within the headquarters building. The new building on State Street is open to the public seven days a week, without charge, and in addition to the material on the Knights of Columbus and its activities, it has brought world-class exhibits to New Haven. Exhibits such as 'Creating St. Peter's,' which included Michelangelo's wooden study model for the dome of St. Peter's, the 'Swiss Guard' exhibit, 'Mosaics from the Vatican,' 'Faith and Art of Mexico,' 'Easter Eggs and Art,' the several icon exhibits, and our annual Christmas Creche exhibit all appeal to audiences not limited to Knights or Catholics. They evangelize in a quiet way, as well as educate about the Order's global outreach."

Beyond the museum, Dechant also had the monumental task of sorting through more than three decades of files that he had accumulated from his time working for the K of C. In the process, he gave and loaned numerous artifacts to the museum, where they could be archived as part of the Order's collection.

Ann Dechant's challenges were just as daunting during the couple's final days in New Haven. She had a house to pack up, along with 33 years worth of memories. Beyond that there were moving plans to make, goodbyes to be said, and favorite places to visit one last time.

Shortly before Christmas 2001, the Dechants loaded up their car and left for Kansas. A large truck with their furniture and personal belongings left with them, although the truck driver and the Dechants would take separate routes before their eventual rendezvous in Kansas City. Virgil joked to family members that he and Ann left New Haven "under the cover of night."

The Dechants moved into a Tudor-style house in Leawood, a Kansas

From left: Paul McGlinchey, Lina McGlinchey, Ann Dechant, Virgil Dechant.

City suburb, less than a mile down the street from their daughter Karen Thompson, her husband Bob, and their family. They had considered other retirement locations such as Florida and Arizona, but all along their hearts had pointed the Dechants back to Kansas. Kansas City seemed like the perfect location. They were in Kansas, close to family, and near an active Catholic parish. Not far away was a major airport. And 300 miles due west was La Crosse, home to Dechant's sizeable farming operation and Dechant Motors.

During their first few years in Leawood, the Dechants did not look the part of a recently retired couple. They traveled regularly but mostly on Knights of Columbus business. In some ways it seemed that they were as busy as ever. But gradually their schedule slowed down.

What never slowed down was their participation in parish life at Church of the Nativity, their new parish. "Virgil and Ann are such faith-filled parishioners here, putting the Eucharist at the center of their lives," said Father Francis Hund, pastor at Church of the Nativ-

Architect Kevin Roche and Dechant take a moment to privately discuss another endeavor.

ity. "As pastor, I know his love of God, his participation in parish activities, and his respect and support for all who shepherd the church. Virgil has made generosity and gratitude an abundant harvest throughout his life."

Archbishop Joseph Naumann, the archbishop of Kansas City in Kansas, said the Dechants were among the first to welcome him and encourage him when he succeeded Archbishop James Keleher in 2005. "Virgil is so revered amongst the Knights, but what a humble person he is. He and Ann are so unassuming, in light of the incredible experiences and events that they've played such an important part in. I've often said that I think they ought to declare Virgil a natural resource for the archdiocese; he's just been present at so many important points in the life of the church."

In 2001, Elmer Meder, the longtime operations manager of Dechant Motors, died of complications from a stroke. Dechant had just relocated to Leawood and decided the timing was right to close the book on Dechant Motors. The business cancelled its contracts with Ford and sold

Archbishop Emeritus of Kansas City in Kansas James Keleher, left, and former Kansas State Chaplain Fr. Tom Dolezal, right, officiated a Mass for past state deputies at the Dechant home in Kansas City.

its franchise rights back to the company for a nominal sum. Over the years, the business had served the small community of La Crosse well. It was a steady employer, community partner, and provider of implements for the agricultural-based economy of La Crosse.

In 2002, Dechant's longtime farm manager J. Arthur Herrman retired. Dechant selected Eddie Herman, who had 25 years of experience as a crop management specialist, as his replacement, and the business continued to prosper. When Herman retired, he was replaced by Steve Befort, another native Kansan. In 2003, the Dechant farm partnership was reorganized as Dechant Farms LLC. After gradually parceling out units of the partnership, today Virgil and Ann's children own a controlling interest in the operation.

After years of failing health, much of which was played out in the public eye, Pope John Paul II, age 84, died on April 2, 2005. In the early years of his papacy, John Paul II had been the picture of fitness: an avid outdoorsman, hiker, and world traveler. Those images were replaced in his final years by those of an aging man, stricken with Parkinson's disease and speech difficulties. Bravely, he continued on, meeting his

The extended family of Virgil and Ann Dechant, pictured at a holiday gathering in Kansas City.

duties as leader of the worldwide church with whatever vigor he had left.

Dechant's last visit with John Paul II came in June 2004. The Knights of Columbus, in partnership with the Pittsburgh Philharmonic Orchestra, sponsored a concert of reconciliation in the Paul VI audience hall in Rome. Following the concert, Dechant and others were received in private audience by the Holy Father.

"As feeble as he was, when he saw us, he came up with a big grin," Dechant recalled. "That's the last time I saw him."

Enrico Demajo, grandson of Count Enrico Galeazzi, suggested Dechant's legacy and the legacy of John Paul II were intertwined through decades of collaboration, all on behalf of the church. Demajo said, "There are men who have written the history of the world, and you don't always see them. They are behind the scenes, writing history. At least a part of history. Virgil Dechant would never tell you all he did, he's so humble. For instance, if you think about the fall of communism and how much John Paul II helped with that, then think of how much Virgil Dechant helped John Paul II."

The pope's death was followed by a week of mourning and visitation, finally concluding on April 8, 2005, with his funeral Mass. Millions of people converged in Rome that week to celebrate the life of the pontiff.

Dechant played an important role in the funeral, serving as a Gentiluomo, or Gentleman of His Holiness. Wearing a black tuxedo (known as "full dress with tails") and numerous badges of knighthood, Dechant had the privilege of escorting President George W. Bush and his wife Laura to their seats in St. Peter's Square for the funeral. The previous August, Dechant and Bush had exchanged greetings at the 122nd supreme convention in Dallas, Texas. Bush called Dechant a "family friend." Despite the obvious sadness that hung over the proceedings, Dechant called the moment "the experience of a lifetime." It wasn't until after the

Dechant escorted U.S. President George W. Bush into the 2005 funeral of Pope John Paul II, presenting him to Cardinal James Harvey.

funeral had ended and he had time to reflect that one oddity occurred to Dechant. More than 200 countries had sent heads of state or representatives to the funeral. The Bushes, for security purposes, were the last dignitaries to be seated before the service began. As it was an outdoor affair, Dechant suspected the president was wearing a bulletproof vest underneath his suit coat and shirt. In an era of global terror, such a precaution would seem reasonable. Dechant, however, was afforded no such luxury. Yet he was there, right beside the president, on the world stage.

A little more than two weeks later, Dechant was back in Rome for the installation of John Paul II's successor, Cardinal Joseph Ratzinger, who took the name Benedict XVI. On this occasion, Dechant escorted Bush's brother Jeb, whom the president had sent on his behalf as a U.S. representative, into the ceremony. Dechant and Ratzinger were well acquainted because the cardinal had kept an apartment in the same build-

Pope Benedict XVI, left, referred to Dechant as "neighbor" in their conversations together.

ing as the Knights of Columbus office in Rome, near the Vatican. His apartment was two floors above the K of C. On the occasions Dechant met Pope Benedict, the pontiff called Dechant "neighbor."

In evaluating the legacy of Virgil Dechant, one cannot overlook his contributions to the Catholic Church. He accomplished more in one lifetime as a layperson than many would ever think possible. His involvement continued long after he left the office of supreme knight. As of this writing, Dechant is still serving as a Consiglieri to the Vatican City State, along with eight other lay persons.

A survey of the hierarchy of the Catholic Church, more than a decade after his retirement, says much about the legacy Dechant has left in his wake. Cardinal Timothy Dolan, archbishop of New York, called Dechant a "Catholic gentleman, whose vocation as a husband and father was his greatest priority." Cardinal Dolan also called Dechant "a man's man,

Pope Benedict XVI, right, resigned from the papacy in 2013.

who was as much at home with a cardinal as he was with the janitor at the local Knights of Columbus hall."

Newly elevated Cardinal Blase Cupich said of Dechant, "It is worth noting that Virgil was 100 percent in support of the Holy Father, no matter who the pope happened to be." Cupich also referred to Dechant as a patriotic American who knew how to weigh in on important political matters without being partisan.

Most Reverend Charles Chaput, archbishop of Philadelphia, called Dechant "an exemplary lay apostle and an inspiration to me and to the other bishops and all the clergy."

James Cardinal Harvey, arch-priest of the Basilica of Saint Paul Outside the Walls in Rome, noted three distinct characteristics that made Dechant the man and leader he was. "Virgil Dechant was successful and esteemed because he was dependable, discreet, and dignified," Harvey said. "Throughout his many years of leading the Knights, Virgil proved himself time and again to be a man of his word. In the course of his involvement with many projects that the Knights of Columbus sponsored or were asked to participate in, superiors in the Vatican learned from dealing with Virgil that he was always willing to listen and was realistic and

Ann Dechant, right, was honored with the Catholic Church's Pro Ecclesia Et Pontifice award. Pictured with her and Virgil is Archbishop Emeritus of Hartford Daniel Cronin.

concrete in responding to requests for assistance, financial or otherwise.

"Over the long run, this reputation for dependability helped the Knights of Columbus as an institution grow in prestige and esteem in the eyes of many high-ranking Vatican officials.

"This reputation for being dependable was always accompanied by an intentional desire on Virgil's part to be discreet in his dealings with the interested Vatican parties. There was no need for fanfare with Virgil. Credit to the Knights for their assistance and generosity was always acknowledged, but it was done in a way that was appropriate and judicious:

appropriate, since as head of the Order he was in some way accountable to the membership, which rightly expected a certain acknowledgement of gratitude for good works performed; yet judicious so that no unsuitable publicity would result for the Vatican or the Knights.

"Finally, in all of his worthy undertakings, Virgil personally comported himself with great dignity, which only redounded to the honor and esteem of the Order, of which he was the public face, so to speak."

Russell Shaw, whom Dechant hired to oversee the Order's public relations in the late 1980s, concluded that the quality which separated the Knights of Columbus from other fraternal organizations that floundered in the 20th century was the steady hand of the man in charge.

"Virgil guided the fortunes of the Knights of Columbus through a very difficult period of history in general and in the history of the Catholic Church in this country," Shaw said. "Over those years a lot of church-related organizations just went out of business or shrank to the point of near-invisibility. The Knights of Columbus didn't. They somehow had a formula for success, and they had the kind of leadership which would see the strong

STATO DELLA CITTÀ DEL VATICANO

CITTÀ DEL VATICANO.

GOVERNATORATO

IL CARDINALE PRESIDENTE

495808

3 July 2010

Dear Mr. Dechant,

I am pleased to forward the enclosed document in which the Holy Father, Pope Benedict XVI, confirms you for five years as *Consigliere* for Vatican City State.

I congratulate you on the Holy Father's renewed act of trust on your behalf.

As for my part, it is my pleasure to acknowledge the constructive support you have offered the Governatorato of Vatican City on important issues regarding the State during your past tenure. I am confident that in the coming years our relations will continue developing in the same spirit of trust and collaboration which has characterized it in the past.

With sense of high esteem, please accept my very best wishes,

G. Card. Lajolo

Giovanni Card. Lajolo

enclosure

Mr. Virgil Dechant
11409 Meadow Lane
Leawood, Kansas 66211
U.S.A.

Dechant and Supreme Knight Carl Anderson, pictured, had the pleasure of meeting Pope Francis.

PHOTO USED WITH PERMISSION OF L'OSSERVATORE ROMANO.

points in the K of C program and capitalize on them to keep the organization alive and growing and strong and healthy. The K of C has been blessed in the leadership that they've had, at least in the years that I've been associated with it. By comparison with other Catholic organizations, a lot of which have simply died in the last 40 years or so, the K of C is some kind of miracle."

Knights of Columbus Supreme Secretary Michael O'Connor echoed Shaw's assessment of Dechant's leadership qualities. "Virgil has business expertise, but at the same time, he's also a fraternalist. He loves interacting with people. You can be all business and not have any fraternal skills, or you can be a fraternalist and not good at business. He's got both, which is really unique. It's also important to be able to take the temperature of what's going on in the field and knowing what members will accept as change. That's hard to come by, to know what the field is looking for. I call that emotional intelligence."

In retirement, Dechant stayed actively involved in the Knights of Columbus, becoming a valuable resource for the Order, particularly for his institutional memory. In 2012, Dechant served as chairman of a committee that decided—yet again—to take a fresh look at the Order's ceremonials. The revisions that the committee instituted are still in place today.

From left: Tom Dechant, Virgil Dechant, Bob Dechant in Dallas for the Gaudium Et Spes award ceremony.

In the years after leaving the office of supreme knight, one initiative captivated Dechant's interest more than any other, the cause for beatification of Father Michael McGivney, the founder of the Knights of Columbus. Ironically and intentionally, Dechant chose to take a hands-off approach as the cause moved forward. He felt that any intervention on his part could be viewed as confusing; thus he opted for near-silence. However, during a trip to Rome in March 2008 for a Vatican Bank board meeting, Dechant felt the urge to visit the office of the Congregation for the Causes of Saints to check if any progress had been made.

Much to his pleasure, Dechant was informed that just a few days prior, the theological consultors presiding over the cause had declared that McGivney "cultivated both the theological and cardinal virtues as well as those joined to them and did so in a heroic manner."

Virgil and Ann Dechant pay their respects in private at the tomb of Pope John Paul II in the grottoes of St. Peter's Basilica.

On the morning of Dechant's visit, Cardinal Prefect Joseph Saraiva Martins presented the information to Pope Benedict XVI, who received and approved the report. Pope Benedict declared: "Concerning the theological virtues of Faith, Hope, and Love both toward God and neighbor as well as the cardinal virtues of Prudence, Justice, Temperance, and Fortitude, and those others joined to them, they existed to a heroic degree in the Servant of God Michael McGivney, Diocesan Priest and Founder of the Fraternal Order 'The Knights of Columbus,' in the case at hand and for the end thereof."

The decree was made public. In substance, Father McGivney had been made venerable. It was an important step in McGivney's path toward sainthood.

Dechant was pleased.

* * *

On November 16, 2012, at the Gaylord Texan Resort and Convention Center in Dallas, Texas, former Supreme Knight Virgil C. Dechant was honored with the Gaudium Et Spes award, the highest honor granted by the Knights of Columbus.

Calling Dechant "the model for Catholic fraternalism for an entire generation," Supreme Knight Carl Anderson presented Dechant with the award while Supreme Chaplain Archbishop William Lori read the citation.

In receiving the award's gold medal, Dechant told the crowd in attendance that night that he would be donating the $100,000 honorarium to a Knights of Columbus scholarship fund for the education of seminarians.

Dechant confessed to feeling "totally inadequate" and "humbled" by the award.

Perhaps he hadn't felt such humility since the time when, as an 18-year-old boy, he was confined to an uncomfortable hospital bed in Kansas after a car accident that could have ended his life. No, it wasn't the car accident that had humbled that young boy from the Kansas plains. It was the humility he had felt in the presence of his fellow Knights of Columbus, many of whom he barely knew, who kept coming to visit throughout his recovery.

Dechant had decided, then and there, "if that's what the Knights of Columbus is all about, with that sort of fraternal spirit, I should become more involved." And he had vowed to himself to give more of his time and energy to the organization.

Boy, did he ever.

ACKNOWLEDGMENTS

This project would have been nearly impossible without the cooperation of many people. That list starts with Virgil and Ann Dechant, who generously agreed to spend considerable time with me developing material for the book.

Members of the clergy who assisted in my research included Cardinal Leo Burke, Cardinal Timothy Dolan, Cardinal James Harvey, Cardinal Adam Maida, Cardinal Ted McCarrick, Cardinal Edwin O'Brien, Cardinal Justin Rigali, Cardinal Donald Wuerl, Cardinal Blaise Cupich, Archbishop Charles Chaput, Archbishop Emeritus Elden Curtiss, Archbishop Emeritus James Keleher, Archbishop William Lori, Archbishop Joseph Naumann, Archbishop Daniel Cronin, Archbishop Leonard Blair, Archbishop Carlo Vigano, Bishop John Brungardt, Bishop Carl Kemme, Bishop Edward Weisenburger, Rev. Francis Hund, Rev. Monsignor John Meyers, and Rev. Monsignor Christopher Schreck.

Others who contributed to this process include Sue Brosnan, Enrico Demajo, Russell Shaw, Mary Lou Cummings, Paula Forni, Joe Mauro, Tom Smith, Ron Tracz, Charles Walden, Tom Zarda, Bob Lane, Bob Wade, Paul Lenherr, Don Kehoe, Charlie Foos, Lou Mautino, Kathy Cogan, John Howard Sanden, Tom Dechant, Dan Dechant, Bob Dechant, Karen Thompson, Maggie Dechant, Gina Dechant, Bob Thompson, Michael O'Connor, Stephen Feiler, Dennis Savoie, and Alton Pelowski.

Throughout my research and writing, the staff of the Knights of Columbus Museum was incredibly helpful. I encourage everyone who reads this book to pay the museum a visit on your next trip to New Haven.

During my work on *The Fraternalist*, colleagues and family members alike asked me, "What aspect of your grandfather's life have you most enjoyed learning about?" Others asked me, "What part of his story came as a surprise?" I'll attempt to answer both questions with one answer: it was the time he orchestrated moving the Knights of Columbus into its new headquarters in New Haven in 1970.

When he told me that story, I first considered it a throwaway. After some reflection, I realized how much that little anecdote said about my grandfather. In any organization, how do you rise to the top? How do you become a leader? You make yourself indispensable. And you pay your dues by handling any task, large or small, that others either cannot handle or are unwilling to take on—like moving a company into its new headquarters in less than a week!

My life began in the early 1980s, so it was about 1990 before I was old enough to form any sort of opinion about who my grandfather was in the world. At that point, he had been supreme knight for more than a decade and had been living in New Haven for more than two decades. So for my entire life, my grandfather had always been supreme knight: the man in charge, the one to whom others looked for leadership.

How had he gotten to that point? It wasn't something that was handed to him. He had to earn it, and he did so by taking on any task that the Order needed. By 1990—that landmark point of my young life—Virgil Dechant was one of the oldest employees working at the Knights of Columbus headquarters in New Haven. Consider all the experience he had accumulated by that point in his career. He wasn't some detached CEO, insulated in his office on the top floor. He knew where every file cabinet and storage room was in the building because he was there on the day the company moved into the place. Similarly, he had learned the Knights of Columbus from the inside out. He had been there

Virgil Dechant, center, was there on the day the four towers were topped off at the new K of C headquarters.

to call Bingo games and serve fried chicken at parish halls on freezing cold nights in the dead of winter; he had picked up the phone when a concerned widow called to ask about attending a council function; and he had visited his brother knights in the hospital when they were most in need—just like they had once visited him.

Indeed, Virgil Dechant was the ultimate student of the Knights of Columbus—you might say a fraternalist.

Ah, yes, hospitals—as you read, you'll notice that many important scenes in this story took place in hospitals. So I suppose it's only fitting that my grandfather was confined to a hospital during the twilight of this project, battling some health problems that most men his age wouldn't have had the courage to fight. But he fought, and he got better, and in the process, at a time when we, the members of his family, should have been giving him the strength to heal, he was the one giving us strength. He was the one making us proud. And, as you might expect, among his visitors to the hospital were a few of his closest friends from the Knights of Columbus, including brother knight Tim Plank, Cardinal Leo Burke, and past state deputies Tom Zarda, Dave Leiker, and Don Wagner. And, of course, his wife Ann.

I guess some things never change.

– John Dechant
Fall 2017

My grandfather asked me to extend his appreciation to those who assisted him to help leave the Order better than they found it. Without the men in the field who work so diligently to promote the good works of the Knights of Columbus it would be impossible to live up to the vision of its founder, the venerable Father Michael McGivney. He also feels it takes a team to lead the members in their mission, and in this regard he gives credit to the entire leadership of the Order, including officers, chairmen, insurance representatives, grand knights, faithful navigators, district masters, vice supreme masters, state deputies, general agents, supreme officers and directors.

His wish is to pay tribute to the following supreme officers, supreme directors (shown in the highest position attained), and assistant officers that he had the privilege to work with since 1963, when he was first elected to the board of directors in Milwaukee, Wisconsin.

Supreme Knights: Luke E. Hart, John W. McDevitt, Carl A. Anderson

Supreme Chaplains: Most Rev. Charles P. Greco, Most Rev. Thomas V. Daily, Most Rev. William E. Lori

Deputy Supreme Knights: Dr. John H. Griffin, M.D., Charles J. Ducey, Ernest J. Wolff, Frederick H. Pelletier, John M. Murphy, Ellis D. Flinn, Robert F. Wade, Jean B. Migneault, Dennis A. Savoie, Logan T. Ludwig, Patrick E. Kelly

Supreme Secretaries: Joseph F. Lamb, D. Francis Sullivan, Richard B. Scheiber, Howard E. Murphy Sr., Charles P. Reisbeck Jr., Charles H. Foos,

Robert J. Lane, Donald R. Kehoe, Emilio B. Moure, Charles E. Maurer Jr., Michael J. O'Connor

Supreme Treasurers: Francis J. Heazel, Daniel L. McCormick, William J. Van Tassel, Deacon Kenneth N. Ryan, John W. O'Reilly Jr., Ronald Schwarz

Supreme Advocates: Harold J. Lamboley, W. Patrick Donlin, Ricardo H. Garcia, Patrick A. Cipollone, Paul R. Devin, John A. Marella

Supreme Physician/Medical Directors: Dr. Gerald J. Lunz, Dr. John O'Neill, Dr. Eugene Rotatari, Dr. Michael Conforti

Supreme Masters: Frank E. McGillen, Alfred N. Nicolas, Hilary F. Schmittzehe, Darrell W. Beck, Nestor V. Barber, Joseph P. Schultz, Lawrence G. Costanzo, Dennis J. Stoddard

Supreme Directors: Francis Fauteux, Clarence J. Malone, Gerald C. Riley, Charles J. Morgan, Hon. Francis J. Connolly, George M. Turner, Harry C. Pierotti, Henry J. Kondrat, Wilfred T. Connelly, Emmett Burke, N.A. Quintanilla, Lawrence D. Hurley, Leo Soenen, Jose Cardenas Stille, Arthur J. Melka, Charles J. Farrell, Joseph Murphy, Carmen R. Capone, Eugene Marquis, Leo P. Stark, Hon. Thomas M. Kavanagh, T.A. Eason Sr., George B. Brackin, Michael M. Collins, James E. Foley, J. Esmonde Barry, Maurice Perron, Medard R. Yutrzenka, Nicholas P. Lucyshyn, Jose Luis Gonzalez, Leslie D. Lemieux, John F. Barrett, Robert J. Hisel, Harvey M. MacDonald, Julian F. Joseph, Thomas J. Keating, Germain A. Fortier, John R. Plunkett, Albert V. Fortunato, Edward J. Buckley, Luke J. Farrell Jr., Frank R. Pulice Jr., George B. Simon, Count Enrico P. Galeazzi, Bernard G. Gerke, Basil A. Desiderio, Dr. Ernest J. Cook Jr., Newman A. Flanagan, Eugene L. Cherwick, Tim

Von Dohlen, Frank M. Jackson III, John E. Nickolas, Gayne J. Maloney, A.L. DeWitt, Mardonio R. Santos, Enrique Rivera Santana, Michael E. Waltz, Gerry Glavine, Albert J. Benedetti, Joseph R. Mauro, Grant R. Ertel, Jules A. Lacoursiere, Albert J. Castello, James W. Murphy, Thomas H. Shaughnessy, Allen J. Langley, Robert C. Stebler, William P. Barr, Louis A. Mautino, Vicent Di Leonardo, Edward J. Mullen, Gregory L. Baltz, Patroncinio R. Bacay, Robert J. Fallon, Ronald H. Tessier, Ronald L. Gay, Philip J. Zakoor, Javier G. Najera Cabrales, Alberto P. Solis, John A. Harrison Jr., Fred J. Abraham Jr., Robert F. Cayea, William J. White, Thomas P. Smith Jr., David A. Bellendier, John P. Wainscott, Ronald B. White, Yves Duceppe, Thomas M. Wegener, Javier S. Martinez, Daniel J. Baker, Reginald F. Beckett, Alonso L. Tan, Michael G. Conrad, Michael T. Gilliam, Paul J. Lambert, Meclea L. Casavant, Brian W. Simer, Arthur J. Harris, James R. Scroggin, Scott A. Flood, Natale L. Gallo, Kenneth E. Stockwell, Michael Wills, Daniel Rossi, Tommy C. Harger, Larry W. Kustra, Graydon A. Nicholas, Arthur L. Peters, Jose C. Reyes Jr., Colin R. Jorsch Jr., Carmine Musumecci, Patrick Mason

Supreme Wardens: Edward J. Bell, Robert E. Dawson, W. Kenneth Johnson, James D. Brackett, Harold G. Westby, Harold V. Welling, John R. Plunkett, Harry J. Tucker Jr., Michael T. Peak, Paul J. Staskey, Eugene R. Thomas, Peter L. Balestracci, Robert H. Ostdiek, Clarence J. Fischer, Joseph M. Behnke, Terrance J. Archbold, E. Price Hatcher, Francisco R. Gomez, George W. Hanna, Michael P. Victorino, Francis G. Drouhard

Assistant Supreme Secretaries: William Piedmont, George Humphrey, Ron Tracz

Administrative Assistant to the Supreme Knight: Edward J. Maloney, Paul McGlinchey, Terrance Lescoe, Stephen Feiler

VIRGIL CHRYSOSTOM DECHANT

Born September 24, 1930
(Antonino, Kansas)

Education

- St. Joseph parish grade school
  (Liebenthal, KS)
- Pontifical College Josephinum
  (Worthington, OH)
- St. Joseph Military Academy
  (Hays, KS)
- Salt City Business College
  (Hutchinson, KS)

Professional Career

- Dechant Motors, owner (1956-2001)
- Farmer (1948-present)
- Kansas State Council, state deputy
  (1960-1962)
- Knights of Columbus, assistant
  supreme secretary (1966-1967)
- Knights of Columbus, supreme master
  of the fourth degree (1966-1967)
- Knights of Columbus, supreme
  secretary (1967-1977)
- Knights of Columbus, supreme knight
  (1977-2000)
- Knights of Columbus, board of
  directors (1963-present)

Honorary Degrees

- St. Anselm's College (Manchester, NH)
- St. Leo's College (St. Leo, FL)
- Pontifical College Josephinum
  (Worthington, OH)
- Mount St. Mary's College
  (Emmitsburg, MD)
- Benedictine College (Atchison, KS)
- St. John's University (Staten Island,
  NY)
- Providence College (Providence, RI)
- Sacred Heart University (Bridgeport,
  CT)
- Pontifical University of Santo Tomas
  (Manila, Philippines)
- Assumption College (Worcester, MA)
- Albertus Magnus College (New Haven,
  CT)
- St. Thomas University (St. Paul-
  Minneapolis, MN)
- Kansas Newman College (Wichita, KS)
- Franciscan University (Steubenville,
  OH)
- St. Thomas University (Fredericton,
  NB)
- Dallas University (Dallas, TX)

Distinctions

- Knight Grand Cross in the Order of St.
  Gregory the Great
- Knight Grand Cross in the Equestrian
  Order of the Holy Sepulchre
- Knight Grand Cross in the Order of
  Pius IX

- Knight of the Sovereign Military Order of Malta
- Knight of the Heraldic Order of Christopher Columbus
- Gentiluomo, or "Gentleman of His Holiness," a member of the Pontifical lay family (1987-present)

Awards and Honors

- Joanine Award, Diocese of Dodge City (1963)
- Gold Medal, St. John's University (1979)
- President's Patronal Medal, Catholic University of America (1981)
- Fr. Michael J. McGivney Award, Connecticut State Council (1982)
- Benemerenti Medal, The Order of Preachers (1986)
- The Lantern Award, Massachusetts State Council (1986)
- Holy Land Medal, Custos of Jerusalem (1986)
- President's Medal, International Order of Catholic Knights (1987)
- Outstanding Alumni, 100th anniversary of the Pontifical College Josephinum (1987)
- National Right to Life's Proudly Pro Life award (1988)
- President's Medal, Assumption College (1993)
- Columbian Order of Merit, Quebec State Council (1994)
- Pro Vita Award, Diocese of Brooklyn (1995)
- Pro Fidelitate et Virtute Medal, Institute for Religious Life (2001)
- Guadium et Spes Award, Knights of Columbus (2012)

- Pope Leo XIII Award, Pontifical College Josephinum (2014)
- Lumen Vitae Medal, St. Benedict's Abbey (2016)

Noteworthy Appointments

- Pontifical Council for the Family (1982-2003)
- Auditor at the Extraordinary Synod of Bishops to commemorate the 20th anniversary of the close of Vatican II (1985)
- Member of the U.S. Christopher Columbus Quincentenary Jubilee Commission (1985-1992)
- Auditor at the Synod on the Laity (1987)
- Honorary consultor of the Pontifical Commission for Vatican City State (1988-2001)
- Consultor for the Pontifical Council for Social Communications (1990-2006)
- Board member (and vice chairman) of the Vatican's Institute for the Works of Religion, or "Vatican Bank" (1990-2009)
- Consultor to the Pro-Life committee of the National Conference of Catholic Bishops (1993)
- Auditor to the Synod for America (1997)
- Councillor to Vatican City State (2001-present)
- Board member of the National Catholic Educational Association
- Board member of the Catholic University of America
- Board member of the National Shrine of the Immaculate Conception
- Board of trustees of Pontifical College Josephinum
- Board of trustees of Albertus Magnus College